KEANE
ORIGINS

EOIN O'CALLAGHAN

MERCIER PRESS

To Joan, who I miss dearly.
For Lyndsey, who I don't deserve.

MERCIER PRESS
Cork
www.mercierpress.ie

© Eoin O'Callaghan, 2020

ISBN: 978 1 78117 731 0

A CIP record for this title is available from the British Library.

Printed and bound in the EU.

CONTENTS

PROLOGUE

February 1990.

A Sunday morning.

A bitter one, with frost on the ground.

The sun glints through a windscreen heavy with condensation. Soft heads, sore eyes, warm bodies. The zips on their tracksuits pulled high, their temples resting on the windows.

Another trip to Dublin.

Belvedere again.

A replay.

Typical.

The first game was a nightmare. At St Colman's Park, he'd put Cobh Ramblers in front with twenty minutes left and a massive win was theirs. Surely. Then a cross came in, the goalkeeper didn't get there.

An equaliser.

A fucking mess.

The usual.

As the bus rattles along, Roy Keane stares into the abyss.

Frustration.

The relentless grind. And for what? The League of Ireland First Division? He'd spent the season with Ramblers' first team and experienced enough shit-hole venues and bitter old veterans to last him a lifetime. He'd left Rockmount to test himself at a higher level. But this was a joyless, aimless, long-ball dirge. They'd tap him on the shoulder and say, 'Fair play, Roy. Character building.' Bullshit. He was a midfielder. Young. Creative.

Quick. He spent most games dodging the craters in the ground and wild lunges from fellas twice his age. Occasionally, he'd meet a kindred spirit on the other team. They'd share a knowing glance. This was no place for them. But what else was there?

He'd gotten a taste of it underage. Pulling on a green shirt. People knowing his name. And then it went away. Turned out he was forgettable. Faceless. Confidence, that innate local swagger, was always second nature, but it was harder now. Friends were cross-channel, signed to proper clubs. They were on a path. And he was worried. Worried about what was next, if it didn't work out. There was a pressure, a fear.

The FÁS course, the government football scheme he'd signed up for five months earlier, was coming to an end. He'd loved it. There was a purpose. He felt like a full-time athlete. He was improving. He was getting stronger. He was earning a few bob. But he was down the pecking order. Others were better than him. And there were still no trials, no phone calls, no interest. Would it have been different at Cork City? Maybe. But they'd annoyed him. They hadn't even cared enough to get him registered properly. Another let-down.

But Cobh had backed him. They wanted him. They were there. They were loyal.

Their youth coach, Eddie O'Rourke, had watched him play as a kid. He'd waited years to get the chance to sign him. And Roy enjoyed playing for him. There was a freedom to the underage side. He could be himself. He could influence. He could dictate.

Today was Fairview Park, one of those heralded Dublin football spaces. With its litany of pitches and freshly manicured surfaces, it reeked of privilege. There was the multitude of whispering 'insiders' on the sidelines too, the Stepford Wives, all dreary anoraks and immersed in the incestuous workings of schoolboy football in Ireland. The decision-makers. The centralised stakeholders. Funnily enough, you'd never see them at a First Division game.

Fuck them too. This was for Eddie and those who believed in him. Those who knew his talent. Those who wanted him to succeed.

PART 1

'If cities are sexed, as Jan Morris believes, then Cork is a male place. Personified further, I would cast him as low-sized, disputatious and stoutly built, a hard-to-knock-over type. He has a haughty demeanour that's perhaps not entirely earned but he can also, in a kinder light, seem princely. He is certainly melancholic. He is given to surreal flights and to an antic humour and he is blessed with pleasingly musical speech patterns. He is careful with money. He is in most leanings a liberal. He is fairly cool, usually quite relaxed, and head over heels in love with himself.'

Kevin Barry

1

THE FIRST HALF

Dublin lets on to be a capital, Frank O'Connor once said. Keane had a difficult relationship with the place.

In 1982 *The Late Late Show*, RTÉ's agenda-setting Friday night television production, headed south and used the Cork studios for a particularly memorable episode. At one point there was a light-hearted vox-pop segment, where a reporter took to the streets of Dublin and asked the locals how they felt about Cork.

'I think they're a nice race of people,' one man warmly offered.

There was never any malice intended. There was merely an assumption from Dubliners that anywhere outside of their cocooned existence was a kind of rural, agricultural wasteland with an array of madcap characters immersed in various kinds of buck-toothed buffoonery. Cork, the country's second-biggest city and a place boasting huge historical influence, cultural resonance, a proud sense of identity and an acerbic wit, always took this worst. The ignorance, indifference and flippancy grated.

Keane was from Mayfield, at the heart of Cork city's northside. He was in his early teens when his city was decimated, the heavyweights – Ford, Dunlop and Verolme – all shutting down their operations in the space of eighteen months from 1983 to 1984, deciding they didn't need Cork any more. Thousands of fathers, including his own, were left to beg, borrow and barter for bits and bobs. When the country was gripped by recession in the late 1980s, it felt like Cork had already been battling it for a decade.

The city informed Keane, certainly. That runt of the litter mentality. They may not have had much, but what they had was special.

As it turned out, Dublin didn't particularly like Keane very much either.

In 1987 he'd lost to Belvedere, an intimidatingly well-run and highly acclaimed club from the northside of Dublin, in an Under–15 national final in miserable circumstances. After forcing a draw in the capital, his Rockmount team surrendered a two-goal lead and lost 3–2 in the replay back home, missing out on a first Evans Cup success in twenty-five years.

He was there too for Ireland Under–15 trials but was ultimately ignored, deemed too small by the selectors. His Rockmount teammates Paul McCarthy, Damian Martin, Len Downey and Alan O'Sullivan all made the grade, which irritated him further. It had always been a solid quintet, a group made famous by the Kennedy Cup photograph taken when all five represented Cork at the Under–14 national tournament in 1986. Keane had captained that side to their first title in a decade as they annihilated an Offaly selection 10–1 on aggregate. Replete in their red and white, Downey is a towering presence on the far left of the picture. Second from right is McCarthy, already a powerful unit. Martin and O'Sullivan are a strong, commanding pair. All four have their shoulders back, chests out and hands clasped firmly behind their backs. A miniature Keane is dead centre, hands draped in front like he's defending a free kick. His posture makes him seem even smaller, a world away from adolescence. Just a boy. But they were all in it together. Written off, abused, criticised. Only Rockmount. Still, the five of them got there. And the Ireland team was next.

But not for Keane. Yet.

He was already known as an elite schoolboy player, which made the snub all the stranger. At the country's most influential football nurseries, the top brass were well aware of Roy Keane. And many of his fellow players and rivals were becoming aware of him too.

'It would've been Under–12 or Under–13 level and I was with Home Farm,' Tommy Dunne says. 'We played that Rockmount team so I was up against Roy throughout the game. At that stage, he was sharp in his mind. A little bit ahead of his years in a way. His movement was really good. And I remembered him, even back then.'[1]

The memory is etched in Richie Purdy's mind too, who also featured that day. 'It was an All-Ireland game up at Mobhi Road on Dublin's northside – it could've been a quarter-final or a semi-final – and there was this tiny little fella. Rockmount had a really good side at the time but he was the standout. His aggression was unbelievable. He was whingeing and kicking. So he hasn't changed much. Then I met him again at Ireland trials, but he didn't get picked because he was too small and that was a bit of a shock.'[2]

At Rockmount, the coaches had famously called Keane 'The Boilerman'. The guy who got things going. The playmaker. But there was another alias too, owing to just how diminutive he was.

'His nickname was The Dot. A full stop, like,' says Noel Spillane, the long-time soccer correspondent for Cork's *Evening Echo* and *Examiner* newspapers, who covered Keane's ascent in detail. 'That's what the lads would say during the games. "Give it to The Dot." That's what he was known as.'[3]

Keane was aware of his physical shortcomings, but that was out of his hands. So he turned a laser-focus to things he could control: fitness, proficiency on the ball and a dedication to the game that seemed out of sync with the moodiness and restless energy of hormonal teenage years.

'A few years after first playing against him, there was a week's camp at The King's Hospital in Dublin and Roy was part of the Cork group invited to attend,' Tommy Dunne says. 'There were two things that stand out. He might talk now about hard work and attitude and how it's not about technical ability, but at that time, Roy won the award for most technical player in our age-group. And the other thing I remember was that we were a load of young lads away at a camp. The King's Hospital had dormitories because it was an old Protestant college. We were there in the summertime and, with the exception of one person, everyone was always messing around. That person was Roy. And the reason? He was resting up because the next day was all about training. I'll never forget it. I used to go into the dorm where the Cork lads were and he was just chilled out.'

Darren Barry was an underage teammate of Keane's at Rockmount.

'Gene O'Sullivan, the manager of Rockmount schoolboys for years, and who was a lovely man and who, sadly, didn't get to see Roy make it, told me one time about him,' he says. 'It was the day of Roy's Confirmation and Rockmount had training. But he still came down to train. He just loved playing that much.'[4]

Keane did eventually get a call-up to the Irish Under–15 squad for a game against France at Bray's Carlisle Grounds in June 1987. But he didn't make the match-day squad, something he'd quickly get used to.

Still, there was a better experience in September, when Keane was named in the Under–16 panel. In a crucial draw with Northern Ireland, he earned an especially rave review and was subsequently included in Joe McGrath's squad for the European Championships in Spain the following summer.

'I suppose we will be out there as underdogs,' coach Maurice Price admitted at the time, before outlining the players he felt could catch the eye. 'It will be a great opportunity for some of the lads not with English clubs to impress. Paul McCarthy from Rockmount looks to be a terrific prospect and so do Richard Purdy and Jason Byrne.'[5]

Keane wasn't afforded a mention but, considering what followed, it was hardly surprising.

In Spain, the Irish team turned in a superb performance and went undefeated in an immensely tough group. They held Portugal, who'd go on to reach the final against the hosts, to a scoreless draw in their opener and then drew 2–2 with Switzerland. Qualification for the semi-finals was still possible heading into their last fixture against Belgium but, despite winning 1–0, the Portuguese did enough in their game against the Swiss to pip Ireland to top spot.

Keane was a spectator for the entire tournament.

From the sixteen-man group, he was one of only two players, the other being the reserve goalkeeper, who saw zero game-time. Even in a brief newspaper report that offered an overview of how the Irish team had fared, he was literally an afterthought: 'Also in the squad were Roy Keane (Rockmount) and John Connolly (Hillcrest).'[6]

Purdy remembers Keane's disgust when McGrath was forced to make changes for the clash with Belgium but still decided against using him. 'It always sticks out in my memory,' he says. 'We had a few injuries after the second game against the Swiss, including myself, so there were some changes for the final fixture against Belgium. I saw Roy's face in the dressing room when he knew he wasn't involved and he was like a demon. I remember looking across at him. I knew by his demeanour that he was devastated at not getting a run. And that was our last game because we didn't qualify for the next stage.'

Keane was badly burned and there'd be plenty of scar tissue. The entire experience – supposedly a proud achievement – was underwhelming.

It didn't help that, despite the FAI seeing a substantial windfall for the senior team's historic qualification for the 1988 European Championships, there was a remarkable occurrence before the Under–16s group departed for their own Euro adventure.

In the middle of May, Keane had appeared in *The Cork Examiner* alongside Downey, McCarthy and Rockmount chairman Jim Deasy. Also in the photograph was Teddy Barry from the New Furniture Centre, the team's main sponsors. Barry was handing over a cheque to 'help with expenses' for the players' forthcoming trip to Spain.

According to the *Evening Herald* later that month, the Irish Under–16s had to contribute £40 each towards the cost of their uniforms. 'We had a very generous sponsorship for both our Under–15s and Under–16s but it is custom and practice to ask the boys to contribute to the cost of such items,' FAI board member Frank Feery told the paper. 'The boys were consulted as to the style of clothing and as a result, they looked extremely smart. Just as important, it was Irish-made.'[7]

Forty-eight hours later, another photograph appeared in the *Herald*. It was of the entire squad, before they had left for Spain, looking refined in their dark blazers and beige slacks.

'The Republic of Ireland Under–16 side kitted out in their Castle Knitwear,' the accompanying caption read.

It was PR fluff and, inevitably, Keane is front-row and glum.

'The FAI were a joke,' Purdy says. 'They'd give us tracksuits to wear if we were playing games or at tournaments, but we'd have to take them off in airport toilets and hand them back.'

By the start of the 1988/89 domestic season, it seemed everyone was moving on and stepping up. Price was right about the Euros acting as a shop window for some of the Irish underage group. Alan O'Sullivan had signed for Luton Town and McCarthy was picked up by Brighton, along with Derek McGrath. Selected for Maurice Setters' Irish youth squad, Keane was now envious of those around him. David Collins was already appearing for Liverpool's reserves. The likes of Kieran Toal (Manchester United), Jason Byrne (Huddersfield) and Paul Byrne (Oxford) were all cross-channel too.

The steady migration of his peers was harming Keane's progress.

In October 1988 the Cork Gaelic football team lost an All-Ireland final replay to Meath at Croke Park by a point. A few days later, Keane would feel a similar sense of bitterness.

'At last, Cork people have something to smile about,' went the GAA-inspired opening line of an *Irish Press* report on the Ireland youths' win over Iceland in their first European Championship qualifier.[8]

But the reference wasn't to Keane. It was to O'Sullivan, who scored twice in the space of four minutes at Dalymount Park. Keane had been named in the initial twenty-two-man squad but failed to even make the bench for the game. Meanwhile, his Rockmount teammate Downey suffered ignominy too, being replaced after half an hour.

When Setters later named an eighteen-man group for a winter tournament in Israel at the end of the year, McCarthy went, O'Sullivan went and even Downey went. Keane was ignored completely.

From the seven home-based players included in the squad, six were from Dublin.

The usual.

Cherry Orchard.

Home Farm.

Belvedere.

For Keane, it was embarrassing. It hadn't been long since some glittering newspaper reports described how he'd 'shone in midfield' in the Under–16 Euro qualifier against Northern Ireland. Now, still stuck at Rockmount, he was being left behind.

There was a pattern. The perception seemed to be that he was good but not good enough. Turning the corner into 1989, there seemed a genuine chance that he could just slip through the net.

McCarthy, through his father, tried to engineer a trial for Keane at Brighton but, mysteriously, it never materialised as the same well-worn excuses were wheeled out.

'The night before I was due to leave, Paul called to say the trial was off,' Keane said years later.[9]

McCarthy went into more detail when he appeared in the RTÉ documentary *Have Boots, Will Travel* in 1997, which charted Keane's rise.[10]

'He was a very small young fella,' McCarthy recalled. 'If you saw a picture of him when he was fifteen, you'd never think it was the same fella. A lot of scouts would have looked at him, seen the size of him and that would've put them off. He was meant to come over to Brighton – my dad set it up. But in the end the Irish scout put the Brighton manager off it because he questioned his temperament and his size. But his ability was unbelievable. He never gave the ball away. He scored a lot of goals. He was only tiny, but he'd never be knocked off the ball and if there was any trouble, he'd be there and would never back away from anything.'

Decades later, Harry Redknapp alleged a different version of the story. He detailed a second-hand yarn – passed on to him by a pal – of how then-Brighton manager Barry Lloyd had agreed to watch Keane play in an Ireland youth international upon a recommendation from an unnamed scout.

'The scout went to see the [Ireland] schools manager and explained the situation – that this was Roy's big break and he could become an apprentice at Brighton if they liked the look of him,' Redknapp writes in *A Man Walks On To A Pitch: Stories from a Life in Football*. '"He's been in every squad but he hasn't played a minute of any game," he [the scout] said. "Can you make sure he's involved on Tuesday?" The coach said no. "We're not here to showcase kids, we're here to win football matches," he said. Keane never played and Brighton didn't take him.'[11]

The scout in question was Brian Brophy, who offers up a slightly different version of events.

'The Under–16s had qualified for the European Championships and Barry [Lloyd] asked me to go over to Spain to have a look at Roy,' Brophy says. 'So myself and two representatives from Brighton – their youth officer, Ted Streeter, and youth coach, Colin Woffinden – turned up. The first game was against Portugal and he didn't play. Then it was Switzerland and he didn't play. And the third game was against Belgium and he wasn't playing. We had gone there purposely to watch him. And we were probably the only club out there. We already had Paul McCarthy and Derek McGrath, and Brian McKenna's parents wanted him to do his Leaving Cert before joining us, so he stayed in Dublin for a while longer. Anyway, we approached Joe [McGrath] and asked him to put Roy on. And he said, "No, no. He's not good enough." And we said, "Look, we've come all this way." But, he never played. Roy and the sub goalkeeper, John Connolly, never got on the pitch.'[12]

Brophy continues, 'With regards to the story of Paul McCarthy's father arranging for Roy to go for a trial, I didn't know anything about it. So I wouldn't have been in a position to tell Brighton, "No, don't take him." I don't know if it was genuine or if somebody else had arranged it or what happened. But it certainly had nothing to do with me.'

According to Ted Streeter, his motivation for going to Bilbao was to watch McGrath and McCarthy, Brighton's two recent acquisitions.

'I hadn't heard anything about Roy,' he says. 'Obviously with his boy having joined us, Joe [McGrath] was keeping an eye on some of the [Irish] lads. But he never mentioned Roy. He was quite small and Joe never recommended him. So Roy was just another member of their squad. We thought Joe just didn't fancy him and that's why he didn't play him. If I had seen him and fancied him, I would've made arrangements for Roy to come over. I don't judge a player on their size and Derek [McGrath] was quite small. So there was no follow-up from me. Also, I certainly don't remember offering Roy a trial at Brighton and then cancelling it afterwards. I wouldn't ever call off a trial anyhow. So that wasn't me. Unless something had been done through Barry Lloyd, the manager.'

Lloyd shatters the myth a little.

'I don't think we were even close to bringing Roy over,' he admits. 'I was told he wasn't the biggest and it's a real difficult one for me. History says we missed out on him, but that's the name of the game, isn't it? And in some respects we were happy in our ways because we brought a few boys over from Ireland in that era.'[13]

And the trial that never was. Does it ring a bell?

'No, not at all. In principle, we travel to see the player in their own environment. We find it more beneficial than the player being amongst a group of boys they don't know.'

Those at Rockmount remained perplexed by Keane's continued absence from the Irish team and his inability to land a trial with a cross-channel club.

'It was bizarre,' says Darren Barry, Keane's midfield partner at Rockmount for three seasons. 'It was bizarre that he wasn't being picked up by English clubs because other players in Cork were. He captained the Cork Under–14 Kennedy Cup team that destroyed Dublin in the semi-finals and then went on to win the national trophy. Therefore, they were the best team in the country and Roy was the skipper. Rockmount were one of the best teams in Ireland at the time too. So he was well known to everyone. Anybody who saw him play at that time would have said he could play professionally, without a doubt.

'It would certainly have been discussed by players, parents and anyone who was watching that Roy wasn't getting the rewards that his talents deserved. Alan O'Sullivan was a magnificent schoolboy player and probably the best in our team. But people were putting Roy's name forward to the Luton scout, who was Eddie Corcoran. But he said Roy was too small, which was ridiculous. Regardless of his size, he was still outstanding. I remember in an Under–15 game, he scored a goal very similar to the one he got in Turin for Manchester United in the Champions League semi-final in 1999. He wasn't very big but he rose up above everyone and headed it across. You rarely saw that at schoolboy level – a player heading the ball like that and particularly somebody who wasn't tall. It was purely based on timing and rising to meet the ball. He had no height advantage.

So I'd seen him do that and knew he was that good in the air even then.'

'Clubs in England kept giving him the excuse that it was his height, because he was four foot nothing when he was fifteen,' says Jamie Cullimore, who played alongside Keane in the Kennedy Cup team and faced him constantly at club level. 'I've no doubt it played on his mind. I don't think it sat very well with him because there was a fight in him from day one. A fifty–fifty header and he'd win it every time and he was half the size of me. It was in him. His timing was superb, his leap. And I don't remember him ever getting a smack either because his timing was so good. I had about six inches on him when I was underage and I don't think I ever won a header against him. And it was that attitude. Nothing was going to stop him getting to where he wanted to be. Full stop. He was tenacious.'[14]

But the local support mattered little, and by the summer Keane was despondent. The season had started with international involvement but that evaporated quickly.

When the Irish youth team beat Northern Ireland in a May friendly, O'Sullivan and McCarthy were both involved, but Keane, snubbed again, was back in Cork instead. A few days earlier, he and Downey featured in the Munster Youth Cup final for Rockmount at Turner's Cross. They came from behind twice to draw 2–2 with Limerick City.

Another replay.

Typical.

And, as the Irish underage group was beating Malta in a crucial Euro qualifier at Dalymount Park at the end of the month, Keane's focus was on something a little lower-key. On the June Bank Holiday Monday, Rockmount traipsed down to the old Priory Park to face Limerick again. They lost in a dramatic penalty shoot-out.

Another season over, another year gone and Keane was right where he had started. The local team. Small time.

***

Desperately in need of a reset that summer of 1989, the League of Ireland offered Keane a chance of better exposure and some extra cash. Rockmount, whose senior side played in the Munster Senior League, could provide neither. Approaching his eighteenth birthday, it wasn't a difficult decision.

And when Brian Carey signed for Manchester United from Premier Division side Cork City that summer, it proved to Keane that maybe it wasn't too late. Carey had never even featured at underage level for the Republic of Ireland. He'd grafted in the local leagues and enrolled in college to study construction economics, impressing as a commanding centre-half when City came calling. He was getting a high-profile move at twenty-one, and there had been plenty of other interest too, from the likes of Celtic and Arsenal.

By late June, it seemed Keane would be a Cork City player too and a report in *The Cork Examiner* detailed how he, Downey and another young prospect, Fergus O'Donoghue, had all agreed terms. But then everything went quiet and for good reason.

There are many local myths regarding Keane, and two pertain to how Cork City managed to squander his signing. One version is that a City employee failed to make it to the post office in time one Friday afternoon to send Keane's documentation to the League of Ireland headquarters. The other is that instead of posting Keane's application to Dublin as soon as he signed it, City waited until they had Downey's and O'Donoghue's too and could send all three in the same envelope.

'For a 28p stamp, Cork lost a potential star,' *The Irish Press* claimed later.[15]

The truth? 'It was just one of those things,' said then-City secretary Seamus Casey afterwards. 'I decided to wait until July 1 to send it off. I was trying to be businesslike.'[16] It wouldn't have been an issue if City were Keane's only suitor, but unbeknownst to them, Cobh Ramblers were also claiming Keane as their player and managed to submit their paperwork before the weekend. It was a sliding doors moment. And considering another crucial administrative occurrence later in Keane's career when Blackburn Rovers attempted to complete his transfer from Nottingham Forest in the summer of 1993, quite the coincidence.[17]

In his first autobiography, Keane says he completed a form committing himself to Cork City and that Cobh Ramblers, who played in the League of Ireland's second tier, only came in for him afterwards. 'Cork City hadn't bothered to send the form I'd signed,' Keane wrote, simplifying the entire episode.[18]

In reality, it was messier than that and contrasted significantly with what Cobh would eventually tell the league.

The stand-off between Ramblers and City over Keane actually continued into February of the following year, when his first league campaign with Cobh was inching close to completion. Described as a 'transfer wrangle' and an 'ongoing saga' in the local press, there was even a meeting arranged involving the clubs, League of Ireland officials and Keane himself to find a satisfactory resolution. According to the report, City wanted a 'substantial fee' as compensation. But John Meade, the Ramblers' secretary, maintained that Keane had signed for them earlier in the summer and then subsequently signed for City too. More importantly, Cobh argued, they were first to register Keane with the league.

Still, City were the bigger club. They played top-flight football. They had reached the FAI Cup final the previous season and, despite their loss at Dalymount Park in the replay to Derry City that day, still qualified for another European competition. Earlier in the 1989/90 campaign, they'd faced Torpedo Moscow in the first round of the Cup Winners' Cup and, though they were ripped to shreds over two legs, it was clear they were operating at a different level to Ramblers. With Carey having secured a move to England owing to his performances for City, maybe more cross-channel teams would be monitoring Noel O'Mahony's side? If Keane was looking for a platform, City presented him with the biggest one. But, despite all of that, despite having to repeatedly trek all the way from the city to a small harbour town and back again, despite his close friend Downey already being at Cork City, Keane didn't appear too interested and seemed stung that City had been so flippant regarding the administrative side of things.

When *The Cork Examiner* reported on Keane's situation, the final line was short, simple but revealing.

'It's understood that Keane wants to continue playing with Cobh Ramblers.'[19]

It really was that simple. Cobh had been good to him. They wanted him. They'd never messed him around. And by February 1990 – unlike Downey at City – he was playing regularly at an elite level. And making that step up had been his biggest motivation to walk away from a club he'd been at since he was eight years old.

'He loved Rockmount and he could've joined their senior team at eighteen,' says Jamie Cullimore. 'But already he was looking to push himself at a higher level. He said goodbye to all of his buddies to go down and play with Ramblers.'

Cobh had got the deal done through youth coach and local carpenter Eddie O'Rourke, who'd been mesmerised by Keane the first time he watched him play in 1985.

'I never in my life saw anything like him,' O'Rourke said later, speaking in exalted terms about the rampaging 'dot' who consistently inflicted so much damage upon various local teams, including Cobh youth club Springfield. 'It was like looking at a salmon. He would leap to head the ball from his own area; next minute he'd be up the other end making the final pass. I made up my mind that if ever I got the job as youth manager with Cobh, I'd go after him.'[20]

He succeeded and Keane was quickly promoted to the senior team for a high-profile pre-season friendly against West Bromwich Albion at St Colman's Park, where there were a couple of familiar faces in the home dressing room that calmed any nerves.

One was Cullimore, who'd battled Keane many times while at Springfield, was a teammate on the Kennedy Cup side and had also been called into Ireland underage squads. The other was Keane's older brother, Denis, a gifted local player for Temple United, who was being courted by Cobh boss Alfie Hale. The fixture against the Baggies was his audition and he passed with flying colours.

'Denis was Man of the Match every second week for Temple,' Noel Spillane says. 'Regarding natural talent, he had more than Roy. He'd go past four or five fellas, nutmeg the keeper and back-heel it into the net. But he just had no interest in training.'

Keane's debut was solid and largely uneventful against a Baggies side that were on a three-game tour of Ireland. A few days earlier, they'd knocked four past Shelbourne at Tolka Park and they did the same down south. Some footage remains of Keane from that evening, scampering down the right side as Cobh break quickly on a counter-attack. Wearing number eight on his back, it's unmistakably Keane: the running style, the gait, the speed.

In front of a thousand-strong crowd, Cobh put some respectability on the scoresheet with two goals of their own, Cullimore grabbing the second. For the guests, one of theirs came courtesy of Gary Robson, younger brother of Bryan – the player Keane would effectively replace at Manchester United.

Keane went close on two separate occasions, ensuring some mentions in the local press reports the following day. But, in keeping with the sibling rivalry, his big moment was usurped.

'Denis came down for the game and they gave him the Man of the Match award, but I'd have given it to Roy,' Cullimore says. 'I think they were eager to hold on to Denis by giving it to him. He was a class act, but you knew Roy's heart and soul was in soccer and I was never convinced Denis' was. He'd play the ninety minutes, but after that he was out gallivanting with the boys. Roy was happy to do that too, but you felt soccer was always in the back of his mind.

'It sounds really silly saying it, but I always knew there was something special about him. Even underage. At Under–14s he was the smallest fella on the pitch, but he was still our captain. He was thinking faster than other people. When he chested the ball, it was into space. As young fellas you didn't do that. You chested it and just made sure you controlled it. I was playing for Springfield against Rockmount one day and offside was pretty big in the game back in the eighties, obviously. He was coming at us and there was about five of us in a line. And we were like, "Nah, we'll catch him offside if he tries to play one of the boys in." But all he did was dink the ball over the five of us, ran around us and buried the fucking thing in the net. He was a small bit cuter. He always had something that would drive him on further.

'After a game, he'd let you know that he'd won the dual between you and him. There was this constant fight, no matter who he was playing against, that he was going to win that battle.'

2

ALL OUT IN THE OPEN

It was January 1988 when *The Economist* surveyed Ireland for their latest issue. The headline was 'Poorest of the rich' and carried a Dickensian photograph of a woman with a child begging on the streets. The magazine detailed the dereliction, social decay and forecast an immensely bleak future.

They were right.

By the end of the year, Anglo-Irish relations were at an all-time low, as Taoiseach Charles Haughey and British Prime Minister Margaret Thatcher had clashed repeatedly in private meetings. One hundred and four people had lost their lives in The Troubles – the highest number of fatalities since 1982. The unemployment rate was over sixteen per cent while 60,000 people emigrated.

There seemed an air of weary resignation.

The melancholy had a wider cultural resonance too. This was the era when contemporary laments were chart successes in Ireland. Jim McCann sang about Grace Gifford, the forgotten wife of Joseph Mary Plunkett, the youngest of the 1916 revolutionary leaders. Both The Wolfe Tones and Dublin City Ramblers had simultaneous top-ten hits with 'Flight of Earls', an ode to an entire generation's forced departure. And Jimmy MacCarthy's 'As I Leave Behind Neidín', a song about parting lovers, carried that haunting, desperate, metaphorical refrain of 'Won't you remember me?'

'The Irish Rover', an age-old folk song, was given a rebirth too as The Pogues partnered with The Dubliners for a number one single. The country seemed stuck between the past and present, probably because the future seemed so out of reach.

An RTÉ television news report looked deeper into the mass exodus and spoke to a group of young men heading to England in search of work.

'Are you trained in any particular skills, lads?' they were asked.

'No, none whatsoever.'[1]

Also in 1988, a government initiative had been announced: Foras Áiseanna Saothair, or FÁS. Effectively, it was a state training agency put in place to try and stem the bleeding as Ireland buckled under the stress of economic collapse. FÁS translates as 'growth' and the organisation's purpose was to provide people on the unemployment register – in particular those in their late teens and early twenties – with educational courses and schemes that could subsequently better their chances of finding a job.

It wasn't a radically new idea. Before it, there had been An Chomhairle Oiliúna (The Training Council), or AnCo for short. Still, it was a rebranding exercise that enabled the Fianna Fáil government to show they were tackling a devastating social problem and not simply paying it lip service.

Enrolling in FÁS meant coming off social welfare and walking into a classroom. But some felt it was a smokescreen, that those in power were merely fiddling the numbers to make themselves look better.

After a multitude of FÁS schemes were announced for East Cork in the summer of 1989, one local Fine Gael politician, Paul Bradford, likened the strategy to putting band aids on the *Titanic*.

Roy Keane later described FÁS as 'one part well-meaning, three parts cynical', but, regardless, it proved a seismic experience for him.

In late June 1989 two jobs were advertised in a variety of national newspapers. Under the name Football Apprenticeship Programme, the full-time roles for Programme Director and Assistant Programme Director were outlined and applicants were encouraged to send their details to the League of Ireland offices at Dublin's Merrion Square.

The Cork Examiner filled in some blanks and in a brief report on the pending scheme revealed that every League of Ireland club would be entitled to nominate one of their players to take part in what was a full-time training opportunity.

FÁS would offer a nominal weekly payment plus expenses and, given the fact that the best young players in the country were either first-team squad members or on the cusp of a breakthrough, it meant two separate football incomes. It wasn't much, but it was certainly better than the dole queue.

By mid-August, the programme was officially launched at an event in Dublin. Maurice Price, one of Keane's underage coaches at international level, was unveiled as the director, and Larry Mahony, then in charge of St Joseph's Boys, confirmed as his assistant. Overseeing everything on behalf of the FAI was another figure Keane knew well, the national team manager of Ireland's Under–16s, Joe McGrath.

'We're breaking new ground,' said League of Ireland president, Enda McGuill, at the time. 'While the benefit may not be immediately evident, I'm certain the long-term effects will be of tremendous importance in the development of the game in this country.'[2]

A report in the *Sunday Independent* described the course as McGrath's 'brainchild' and added it incorporated 'the best features of the English YTS scheme with some improvements'.[3]

The Irish Press went into more detail: 'The objectives of the scheme, which will operate initially for a year, are to provide opportunities for young players to receive full-time training in their own country – in addition to bringing about an improvement in players' technical skills, plus the chance to obtain a basic education, including acquiring a foreign language and experience in technology and computer programming.

'The duration of the programme is forty-eight weeks and players interested in the scheme should be between sixteen and twenty. Players joining the scheme from provincial clubs will live in approved accommodation in the Palmerstown area, while the participants will be given the standard FÁS allowances.

'Clubs with players taking advantage of the scheme are expected to contribute nominally to the running costs and development of the programme.'[4]

The initial idea of each League of Ireland club – from both the Premier and First Divisions – enrolling one young player quickly changed. Reigning champions Derry City, as well as the likes of Shamrock Rovers, didn't take up the offer. So, Cobh Ramblers, Cork City, Drogheda United, Finn Harps, Home Farm and Shelbourne all secured two representatives.

In total, twenty players were selected for the finalised group, including two Republic of Ireland Under–21 internationals, Pat Fenlon and Tommy Fitzgerald, who'd been at Chelsea and Tottenham respectively but failed to make the grade. Others, such as Tony Gorman, who'd had an unsuccessful stint at Mansfield Town and returned to sign for Finn Harps, were in a similar boat.

Keane was part of a Cork foursome. Aware of the course starting in the autumn, he had told Ramblers prior to arriving that if they secured him a place, he'd join.

'The deal was if I got him on the course, he'd sign. That clinched it,' Eddie O'Rourke later confirmed. 'Roy was desperate to go.'

Alongside him was his Cobh teammate Jamie Cullimore, while representing Cork City were Keane's long-time pal Len Downey and goalkeeper John Donegan. There were other familiar faces too, including Tommy Dunne and Richie Purdy, the latter having featured in Irish squads with Keane.

The start date was set for Monday 4 September, and the day before, Keane was in Ballybofey for a First Division season opener against Finn Harps. Ramblers were fortunate to only come away with a 3–1 defeat, as midfielder Tony Gorman missed a first-half penalty for the hosts.

Afterwards, Gorman headed for Dublin to get settled before the FÁS course began. He was glad of the victory over Ramblers and especially pleased with having got one over on their mouthy midfielder who was on his case for the entire afternoon.

It was the first time he'd ever met Roy Keane. And his second meeting with him happened a lot sooner than he expected.

'We had a right battle,' Gorman says. 'We kicked each other, had a few unpleasant things to say to each other. There was a lot of effing. He was this and I was that. I was gonna kill him and he was gonna kill me. After I missed the penalty, he was in my face. To arrive into Dublin the following day and one of the first people you see is the guy you were in combat with the day before … You just thought, "Jesus, not him."

'We probably didn't speak all week. When we finally got talking, I told him Cobh's best player was their left-winger, who turned out to be his brother, Denis! Technically, he was really good and skilful and had a bit of pace about him, and I suppose, at that time, Denis looked the better Keane.'[5]

Gorman remembers plenty about that first interaction in Finn Park, but mainly the insults. They continued during the course too. 'Langer was the obvious one,' he says. 'We heard langer a hundred times a day down there [in Palmerstown], between the whole lot of the Cork lads. And d'you know what? I think we started using it ourselves. We'd come back to Donegal and call people langers.

'It was a difficult game against him. Tough. He was quick. He was very good in the air. He was competitive. Some people might say, "We knew he was going to be this or that", but you couldn't have judged from that game. First impressions were that he was physical, a really athletic player and a tough opponent. He had a skinny upper body but I thought his legs were quite big. It was Adidas gear that Cobh had at the time and the shorts were the real eighties kind where they'd cut the balls off you and were really tight. For somebody who I thought was light, he was still incredibly strong, mainly because he was so bloody competitive.'

The FÁS course was ritualistic. The Cork contingent would all meet at Kent Station early on a Monday morning for the train to Dublin. Cullimore, music-obsessed and a budding singer/songwriter, would bring his guitar.

'The Monday morning blues just to get you in the right frame of mind to go up to the second capital,' says John Donegan. 'And c'mere, who doesn't like a good sing-song?'[6]

From Dublin city centre, they'd hop a bus to Palmerstown, walk down the back of Stewarts Hospital and get things started.

With the players involved in club games the previous day and so many of them spending the morning commuting to Dublin, Mondays were usually quite light, but it was a 9 a.m. start for the rest of the week. Because it was a FÁS scheme, the group also had academic commitments, so on Tuesday and Thursday afternoons they'd head for classes, where the curriculum was certainly unique.

'We probably did about two hours each day,' Gorman says. 'We did English and we studied Spanish too, don't ask me why. There was a computer class where we did some basic typing as well. But I remember the book we studied in English class was *To Kill A Mockingbird*. I actually enjoyed it so much, and what we were doing, that I went and got a copy myself because we were only getting through a chapter at a time and I couldn't wait to get to the end of it. We had to read passages in front of everyone and I remember thinking, "Atticus Finch – what a brilliant name." But we didn't have any tests or anything.

'One day, some lad came into us to talk about sex. There was a banana and a condom. It was one of those moments where all the stupid questions started. "How long does it take?" and all of that. So my two abiding memories of the FÁS course are *To Kill A Mockingbird* and some lad shoving a condom over the top of a banana.'

Dunne remembers the classroom stints for a different reason. 'We used to walk from Palmerstown to Collinstown College, which is a decent stretch. And we used to all have these shell-suits on us. They were black but had pink and white and blue on them. We looked like something getting off the latest fucking spaceship, like the *Discovery*. We went into class and we all hated it, but we did have some great characters. There was a guy called Mick Wilson who was from Monaghan, and he was mad. The Liffey ran by where we trained at Stewarts Hospital and any of the balls that went into the river, he'd take off all his gear but leave his boots on and dive straight in to get them. There could've been anything in there. He didn't even know the depth of it but was head-first into it.'

'Those tracksuits were like something you'd wear to a rave,' according to Purdy. 'We were like a load of drug dealers walking around Neilstown. How we didn't get mugged I'll never know. I think Stewarts Hospital actually got robbed one day by some kid and he still left all the tracksuits behind. That shows you how bad they were. Absolutely desperate.'

The coaching staff felt differently. 'The tracksuits were the best of swag at that time,' says Larry Mahony, defiantly. 'It was the best of gear they had. It was shiny but everyone was wearing that style.'[7]

Returning to a classroom brought out an anxiety in Keane and he tried his best to skip the mandatory lessons, regardless of the consequences.

'Roy was a quiet, shy young man in the senior Cobh dressing room and, to be fair, it was a daunting place for an eighteen-year-old as there were a few "less-than-shy" characters already in there,' says Fergus McDaid, an experienced member of the Ramblers squad. 'Liam [McMahon], who was in charge by that stage, had received the usual monthly report from Dublin on Roy's progress. There was no difficulty with ability, effort, performance, etc. Roy was applying himself fully in every sense. But there was an issue with an academic element: attending classes. So, Liam deftly employed the schoolteacher – me – to address this issue with the allegedly reluctant student. When I broached the subject with Roy, the coyness and shyness disappeared. He left me in no doubt as to where his ambitions lay. English First Division football was what he wanted. Academic pursuits were not for Roy and were never mentioned again! Next conversation ...'[8]

Much to his shame, Keane had failed his Intermediate Certificate, and he later admitted that he felt he'd let his parents down as a result. Having just turned eighteen – the age when so many other teenagers were college-bound and taking the first steps towards the rest of their lives – there was some trepidation, perhaps even a fear, of his own future. He'd dedicated himself to football and for what? Some underage caps? He put on a good show but seemed concerned about what was next. One Monday morning, as the train pulled out of Kent Station on its way to Dublin, Keane caught a glimpse of his possible future.

'We passed a load of workers on the side of the railway tracks,' Cullimore remembers. 'And Roy says, "Look at them fuckers out there and they're going like the hammers. I *have* to make it as a footballer." He knew the brains weren't there, in that way, so he had to make it at soccer. He put everything into trying to make it. In Palmerstown, we'd have to walk to get to our classes and Roy would be like a dog. He didn't want to go near computers or have anything to do with them. During the class, Roy would turn his off in front of the teacher and just say, "I don't want to do it, I don't want anything to do with it." But that was Roy. All he wanted to do was play ball. "I don't want to know about computers." That's just how headstrong he was when it came to soccer.'

John Donegan, who'd sit alongside him every Monday morning on the way to Dublin, picked up on the single-mindedness too. 'The fellas working outside on the train tracks had no meaning for him, other than he knew he didn't want to be there,' he says. 'There was only soccer. There wasn't a case of him having a job. There wasn't a case of him doing anything else. This was his path. He was well known on the way up but got overlooked.

And this was another platform for him. He grabbed it. He said, "I'm going to do it." And he did it. Growing up, school for Roy was probably the same as that computer course in Collinstown College – he just didn't want to be there. He probably felt he could've been doing something better, like playing ball.'

Still, Keane had carried that determination and hunger for years and knew from previous setbacks that it wasn't necessarily enough. He admitted to Gorman that watching his former teammates get opportunities in England while he remained at Rockmount was a tough swallow.

'I remember him saying he'd had a few disappointments where lads were going on trials, like Paul McCarthy and Alan O'Sullivan, and he'd come to a junction in the road,' Gorman says. 'There was a road leading him to GAA and another one towards boxing, but he chose the one leading to football and he was going to give it a go. Where other fellas at thirteen or fourteen would still have been playing different sports, he made the choice to concentrate on football.'

The FÁS course became Keane's obsession. It was intense. It was full-time. It was draining. But there was a feeling of accomplishment. Under Price and Mahony, the training was technical and challenging. Regular games against local teams were uncompromising. The gym work ensured he was building himself up. He had never been as fit and strong, and a growth spurt finally added some inches to his frame. He had constant access to a pitch and a ball and he even seemed to consider meal times an inconvenient interruption.

'We'd have a lunch break for maybe forty-five minutes,' Cullimore says. 'But within twenty minutes, Roy had the ball under his arm, was out the door and back down practising free kicks or taking shots. And there wasn't many guys who would do that – give up their lunch break and start fannying around with the ball. But that's all he wanted to do.'

Each weekend, Keane was also getting an opportunity to showcase the improvements in his game. However dismal things were at Cobh and however patchy the general standard of First Division football was, it remained an important education. Many of his peers felt it was a more impactful experience than what cross-channel trainees were being exposed to.

'It wasn't like you were playing underage soccer,' Donegan says. 'When you played, you played. And in the League of Ireland, you had to man up pretty quickly. I'd say that really helped Roy a lot. In my case, Phil Harrington was the keeper at Cork City but got injured just before the start of the season and I played about six league matches. He was still injured when we played Torpedo Moscow, so I was lucky enough to play in a massive European game at just eighteen years of age. And that brought a bit of confidence. Going up to the course, you saw all the good players and you had to do a bit better. But the craic was unbelievable too. So it was really full-time training without the pressure of full-time training. And a lot of boys thrived on it. Maybe in England it would've been a harsher, harder regime, but we worked really hard and enjoyed it as well. There was a good bit of fun in it but we were still going back playing at the highest national level at the weekend.'

Cobh's early season form was alarming. Prior to the opening-day loss to Gorman and Finn Harps, the domestic campaign had started with three successive August defeats in Group A of the Opel League Cup. Away to Kilkenny City, where Keane made his competitive debut alongside Denis, they lost 2–0, but worse was to follow.

A few days later, Keane featured again as Cork City visited St Colman's Park for what proved a tempestuous local derby and where the eighteen-year-old was reminded of just how unforgiving an environment the League of Ireland was.

The fuse was lit shortly before half-time when City midfielder Mick Conroy, who'd already been booked, was involved in an incident with

Cobh's Ken O'Neill. Referee Pat Kelly decided against taking more action against the ex-Celtic player, and Cobh boss Alfie Hale stormed onto the field to remonstrate. He was subsequently sent to the stands, which fuelled the home side's sense of injustice.

With the interval approaching, Cobh's goalkeeper and assistant manager Alex Ludzic – whose mistake earlier in the half resulted in a debut City goal for Cormac Cotter – thumped the ball out of the ground in frustration after Kelly whistled for a City free kick. As Kelly reached for a yellow card, Ludzic unleashed a volley of abuse and was sent off instead. Trudging towards the dressing rooms, Ludzic whipped off his jersey and threw it at Kelly in disgust.

The story made the front page of the following day's *Cork Examiner*. 'Conroy's tackle was the nearest thing I have seen to physical assault in a football match,' an incensed Hale told reporters afterwards.[9] But, his protestations mattered little and he was handed a four-week dugout ban by the FAI.

By the middle of September, however, Hale had walked away. Based in Waterford and running his own business, the commitment and commute proved too much, so, after a 1–0 away defeat to Sligo Rovers, he stepped aside and Ludzic was promoted to player-coach.

Still, the miserable run continued. The evening before Cork played Mayo in the 1989 All-Ireland football final, Cobh were in the shadow of Croke Park themselves to face Home Farm. They lost 2–0. Keane, by that stage on the FÁS course for a fortnight and with only a handful of competitive league games under his belt, wasted little time in getting acquainted with the home side's goalkeeper, Aidan 'Jacko' Smith.

'We would've known about him because the FAI course was in its first year and was a big thing – full-time coaching for the best young lads in the country, including my two full-backs that night – Richie Purdy and Tommy Dunne,' Smith says. 'I came out to pick up a ball and Roy went for it and got a piece of me. There was no malice. It was basically the two of us colliding. It probably looked a lot more serious than it was. I got straight up and played on and we had a little laugh to each other. There was nothing in it. And, in fairness to Roy, you'd expect that. He never pulled out of a challenge and he wasn't going to start then. So maybe that was a sign of things to come. He was going to fight and get stuck in and take the chance he was given by Cobh to play first-team football. Because there weren't that many kids playing in the first teams. It was a tough, tough league. For an eighteen-year-old to play on a regular basis, he must have had something. You'd have had a lot of experience, a lot of tough heads. They'd have taken no prisoners. In those days, you grew up very quickly if you were a young fella and playing in the first team.'[10]

Despite Cobh's on-field issues, Keane rolled the sleeves up. But Cullimore found it hard to keep the spark going. Moving from the youth side to the first team seemed a bit underwhelming. The FÁS course was a full-time commitment. Then there were Cobh games at the weekend and some never-ending bus journeys to the deepest corners of the country.

'I found it kind of awkward,' he says. 'The First Division was a load of bollocks back then. Sometimes you were togging off in cow sheds, for God's sake. It was really poorly looked after. But Roy would shoot from the hip when he had to. And there was no love lost between him and Irish soccer. There was always that underlying problem with the FAI. He was ready to jump into the middle of things and get stuck in, and when it came to saying something he'd say it. But it was strange. You were up to Finn Harps, which was a six-hour drive. You were getting £30 a week. Your whole weekend was gone. You needed to have the love for it. My love for it was already waning but it didn't bother Roy – he was happy to go everywhere and anywhere with the team and it did him no harm.'

Keane's hard work was evidently paying off because he was handed another boost later in September and travelled to Orleans with the Republic of Ireland youth side for a friendly against France. He came on as a second-half substitute and, although the game ended in a 1–0 defeat, he was glad to be back in Maurice Setters' squad. With three Euro qualifiers scheduled between the end of October and November, the timing of his return was ideal.

On Halloween night, he made another impressive cameo. Coming off the bench with twenty-five minutes left, he set up a third goal for Kieron Brady as the Irish side breezed past Bulgaria at Dalymount Park. It was a 'spellbinding performance' from the hosts, according to *The Cork Examiner* and, with the team well-placed to reach the European Championships the following summer, Keane was right back in the mix.

However, there was some trouble ahead.

Keane was included in the Ireland squad for their trip to Malta in mid-November and, as a result, was excused from Cobh's league clash against Sligo Rovers. Understandably, there was a buzz around the club. Keane's involvement with his country and the prospect of him getting to play at a major underage tournament was an exciting prospect.

'It's a nice boost to have an international player in the club again,' admitted Liam McMahon, who had agreed to a second stint as Ramblers boss the previous month.[11]

Victory at the Hibernian Ground in Corradino would effectively secure qualification. But what added to an already-special atmosphere was the fact that the Republic of Ireland senior team were also in Malta for a crucial World Cup fixture. A win for them in Valletta the following afternoon would confirm their place at Italia '90. This meant that there was a capacity crowd of over 2,000 people watching the youth side, including Jack Charlton and his players. But there was little in the way of stage fright and the kids stuck to the script perfectly by easing to a 3–0 victory.

'Cork aces pave the way for Irish Youths' win' was the headline in the next day's *Cork Examiner* as Noel Spillane's match report detailed how the local 'double-act' of Paul McCarthy and Alan O'Sullivan both got on the scoresheet. At full-time, the jubilant players ran to the stands, whipped off their jerseys and threw them at fans.

But Keane cut a desolate figure. And for good reason. Again.

'There were seventeen players that went to Malta but only sixteen were in the match-day squad and Roy was the one left out,' recounts Tommy Dunne, who started the game. 'During the warm-up, I remember [Maurice] Setters telling him to go and get the balls behind the goal. Inside he must have been tearing himself apart. Of course you would've seen some of it, but he wouldn't have shown his absolute disappointment. When Setters asked him to do it, he just did it. He was disciplined. To be honest, I would've thought that incident and that situation would have made him even more determined and even stronger. You can go either way but he was of the mentality that he was going to play harder and work better. He would've knuckled down, trained and played.

'Of course he might have had it in his mind that he wasn't getting a chance, but the one thing about Roy was that when he did get his chance he took it. At the time he was playing really well for Cobh. We were training twice a day on the FÁS course and some of us were absolutely shattered by the end of the week. But it looked to me like Roy was getting stronger. He was ready. For a lot of people, when the opportunity arises, it's about being ready for it. And he was absolutely ready.'

Purdy, who was also in Malta, maintains Keane wasn't being victimised and that him being left out had more to do with the club he played for. 'It was just ridiculous,' he says, referring to Setters' ostracising of Keane. 'It wasn't personal, but I think that unless you were in England, you weren't deemed good enough by Maurice Setters. Myself, Tommy, John Connolly and Roy were the only League of Ireland players in the squad, but a lot of the lads who were in England were still playing youth football. I actually thought we were playing at a higher level, but we hadn't got Liverpool or

Chelsea beside our names, we had Home Farm and Hillcrest and Cobh instead. Roy didn't react to Setters, but you knew he was sick. I didn't get a run that day and Roy didn't even get stripped, so it summed up how much the League of Ireland players were struggling to get a look-in.'

Keane's snub also ensured that history repeated itself in more ways than one.

An interested spectator at the Hibernian Ground that afternoon was Ted Streeter, Brighton's youth development officer. And just like in Bilbao eighteen months earlier, he never got to see Roy Keane involved.

'I went over with Martin Hinshelwood [then Brighton's assistant manager] to watch and encourage Paul [McCarthy] and Derek [McGrath]. I'm absolutely certain that had I seen Roy play I would have at least invited him for a trial. He must have shown some talent at that time. But when you think that neither the Under–16s manager or Under–18s manager fancied him or played him, you wonder what's going on, don't you? Had I seen him – on either occasion – I'm sure I would have recognised talent. And I'm only sorry that I didn't get the chance.'[12]

For all his mental maturity, Keane wasn't above letting his emotions spill over. He had plenty of time to dwell on his latest international humiliation. The unique circumstances of the trip ensured a prolonged stay for the youth squad and when Charlton's senior team made history by booking their place at a World Cup for the first time, there was an inevitable knees-up afterwards. The drinks flowed, the sing-songs started, but Keane was in no mood to celebrate. Tightly wound for over twenty-four hours, the elastic finally snapped.

'We were all having one or two beers with the senior team,' Purdy recalls. 'Roy was pissed off and had had a few drinks. He had a bit of a tongue on him with a few beers, but this was worse because he was pissed off and scooped. Packie [Bonner] was walking past with Mick [McCarthy] and he was always nice and would say hello to us. But Roy slaughtered him.

In that Cork accent, he said something like "You're a shit keeper and only for Gerry Peyton being shit as well, you wouldn't be playing." Packie was looking at him because we all had our tracksuits on, but he just laughed it off. That's what Roy did. He said what he felt. Sometimes I think he should've kept it down a bit.'

Dunne describes the experience in Malta as strange: 'We won our game easily enough and ended up at this function for the senior players. It didn't surprise me when Roy was getting stuck in. When we'd have a few drinks he was quite wild. It was no holds barred. He'd get stuck in from all angles. He was fairly opinionated on the game and he was really, really witty – especially with the one-liners.'

On the FÁS course, players would usually finish up training in late afternoon, head for their digs and relax for the night. But on Thursday evenings, some of the group would meet up, sometimes in Palmerstown but usually in Lucan. A few games of snooker, a few pints and then maybe the disco in the Spa Hotel. So when Dunne, Purdy and Keane all returned from Malta on a Thursday, word quickly got around about Keane's party trick.

'We were all saying, "Jesus Christ, Roy – what were you thinking?"' Gorman says. 'But we also thought it was fucking hilarious. We got some laugh out of it. As a senior Irish player you probably wouldn't even remember some eighteen-year-old. But if he was saying you were shite, you might. Tommy was saying, "He can't even get in the squad of sixteen and he's slaughtering these boys with fifty and sixty caps and telling them they're fucking useless."'

Keane was known for his withering put-downs, particularly of those who weren't used to being on the receiving end. To his mates, it was funny. To others, less so.

'There was a lad from the league that came in on a Friday with our cheques, a nice man involved with Sligo Rovers called Tommy Mullen,'

Gorman says. 'He was always bemoaning Sligo's hard luck. I was talking to him one day and I said, "Well Tommy, no luck last weekend?" And he says to me, "Aye Tony, we were fucking robbed." So Roy pipes up and says, "Don't worry, Tommy. If you've got insurance, I'm sure it'll cover you." And I remember Tommy going ballistic over this cheeky pup. It was one of the main men from the league who you were supposed to be nice to. But Roy didn't give a monkey's.'

'He could be cutting and not very nice,' Larry Mahony says. 'I had a name for him. I'd say, "Here's Mr Charisma in now."'

Occasionally on the FÁS course, the general topic of Irish underage football cropped up, usually following a squad announcement. Gorman remembers one lunchtime when Joe McGrath, such a prominent youth coach and influential figure within the FAI, was present and Keane offered his thoughts on some recent selections.

'Roy always fought the case for the Cork lads,' Gorman says. 'He was on about how Damien Martin and Eric Hogan from Rockmount should've been in the Ireland squad. He was saying the only reason another player was selected instead of Eric was because they were from Dublin. Now, it was never about Roy. He never said he should be picked. We all probably knew that's what he was angling at, but he never brought it up. It was other players he was mentioning. I suppose the other boys around the Ireland squad at the time – like Tommy or Richie – would be saying he should be in the team but Roy didn't bring himself into it.

'What was really interesting was that Roy and Eric Hogan never spoke. Eric was a good lad and I got to know him well because we went on trial together at Derby County afterwards. But him and Roy fell out and they used to walk to Rockmount games on the opposite sides of the road, purposely ignoring each other. On the pitch there was obviously that professionalism because the team was excellent. But I found it so interesting that Roy didn't speak to him and here he was in Palmerstown still saying

Eric should be picked for the Ireland team. I think it was Lenny Downey telling us afterwards, "He wants Eric in the squad and he doesn't even speak to him – they can't stand each other.'"

The falling out with Hogan, generously described by Keane in *The Second Half* as having lasted for a year, was inevitably juvenile. 'He wouldn't go training one night because he got a new skateboard,' Keane told his ghostwriter, Roddy Doyle. 'I fell out with him. "Stick your fuckin' skateboard."'[13]

It didn't exactly shock the rest of the FÁS group that Keane was voicing his displeasure. His opinion about underage squads wasn't outlandish and many of the players agreed with him. Still, to outline his concerns so strongly to McGrath seemed unnecessarily risky.

'It's something I would never have done,' Gorman admits. 'I remember coming down from Donegal and going for Ireland trials and not getting picked and thinking you were as good as those who had made the squad. So you could definitely see where Roy was coming from. But at the end of the day, the city boys – like Roy – played at a higher level than us. Getting picked for Ireland was unbelievable in my eyes and I was just so grateful to get the opportunity. Never in a million years would I question a manager or a coach regarding the merits of why I should get picked or not. I'd be grateful to be there and bust my balls to get in the team.

'But I don't think any of us were surprised when these discussions were taking place because what Roy was saying was all true. And he was having the balls to say it at eighteen years of age, basically calling out the international manager for only picking players based on where they were from. When he was talking – and he was always very honest and open – he could have been cutting people in two with his tongue. But he was saying what the rest of us probably wanted to.'

'I liked that about him,' Purdy says. 'He didn't sit on the fence. He didn't go behind your back and say things. He was very straightforward. If he had an issue with you, he'd say it. He had a great desire to stick up for everyone, especially the Cork lads. But I thought it was a bit anti-Dublin as well. Unless you were an exceptionally talented player from the country, you were just up against it [to get spotted]. He did have a little bit of a chip on his shoulder because he hadn't been picked a few times.'

Keane was forthright, opinionated and prickly but, according to Mahony, never driven by ego. 'It wouldn't have been the macro picture that Roy was thinking about,' he says. 'He would've been thinking about himself. "I'm not getting a chance." But I would never have thought of him as arrogant. It would be more like a display of strength around other people. And it all went into the mix so he could be this guy who could step up and not be fazed. Confident and single-minded. I admire him because he's a no-bullshit type of fella. He was able to see through it. He didn't buy into all this stupidity that goes around the game and was clear-headed enough like that. But I don't see him as being this complex individual. I see him as being very clear-minded and simple in his approach. What suits Roy Keane, what doesn't suit Roy Keane. That's the impression I had of him. Steely in his determination to succeed. I don't see where the complexity is. I don't see Roy being a deep type of fella.'

Keane wasn't on the FÁS course to make friends. He was there to work. It was a means to an end. Something to prepare him for when the opportunity finally presented itself. And he didn't have long to wait.

3

NEVER TOO LATE

In Palmerstown, there was a group of excellent young athletes – some of the best footballers in the country – and so it was an ultra-competitive environment. During games, players battled hard. If levels dropped, you'd know about it. And the loudest voice was usually a Cork one. There were the usual scrapes – plenty of verbals, some pushing and shoving, but nothing too extreme. Occasionally, there was some simmering tension.

'The Cork–Dublin rivalry,' John Donegan remembers. 'We wouldn't be slow to let them know they weren't from the real capital. There was good craic between us but when you did go back to your club and you played any of the boys, you wouldn't spare them – especially if you won.'

'It was always bubbling under the surface,' Jamie Cullimore says. 'The majority of big Irish clubs are based in Dublin so the majority of players are from Dublin. But it didn't bother Roy. He'd love that challenge of taking on the Dubs and sticking it in their face. He lived for that. Proving people wrong. From an early age, he was told he'd never make it because of this or that. He was getting it all through his life. But the bigger the challenge, the more he was willing to stand up and take it. That was the type of character he was.'

During one particularly sodden afternoon session, the Cork–Dublin subplot reached a pretty memorable conclusion.

'It was pissing rain,' Tony Gorman says. 'There was a mini-game going on and it was really competitive. I think Roy caught [Bray Wanderers']

Richie Parsons and there'd already been some verbals between them. Richie either shoved him back or smacked him, but then there were two or three of the quickest punches you'll ever see and Richie was on the ground. The next thing was Maurice [Price] had Roy in a headlock and he was trying to make light of it. Roy was laughing at this stage because Maurice was on top of him and had his face planted in the mud. He was saying to him, "Roy, don't fuck with The Blondie Savage" – that's what he called himself. But poor Richie. It could have been any of us, to tell you the truth. He'd taken a wee combination at that stage. It was pretty impressive to watch. If Roy had taken the boxing path instead of the football, he could have been a great in the ring too.'

Quite a few of the players were impressed by Keane's display of pugilistic expertise.

'He was like Rocky Marciano throwing the digs,' Richie Purdy says. 'It was unbelievable. He had quick hands. They always had a little row, Roy and Richie. The usual handbags. But Roy gave him about three or four digs in the space of a second. Now, Richie was a strong lad as well, but he was on the deck straightaway.'

Keane could be difficult, challenging and acid-tongued but, for the most part, players on the course respected his outlook. He was tough but fair. And consistent. Also, he was loyal to the concept of team etiquette and having the backs of those around him, regardless of any off-field needling.

'We played against a local side one day and I either called a ball and didn't get it or I should have called it and didn't,' Donegan says. 'But I certainly knew about it. We had a good aul' roaring match, the two of us. He wouldn't back down, I wouldn't back down. If it was your job, you had to do it – that was his point. He'd drive you on like that. But on the other side, if anything happened you, he was there immediately. However hard he'd be *on* you, he'd be twice as hard *with* you.'

'I was twice the width of him and probably had a few stone on him, but

I remember him sticking up for me on and off the pitch,' Cullimore says. 'Sometimes I'd look at him and say, "Jesus, Roy, you don't have to do that," but that was him. If somebody got at his friend, he was willing to stand up for him there and then, whether it was necessary or not. I remember a game we played one day in Palmerstown and a Dublin fella kicked me around and I just went away limping. But Roy went up to him and grabbed him by the throat and said, "The cheek of ya." He was looking after his Cork buddy against the Dublin boys who we always thought were looking down on us – "the culchies". It was in his DNA to look after people and stand up for them and be that captain character.'

But as much as Keane would always be ready to jump in and support his teammates, his coaches never saw him as a dynamic leader or motivator.

'I don't remember him ever radiating influence on the pitch,' says Larry Mahony, who was overseeing the sessions every day along with Maurice Price. 'My memory is of him getting on with his own job and doing it really, really well. Tony Gorman would've been the fella to get the lads going, but I can't remember Roy doing that. I have no recollection of Roy motivating others in the group. He would let someone know if they hadn't done their job but is that motivation? It could've been de-motivating, depending on the player. And back in those days, our appreciation of that would've been a lot weaker. He definitely held sway in the group. It would be a bit strong to say he was manipulative but he had a hold over fellas. He could influence people and was strong enough to do that. He seemed to be at the centre of things all the time.'

Despite boasting a solid dynamic with the rest of the group, Keane did not have the easiest of relationships with Joe McGrath. It didn't help that Keane was staying with the McGrath family in Leixlip and that this arrangement proved unsustainable. Dunne remembers an irritated Keane complaining about how he wasn't getting fed enough and it just seemed a bad fit for all parties. Alternative lodgings were quickly sought and arranged, and Keane left. It was Gorman and another Harps player, Damien Dunleavy, who moved in after him.

'Roy stayed with Joe briefly but they fell out,' Gorman says. 'I think there was a wee bit of tension between the two of them and it wouldn't have been a great environment for both of them.'

Given their history, Purdy felt it was a curious idea to have McGrath as Keane's landlord in the first place and that things were destined to boil over eventually. 'I don't think it was a very clever thing to do,' he says. 'Roy was a bit of a hot-head and Joe hadn't picked him for a few squads so there was always going to be a bit of friction there. I don't remember them having a go at each other on the course but I do remember Roy saying he wasn't happy at Joe's.'

But there are different recollections of the same story.

'It wasn't football-related,' says Larry Mahony, suggesting a personality clash rather than something more malicious. 'I don't know if it was a chicken or egg situation. But the fact that Roy stayed with Joe would suggest to me that there wasn't a tension there beforehand. As far as I know, he wasn't an ideal lodger. And in terms of not being fed enough, I remember a specific moment where it was the opposite and he was turning down food. He wasn't taking what he was being given.'

'My boss, Anne O'Brien, was from Cork and she actually took Lenny Downey as a lodger,' remembers Brian Brophy, who was Brighton's scout in Ireland and instrumental in McGrath's son, Derek, signing for the club. 'Joe took Roy in himself but, after a few months, he came down to me one day and said, "Could your boss take another one?" He said that his wife, Florrie, had told him, "Either Roy goes or you go." And after that, Roy went into digs with Anne.'

Keane had been envious of other players' living arrangements, particularly Donegan, who was staying with future Ireland international Jeff Kenna's family. 'He came into my digs one day,' he says. 'I was staying in one of the girl's rooms and there was a picture of Kylie Minogue on the wall. And Roy was thrilled by that because he was mad about Kylie. "Look at you sleeping with Kylie every night."'

Keane didn't enjoy Dublin and missed his home comforts. But it was a good group with plenty of camaraderie.

'On a Friday, we'd get our FÁS cheques and go up to Palmerstown village to cash them,' Purdy remembers. 'I think it was about twenty-five or thirty quid. We'd have a half-day because so many of the boys had to get trains or buses back home, so we'd get a pint or two before they'd head off, usually in the Palmerstown House. One day, I lost all my cash somewhere between Stewarts Hospital and the pub and I was sick. But Roy got me two drinks. I'll never forget it. "No worries, Richie – I'll get you a pint" and he actually got me two. It was class. We were friends on the course but he was a Cork lad, I was a Dublin lad. He kind of stuck to his own and I stuck to the likes of Tommy and some of the other Dubs. But he was the only one who said he'd get me a drink. I was sick at losing the money and it was such a nice gesture from him.'

There was a positive mood, in spite of the edge to all of it. Twenty players – many who played the same positions – were chasing the same goal: a move to England. A handful had already been there and were unceremoniously chewed up and spat out. This was their physical and emotional rehabilitation. 'A second chance,' as Gorman puts it.

Ability-wise, Keane offered plenty, but so did every player on the course. The common consensus was that he wasn't the best one there.

'There was a friend of Larry Mahony's – a well-known ex-footballer called Ben Hannigan – who used to come down to Stewarts Hospital and watch the training,' Dunne says, already chuckling at the memory. 'And Ben got in one day for a game. He was on Roy's team, up front and would always be commenting on everything. So, during the game, Roy slips a ball through for Ben to run onto. And Ben shouts, "Give it to me feet."

The next one, Roy picks it up and knocks another great pass through for Ben. And he shouts at Roy again, "For fuck's sake – into me feet!" And then Ben turns around to me and says, "That young fella has no chance of making it."'

'Tony Gorman was the best player on the course by a mile,' says Purdy. 'When we finished up, I still thought he was the best player. When the course had started, I wouldn't even have put Roy in the top three or four and I'd say Roy would agree with that too. But over the last few months, he really seemed to get stronger and fitter. I always remember that his passing was unbelievable. The pace he'd get was something else because he'd always side-foot the ball but he would even do it from twenty yards. He didn't have to drive it. He just had such a lovely strike of a ball.'

'As a player, Roy was neat,' remembers Mahony. 'I wouldn't have thought he was the outstanding prospect on the course. I'd have said Tony Gorman and Pat Fenlon, while Lee King looked very promising at one point too. But over a period of time you could see he would do anything you asked him and was able to do anything you asked him. But the important quality he had was an ability to step up. And that's innate. When we played friendly games, which were very intense, he was never fazed by them. Roy was Roy. He was steady, consistent and could always step into the next level. Each time he made that step, he was the same fella.

'The late Charlie Walker, the former St Pat's manager, was running a course somewhere and we played a game against his lads. Roy was asked to play at right-back and that match always sticks out because he was just so at ease. It took absolutely nothing out of him. And I don't know whether he had any experience of playing there beforehand. He was very, very good at what he did. He was able to simplify his game. He didn't complicate it.

'And the matches were tough. We played Maurice Setters' youth team and Joe [McGrath] said to us beforehand, "Look, no kicking – they're heading off to play in a tournament." And when the first ball came to one of our centre-backs, Lee Power came across and hit him late. It was an awful challenge. And this was after Joe warned us not to be too physical with them. So it turned into a free-for-all. And my memory is that Setters took his players off the pitch and the game didn't finish.'

As Cobh's season headed towards the midway point, Keane was beginning to make an impact. After returning from the dispiriting Malta trip, he gave a standout performance in a return clash with Gorman's Finn Harps at St Colman's Park towards the end of November. He even scored his first goal for the club in a 3–0 win.

'It was a cracker,' Gorman remembers. 'The ball was rolled across the eighteen-yard line, he came onto it and bent one in at the near post.'

'The execution of the goal by young Keane was perfection itself,' commented Spillane in the following day's *Cork Examiner*, adding it was 'another impeccable match from the midfielder'.[1] Spillane also described Keane, perhaps somewhat oddly given his latest omission, as an 'Irish youths star'. But it turned out to be a prescient statement.

At the end of November, the Irish youths had their final Euro qualifier away to Bulgaria. Because of a far superior goal difference, the home side required a comprehensive win. And owing to a spate of withdrawals, Keane was handed a very first start alongside his FÁS course cohorts Dunne and Purdy.

Conditions in Blagoevgrad, a small city 100 kilometres south of Sofia and close to the Macedonian border, were extreme. There were four inches of snow on the ground when the team touched down in the capital and when they got to the venue, the pitch was rutted and frozen.

Derek McGrath was sent off after half an hour, which contributed to some nervous anxiety, but Keane was magnificent throughout. Bulgaria only managed to find the net once and the Irish were through.

'It reminded me a bit of when he played against Juventus in the

Champions League semi-final in 1999,' says Purdy, who scored an unfortunate own goal that afternoon. 'It was like that for Roy against Bulgaria. The pitch suited him, he was winning tackles. And he just got better and better. He was a different class.'

'He could run forever and he was really athletic,' Dunne adds. 'He'd taken a stretch at that stage and as a midfielder he was very dynamic. He played really, really well. We were down to ten men early on. Really difficult conditions. And he was very, very good.'

After returning home, Keane was straight back to Cobh for a league encounter with Kilkenny City that proved memorable for all the wrong reasons. On a bitterly cold Sunday afternoon on 3 December, the home side were 2–0 up after an hour and seemingly coasting. At the time, Price – Keane's coach on the FÁS course – was also in charge of Kilkenny, alongside player/manager Eamonn Gregg. During the first half, Price had been warned about his verbal abuse of the linesman. Shortly after the restart, Price was banished to the dressing-room after another tirade.

'The whole scenario tarnished the image of the game that the League of Ireland are trying to portray and football can certainly do without this type of behaviour,' wrote Spillane in his *Cork Examiner* match report the following day.[2]

So there was plenty of ammunition for Keane at the next day's session back in Palmerstown, especially considering Kilkenny staged a remarkable comeback once Price was dismissed and ended up winning 3–2 thanks to an eighty-seventh-minute winner.

The season was a slog and results continued to be mixed under McMahon, but over the festive period particularly, Keane was involved in some enjoyable battles for Cobh. On Christmas Eve, in a Munster Senior Cup semi-final at Turner's Cross, he had the strange experience of playing against long-time teammate Len Downey, who had waited patiently to make his first-team debut for Cork City. And the centre-forward left an impression too, setting up John Caulfield with a flick-on for what proved the game winner.

Just two days later, Keane was excellent in a family affair away to Longford Town. He set up Denis for an equalising header and saw his own effort crash back off the crossbar early in the second half. With the game level at 2–2 late on, his slaloming run took him past a handful of challenges but his shot rolled agonisingly wide. Afterwards, the Town management said Ramblers had played some of the best football they'd seen at Abbeycartron all season. A rare jolt of positivity in an otherwise languid season, though Keane's emergence was a simmering subplot too.

'We came off after a game and I remember Liam McMahon saying, "That boy is going to be worth millions some day,"' Cullimore says. 'You could see there was something there. Everyone could see. He was tenacious, he was cute, great in the air, great touch. He wasn't super technically gifted but he had enough fight.'

Despite the general turbulence, Cobh confirmed their First Division status early in January 1990 and Keane continued to impress. In horrible conditions at home to Sligo, and while facing the likes of ex-Northern Ireland international Billy Hamilton and a combative trio of Dermot Keely, Gavin Dykes and Declan Bonner – brother of his old friend Packie – it was Keane who stood out and he really should have scored in the 0–0 stalemate. But again, just like in Longford, he failed to hit the target after racing through on goal.

Because Keane still qualified to play at underage level, it meant he was eligible for the national youth cup competition. Come the end of January, the Ramblers' team had reached the quarter-finals and were drawn to face high-profile Dublin outfit Belvedere at home.

Given the magnitude of the fixture, manager Eddie O'Rourke asked Keane to play. So, he took the train home from Dublin on Friday evening and the following day headed for St Colman's Park and the 2.30 kick-off.

The game was one of very few fixtures to go ahead in Cork that weekend. With the exception of four Munster Senior League games, everything else – at senior, junior, youth and schoolboy levels – was postponed as north-western Europe, but particularly the UK, was battered by violent weather during the latter part of the week. Later christened the Burns Day Storm, there were countless fatalities, including children. In Ireland, three men lost their lives while many others suffered injuries as Cork Harbour experienced gales of over 100kph. Thousands of homes were left without electricity and travel was heavily disrupted.

But by Saturday morning, the worst had passed, so the Belvedere youth side hopped on at Heuston Station and began their trek to Cobh.

'It was always seen as that bit of folklore at Belvedere – the goal that made Roy Keane,' Graham Brereton, part of the Dubliners' side that day, begins. 'We knew of him because a few of our players would've been junior internationals, so the name was known but not overly. The game was very competitive and Roy actually scored a great header that day that was reminiscent of his whole career – arriving late into the box, excellent finish, big moment.'[3]

But Cobh couldn't see the game out and it was Brereton, fortuitously, who made them pay.

'I played at full-back and there was about ten or fifteen minutes left,' Brereton says. 'There was a throw-in about halfway into Cobh territory. I threw it to our right-winger, he knocked it back to me and I whipped the ball in. Our centre-forward, a tall lad by the name of Gary Kyle, went up with their goalkeeper and I thought he'd flicked it in so I went over to celebrate with him but he was telling me I'd scored. My goal – the one that "made" Roy – it was a cross, to be totally honest. So it finished 1–1 and we got them back to Fairview Park for the replay.'

There was little time for Keane to dwell on the irritation of a missed opportunity. The following day, Cobh's senior team made the exhaustive trip to Donegal to face Finn Harps.

'The plan was for him to drive up and join the first team afterwards,' according to McMahon. 'We hit the midlands, were engulfed in heavy snow and I remember thinking: "That's the end of Roy's chances." The players were long gone to bed, it was about half-one in the morning and let's just say I was in the vicinity of the bar when the door to the hotel opened and in walked Roy. He just asked where his room was and went straight to bed.'[4]

Two matches in forty-eight hours, one a crucial youth cup fixture and the other a typical League of Ireland war of attrition. Added to that, at least a three-hour train commute from Dublin to Cork on the Friday evening and a six-hour drive to Ballybofey on Saturday evening. From there, about four hours to get back to the FÁS course in Palmerstown on Monday morning. The majority of players looked at Keane's stamina with amazement. It was like he couldn't get enough.

'We'd train twice a day and the majority of us were still only seventeen and eighteen,' Purdy says. 'We'd have matches after a hard day's work. You'd just want to lay the ball off and take it easy because your legs were like jelly. But Roy was still ploughing into people. He still had the pace and energy. And you were actually getting thick with him because you were tired and he was still crunching in. I thought the idea [of the course] was right, but the training was too much. At the weekend, we were legless playing for our clubs. I was at Home Farm under Ray Treacy at the time and, in fairness to him, I wouldn't have to go training on a Tuesday but had to do Thursday nights and then play a game on the Sunday. And I wasn't playing particularly well. I enjoyed the course so much and was putting so much effort into it that I was struggling to perform for my own team.'

While Keane had repeatedly criticised Dublin-based players for having an advantage over everyone else, that wasn't the case on the FÁS course. There, it seemed they carried a slightly heavier burden.

'The course was physically hard on the players and there was very little leeway in terms of the load we put on them and the load their clubs put on them,' says Larry Mahony. 'But that wouldn't have affected Roy because he wasn't going back to Cobh to train during the week. And I do remember friction between the Dublin players, who were working their socks off with us during the day and then having to go training with their clubs at night. A few of them were knackered and there were many instances of that happening. Looking back, the course wasn't planned as well as it could have been. But when everyone else was falling away, Roy stood out. When everyone else started to flag, their interest went a bit, they lost some motivation and dropped their work rate, Roy never did.'

In fact, Keane did make a point of attending one club session per week. After the three-hour train commute from Dublin, he'd grab a quick bite to eat in Mayfield before heading straight out the door again.

'Roy would train with us on a Friday night and I'd pick him up at Silversprings Hotel en route,' says former teammate Fergus McDaid. 'The usual brief chat would ensue as to how things went for him during the week in Dublin and there was the usual small talk. But, to be fair, this was a tricky conversation between a teenager and a thirty-plus schoolteacher so it wasn't exactly an ideal scenario.'

In his next club outing, Keane got the better of both Purdy and Dunne as Cobh managed a 1–0 home win over Home Farm. The following weekend, there was a forgettable 3–1 loss to Waterford United and the league campaign was limping to a sorry conclusion. McMahon was already turning his attention to an FAI Cup tie with Monaghan United in March, while also looking ahead to the following season and trying to make 'a real challenge' for promotion. So, even though Keane had to miss a league fixture with Bray Wanderers on 18 February because of the youth cup replay, it offered some respite from the mundane. It was a chance of making a national semi-final and getting one over on a well-regarded elite Dublin side in their own backyard.

However, things started badly and rapidly got worse. Though there was a small accident on the way up to Fairview Park ('a tip with a car', is how Cullimore describes it), what seemed to properly delay the Cobh squad was the bus driver's lack of local geography once he entered Dublin city centre.

'We were driving all over the place looking for the ground,' says Ken O'Rourke, who was part of the Ramblers' team that day.

This tallies with Keane's own memories, who recounted in his autobiography that the Cobh team arrived with 'only minutes to spare', describing the entire episode as 'a fucking cock-up, Mickey fucking Mouse'.[5]

For Cobh, the game proved somewhat similar.

'We absolutely destroyed them, annihilated them,' Graham Brereton says. 'I don't know if it was 4–0 at half-time or something like that, but it could have been. I remember being very surprised at how easy it was because they had probably deserved to win the first game down in Cobh. Maybe it was because they had to step off a bus and come straight onto a pitch. Maybe that was the problem. But we weren't aware of it.'

As usual, Brereton's father was watching from the sideline that afternoon when a friend arrived on his bike.

'My dad knew Noel McCabe, the Nottingham Forest scout, very well. They were chatting and my dad was actually pointing out Keane to him because the story goes that Noel had actually turned up to look at another player – Cobh's left-winger. But I was right-back and I didn't give him a sniff that day.'

Cobh's left-winger was Jamie Cullimore.

'Before the game, a Ramblers committee member came over and said, "Forest are over here to look at you" and, to be honest, I shat myself and had a poor game,' he says. 'I don't know if Roy knew Noel McCabe was there, but I'm not sure it would've bothered him. That's the type of character he was. And you'd nearly have given him Man of the Match again even though we were thumped 4–0. There was just something special and people were starting to sit up and notice.'

At half-time, McCabe approached the Cobh chairman, John O'Rourke, and asked about 'the number 10'. It was Keane.

Regarding his performance that day, recollections vary. It had been so easy for Belvedere and they dominated all over the pitch. But to some, as Brereton quickly found out, Keane had stood out right from kick-off.

'There was a pub across the road from Fairview Park called Meaghers and any team from the country that would come up, we'd always go there with them after the game,' he says. 'We were buzzing. A 4–0 cup win and on to the semi-finals. Our two midfielders were Liam Dunne and Pat Curran, both smashing players. But my dad said to us, "That guy in the middle, Roy Keane, he's some player." And we were all like, "What? Sure, he did nothing." But when you're on the sideline, you see a lot more than when you're in the thick of the action.

'He certainly wouldn't have come into our minds as being special. I felt our players were just as good. He played well but you weren't asking, "When is this player going over to England?" But back then, you could see how competitive he was. My dad tried to talk to him in the pub and just tell him he'd had a great game and to keep going, but he got the impression Roy didn't want to be spoken to and didn't want people annoying him. He just wasn't very talkative.

'When you look at it, after beating Cobh 4–0, how come our players weren't picked up that day as well? Noel McCabe was looking at the Cobh winger and I didn't give him a kick, so why didn't I get a shout, y'know? But that's a scout's job. Football can be a bit of luck, can't it? Right place, right time.'

But McCabe wasn't the only influential figure there that day. The feeling at the time was that young talent didn't get spotted unless they played at Fairview Park or Albert College and, given the fixture was a national cup quarter-final with some well-regarded players on show, there were plenty of magpie eyes hungry for the prize.

'There was every kind of scout there that day, including Boy Scouts,' Eddie O'Rourke recalled years afterwards. 'I will always wonder what the others were watching.'[6]

'Noel McCabe is the luckiest man in Ireland that the replay went to Dublin,' O'Rourke later told *The Independent*. 'Scouts here are lazy – they think Ireland means Dublin. I'm not saying Roy wouldn't have risen, mind, because he was very good.'[7]

McCabe's scouting report provides a fascinating insight. It indicates that Keane's overall profile was what caught the eye, not anything specific. Certain phrases jump off the page: 'finding players', 'involved in all activities' and 'progressive with his tackling'. There are additional references to him taking responsibility on the ball and McCabe doesn't express a single concern about his size. In fact, he singles out Keane's physical conditioning for praise, describing a 'broad upper body'. But it's the last line that draws the most attention and reflects the immediate impact Keane had on McCabe that Sunday afternoon: 'In my opinion, a player to go on trial with Forest. Right away.'[8]

Keane was made aware of McCabe's interest immediately after the game. Years later, he claimed he wasn't particularly excited by the news, the collapsed Brighton trial from a few years prior giving him reason to be sceptical. But he did seem buoyed when he met Tony Gorman later that night.

'Finn Harps played Waterford United on the Sunday so we stayed in Dublin,' Gorman says. 'There were a couple of us that met up and Roy was there. I remember sitting down and him saying, "You won't believe this but we got beaten 4–0 and I didn't even play that well but some lad asked me to go to Nottingham Forest for a trial afterwards." He was surprised because they were beaten and in his eyes he didn't play well. But obviously he'd kept going for ninety minutes and there was that never-say-die attitude. I had come back from Mansfield the previous year and I would've known a lot of the Forest boys. So I told him about some of the players and the likes of Liam O'Kane and Archie Gemmill who were coaching. It was a wee bit of a heads-up for him. Just going through the playing squad, where Forest trained, that type of stuff.'

Later, McCabe met with Keane at the Aisling Hotel, across the quay from Heuston Station, to formalise arrangements for a trial.

'Immediately I was impressed by his attitude,' McCabe said years later. 'He gave me the impression that he'd nearly swim over to England to become a footballer.'[9]

Dovetailing with the development of a Forest trial and an opportunity he had craved for so long was some more recognition of his progress. In late February, Keane was honoured, along with twelve other young athletes, at The Munster Youth Sports Awards, an annual shindig sponsored by *The Cork Examiner* and held at the Imperial Hotel.

A different kind of team group photo made the paper the following day. In the front row, seated next to his mother, Marie, is Keane, all suave and slick in a tuxedo, the almost-rockabilly haircut carefully moulded and finessed. Directly behind him are two beaming faces: his father, Mossie, and his uncle, Pat Lynch. Other award-winners that evening offer up big grins for the camera, but while Keane doesn't appear glum, he's certainly disinterested. He stares right down the barrel of the lens. Emotionless.

Outside of Bishop John Buckley, the guest of honour that night was Tipperary hurling icon Nicky English. His speech was curious and compelling, devoid of the usual platitudes. He told the award-winners that being acknowledged as the best was something to be proud of, but that it dictated what came next for them too.

'It creates its own pressure and responsibility,' he said. 'People like to knock those who have been chosen as the best. And, you will soon realise that your performances will have to keep improving if you want to stay the best. That should always be your ambition and if you remain committed, your performances will improve.'[10]

It was a reminder to Keane that despite the glad rags and the accolades, he'd achieved nothing yet and the real work was still ahead.

**

By early March, the pending trial was noted in the local Cork press. As usual for a Saturday edition, the back pages of *The Cork Examiner* were dominated by cross-channel previews – how Arsenal's away form needed to improve if they wished to retain the First Division title and Alex Ferguson's defiance ahead of Manchester United's relegation battle against Luton ('We'll fight like tigers to stay up'). Buried in a sidebar, the paper revealed that Keane was heading to Nottingham: 'Roy Keane of Cobh Ramblers is on his way to Nottingham Forest for a week's trial, which could result in a full-time professional career for the talented midfield player,' wrote Mark Woods.[11]

But due to commitments with Cobh, it wasn't until later in the month that Keane made the trip. He played in Ramblers' final league match of the season – a 3–0 win over Newcastle West – and appeared in the following week's FAI Cup clash with Monaghan too, where Cullimore came off the bench to grab a late winner and book a home tie with non-league St Francis in the next round.

Cobh's manager, Liam McMahon, was agitated that the First Division season was already completed and complained that the cup was heavily geared towards top-tier teams because of their six weeks of extra league action. Instead of games coming thick and fast, Cobh were now left trying to arrange weekend friendlies to keep players on their toes. More importantly, they were also losing out on income while still having to pay their squad.

While a decent run in the cup was always an aspiration, it seemed to carry a greater importance this time around. And despite St Francis having got the better of Kilkenny City in the first round, they were still a Leinster Senior League outfit and Cobh fancied their chances of reaching the quarter-finals.

Keane began his week-long trial in Nottingham on 19 March and Forest wanted him to prolong his stay so that he'd feature in a youth game against Port Vale that weekend. But Ramblers dug their heels in and ordered him back to Cork. Under the headline of 'Cobh in SOS to Clough', the *Irish Independent* described the situation as a 'tug o' war'.

'Roy is a professional player with Cobh,' McMahon said at the time. 'I'm sure he appreciates his commitments to the club ... and we have told Forest that there is no way that they can hold onto him. It's not the end of the world for Roy. At eighteen, there will be other opportunities; and Forest may well come back to him in the near future.'[12]

Forest did what they were told, and the whole affair wasn't much of a distraction for Keane, who returned to score Cobh's opener at St Colman's Park. But they squandered a 2–0 lead and the plucky underdogs forced a replay. A few days later, at John Hyland Park in Baldonnell – about a fifteen-minute drive from where he usually spent his Thursdays in Palmerstown – Cobh and Keane were embarrassingly dumped out of the competition by the non-leaguers after a comprehensive 3–0 defeat. Remarkably, St Francis went on to reach the Lansdowne Road decider that season, becoming the very first amateur side to do so, but were well beaten by Bray Wanderers.

With his club season over but a move to Forest still very much a possibility, Keane needed games, but they were hard to come by. At the end of the month, he remained in the capital to turn out for the Munster Senior League youth side – along with fellow FÁS players Cullimore and Downey – in a national tournament semi-final against Dublin Schoolboys in Ballyfermot. Trailing 1–0 at the break, Keane was denied a magnificent volleyed equaliser by a goal-line clearance and the team failed to force a replay.

It was mid-April when Forest asked him to return. But Keane had been irked by the previous trip.

'No one seemed to take any notice of me,' he said later. 'I was training with the youth team, then the next thing I was back on the plane. But the coach, Archie Gemmill, apparently said he had seen enough to offer me another trial.'[13] Tony Gorman had mentioned names like Forest coach Liam O'Kane to him. He'd gone through the entire playing staff for both the first team and reserves with him. But Keane had met none of them.

On this second occasion, however, things were different. After a couple of days training, he was selected for a Midlands Senior League game against Tranmere. O'Kane and Forest's chief scout, Alan Hill, turned up to watch him.

'He played in midfield, broke forward, had some shots at goal, headed the ball, stuck his foot in a bit and we thought, "This lad has got something,"' Hill said, recounting the memory years later.[14]

Scot Gemmill, the son of Forest coach Archie, was another witness and recalled Keane's trial period years later. 'I played in the game when Roy came over from Ireland: Scarborough away in a trial game,' he said. 'Roy and I were in midfield. Roy asked to play on the right and I wouldn't let him. Even as a young player he was very demanding, very quick to let you know if standards weren't being reached.'[15]

Keane was back in Cork as the Cobh Ramblers youth side looked to get over their national cup exit at the hands of Belvedere and pick up some local silverware in an MSL League Cup final against St Mary's at Turner's Cross on 13 April. Inevitably, he played a key role. With Cobh 2–0 down, Cullimore pulled one back before sending in a free kick shortly after the restart that Keane headed home. With four minutes to go, Keane turned provider, sending Cullimore through to complete t[...] Darren Fenton added a fourth to ensure a Cobh vict[...]

The match report was carried on page twenty-one [...] *Cork Examiner*, the column inches dominated by tw[...] Stapleton's omission from Jack Charlton's Republic of Ireland squad for the upcoming friendly against the Soviet Union, and the climax to the First Division season in England.

Title-favourites Liverpool were seeking their eighteenth top-flight crown and were preparing for a clash with Nottingham Forest at Anfield. The next time the sides faced each other – a little over three months later – Keane would be playing.

4

LION'S DEN

In mid-May, Keane sat in the living room of his digs in Leixlip, about a twenty-minute drive down the N4 from Palmerstown, and settled in for the evening to watch the FA Cup final replay.

Alex Ferguson had survived as Manchester United manager, just about. They finished five points clear of relegation, but the cup run, which began with a third-round victory over Nottingham Forest at the City Ground in early January, had provided a much-needed distraction. After some more narrow wins and then an exhausting semi-final battle with Oldham that went to a second game, they struggled in the decider against Crystal Palace and required a late equaliser from Mark Hughes in extra time to force a replay.

Keane was joined by a couple of other players from the FÁS course that Thursday night, including Tony Gorman, when the team news filtered through.

'I was a United fan and concerned with how they were going to play after the 3–3 draw on the Saturday, but there was the big shock of Jim Leighton being dropped and Les Sealey coming in as goalkeeper,' Gorman remembers. 'Nobody was expecting that at all.'

Keane sat back in his chair. This was ruthless from Ferguson, who went back a long way with Leighton. Still, not a hint of sentiment.

United had goalkeeping issues because of an injury to regular back-up Gary Walsh, so they'd brought in Mark Crossley from Forest on a month's loan. But when Clough summoned him back, Ferguson signed Sealey from Luton on a temporary deal until the end of the season.

Now here he was, a borrowed goalkeeper, starting United's biggest game in five years. Leighton would never speak to Ferguson again.

As a Tottenham fan and a Glenn Hoddle obsessive, Keane had no vested interest in the game, but he deeply admired Bryan Robson and his style of play, so was happy to see him lift the trophy after Lee Martin's goal gave United a 1–0 win.

Unbeknownst to Keane, he would face them at Old Trafford in September.

Negotiations over his move to Forest had been concluded by that stage and he was making national news as a result.

In late April, Cobh had revealed that they'd turned down an initial offer for Keane, with Liam McMahon telling *The Irish Press* that Forest's suggested price was very much in the 'opening bid mould', while adding that Keane had been impressed with what he'd seen during his trial and wanted to join the club.

The deal was completed just a fortnight later, when a Cobh contingent flew to Nottingham to iron out the details. Inexperienced in the art of the deal, they called in a favour from an old pal.

John Hollins, who'd won an FA Cup and UEFA Cup Winners' Cup during a long stint at Chelsea, and who went on to manage the club between 1985 and 1988, arrived in Cobh in early 1989, as manager Alfie Hale sought to keep his side in the League of Ireland Premier Division by sprinkling some stardust. He added ex-Everton midfielder Andy King to the squad too, but the strategy was remarkably ill-judged. Hollins was forty-two and hadn't played competitively in five years. Inevitably, the extent of his Ramblers career was a seventy-three-minute shift against Athlone Town at St Colman's Park before he was advised to stop playing altogether because of a nagging hip problem.

But when his departure was announced, Cobh revealed Hollins would informally advise and consult for the club from his London base, utilising his various links to Chelsea, Arsenal and QPR. So, when Ramblers were required to discuss the terms of Keane's proposed transfer to Forest in person, Cobh executives John O'Rourke and John Meade asked Hollins to be involved. But his presence carried little influence on proceedings.

The Cork Examiner and *Irish Independent* reported an agreed fee of £10,000, but the *Evening Herald* suggested it was triple that amount, while they also ran quotes from McMahon claiming late interest from two other First Division teams.

'Roy is a mature lad and he'll be signed on a two-year professional contract,' McMahon said. 'He had his mind set on Forest for a long time even though Tottenham and Luton were both interested in making a bid and I'm very happy to see him getting his wish. You will find very few finished players aged eighteen and Roy still has a lot to learn. But he always showed the potential to be a great player and he couldn't work under a better teacher than Brian Clough.'[1]

The negotiations were suitably strange. Keane was present in the room as the Cobh delegation sat down with Ron Fenton, Clough's right-hand man, to talk money. The atmosphere was already strained when Clough made his entrance.

'He came into the room in his green sweater,' O'Rourke recalled in RTÉ's 1997 documentary about Keane, *Have Boots, Will Travel*. 'The first thing he asked: did we get a drink? I told him we hadn't and he turned around and said, "Ronnie, what are you doing? You never offered these lads a drink?" So he opened his cabinet and everything was there. We got a drink and then he turned to Ronnie Fenton and said, "Is this lad any good?" And Fenton said, "Oh, yes. The potential is there."'

Then, Clough turned his attention to gauging whether O'Rourke and Meade were morally upstanding. 'Clough asked why we wanted the money,'

Meade said. 'John said it was for the club and Clough said, "How am I to know it's for the club? How am I to know that you won't put the extra money into your pockets, as has happened with some of the players that I have here?" We said we were doing it for the club, not for ourselves and that we had to take a day's holiday from work [to travel to Nottingham].'[2]

Satisfied, Clough gave Fenton a simple order: 'Ronnie, pay them the money.' The arrangement was £20,000 up front and an additional £27,000 in add-ons, if Keane managed at least twenty first-team appearances for Forest and won a minimum of five senior caps for the Republic of Ireland. To sweeten the deal, Forest would also come to Cobh and play a pre-season game at St Colman's Park.

With everything agreed, Clough kissed O'Rourke, suggested another drink and told everyone to call him Brian. Turning to face Keane, he said, 'Except you. You're to call me Mister Clough.'

Meade told him that Keane would make the first team within a year. In fact, it would take him a little over three months. And his ascent was so remarkable that Cobh were due £40,000 of the transfer fee by Christmas. The rest would take two years to come through, with Keane – incredibly – not handed a first Ireland cap by Jack Charlton until May 1991.

But one thing was missing from Cobh's deal with Forest: a percentage of any future Keane transfer fees.

'We got £47,000 over a period of time and it was the fastest period of time you could imagine,' said Meade. 'It's easy to look back today, but, at the time, no one expected Roy Keane to mature the way he did.'

In fact, the majority didn't really expect Keane to make it at all. For whatever reason, they felt he'd missed his chance. Still considered a fringe player by his country, he was playing regular football, but in a backwater which was unable to provide any proper platform to impress. When he was spotted, it wasn't in a League of Ireland fixture but an innocuous youth game that he really shouldn't have been playing in.

'I admit, I didn't see the talent then,' says Noel Spillane. 'But he was playing with Cobh for an entire season and nobody was saying, "He should be going across."'

Richie Purdy suggests the League of Ireland environment at the time, particularly the First Division, wasn't conducive to young players making a mark. The onus was on aggression and physicality, so the likelihood was that the talent – so hell-bent on merely surviving – blended rather than set themselves apart.

'He didn't stand out for Cobh when I played against him,' he says. 'But it was a kicking game in the First Division – a lot of men against kids. But there's that bit of luck too. Roy told me he'd written a load of letters to clubs and never got replies from the majority of them. You might have ten bad games and then a stormer and the scout is there on that particular afternoon. Should Roy have even been involved in the youth game at Fairview Park? Probably not. It was just that the All-Ireland tournament was a big thing years ago. So there's plenty of good fortune there.'

McMahon may have commented previously that Keane would be worth a few million some day but, until then, his monetary value was difficult to appraise.

'He was a talented player and we sold him as raw talent,' McMahon later told RTÉ. 'But what value do you put on talent? He was a player who was going to make it, but we didn't think he was going to make it that soon or burst on the scene the way he did. I certainly didn't.

'We had to take, basically, what Forest offered. What other clubs will learn from this and what Cobh Ramblers have learned is that if you sell a player, you try and get a percentage of his next transfer.'[3]

For Keane, after years of meandering, there seemed a finality to things. His relationship with Cobh Ramblers and his short stint in the League of Ireland was over. And after eight months on the FÁS course, things started to wrap up there too. He'd made the step that so many of the group longed for, but there was no malice, just admiration and support. During the flirtations with Forest, he was treated with kid gloves in Palmerstown, just in case.

'They didn't allow him to get involved in any games because he might injure himself,' Cullimore says. 'He'd be saying, "Morrie [Price], just give me a fucking ball and let me play." All he wanted was to play ball. And he'd pester him, "Just give me a run, let me fall in for ten minutes." But they wouldn't. There was no gloating from him whatsoever about the Forest move. I got this feeling from him that he was thinking, "It's about time." He knew what he wanted to be long before he got to where he wanted to be.'

Still, the feeling was that Keane would be one of a number of players on the course to get a cross-channel opportunity, such was the calibre of the group.

'The course really suited Roy,' says Purdy. 'From where he started seven or eight months before, he was a different player. He got stronger, quicker, more aggressive. Tony Gorman still would've been the best player come the end of the course but Roy definitely would've been the most improved.'

There seemed a mental resolve to Keane. Up to that point, he didn't express or display any degree of nervousness or anxiety. Signing for Forest was greeted with an effective shoulder shrug by him, probably because he knew – as Nicky English said in that astute speech a few months earlier back in Cork – that the path was a long one. This was just the start of another gargantuan slog that offered no guarantees.

'There were probably more talented players on the course,' John Donegan says. 'But was there somebody who wanted it more? Maybe not. He was doing what he wanted to be doing. If he had to go to Timbuktu, he'd have gone there to play soccer. It's always nice to be at home, but in Dublin at least the craic was the same. In a different country with different people and a different culture it might have been more difficult. But he would've gone anywhere to play. And to get that opportunity why wouldn't you?'

'It's a strange thing to say,' Cullimore begins, almost with a sigh. 'But I always felt it with him. Dublin was a good base for guys to be away from home. It wasn't too far away, you weren't in a different country. But I don't think Roy cared where he was. He wanted to play ball, wanted to play at the highest level and knew this was a stepping stone. He'd make these little quips. I used to bring a guitar up with me to Dublin and he'd come in and we'd chat away. I'd strum a few chords or sing a song and he'd say, "Jesus, that's great – I'd love to play an instrument." And he'd sit in and watch me play and say, "C'mere, when I make it as a professional footballer, you can come to one of my games and I'll go to one of your gigs." Little things like that. He was just thinking straight ahead. He knew what he wanted to do and knew what he had to do.'

Keane left for Nottingham, but there wasn't much time to settle in because of a significant international commitment in the middle of July. Named in Maurice Setters' sixteen-man squad for the European Youths Championship in Hungary alongside Dunne and Purdy, his old Rockmount teammate Paul McCarthy, and another member of the FÁS course, Barry O'Connor, things were radically different than before. Now officially a Forest player, Keane was handed a starring role in the Ireland side.

The eight-team tournament pitted the Irish against Spain in their opening game, with the winners facing Portugal or the host nation in the semi-finals. In Gyula, temperatures topped thirty degrees Celsius and despite holding the Spaniards scoreless for seventy minutes, the Irish finally wilted and uncharacteristically shipped three goals late on.

But there was still plenty to play for. With six Euro spots available for the following year's World Youths Championship, and FIFA allocating them based on how teams fared at the tournament (the four semi-finalists plus two more), Ireland faced Hungary in a play-off just a few days later.

In front of around 3,000 locals, Keane was superb, and was widely praised in the Irish media as Barry O'Connor's solitary strike was enough to secure the win. According to the *Irish Independent*, Keane was 'outstanding in the middle of the park'.[4] The *Herald* went into some more detail: 'The man-of-the-match was Nottingham Forest's recent acquisition from Cobh Ramblers, Roy Keane, whose ball control and tireless foraging dominated the central midfield exchanges.'[5]

Setters had never trusted Keane before, except when injuries forced his hand in Bulgaria, and it hadn't been long since he'd humiliated Keane, banishing him behind the goals in Malta to retrieve the balls. Understandably, Keane would never forget, regardless of his upgraded status within the squad.

'Apart from a few clichés about "having a go" and "putting them under pressure", Setters had very little to say,' Keane wrote witheringly about Setters' coaching acumen in his first autobiography. 'The set-up didn't impress me. I smelt bullshit.'[6]

Other players felt similarly, given Keane's newfound responsibility and how it contrasted so starkly with how he'd been treated by Setters while still a Cobh Ramblers player.

'He'd got in because he'd signed for Forest and that's why Setters played him,' Purdy says. 'Roy was the only one who wasn't stripped in Malta and then he was starting in Hungary. It was a joke. He hadn't even settled in England properly yet, but Setters still started him. It was a farce.'

On the journey home, the plane stopped in London so the Irish squad members based in the UK could get off. And it was there that Keane – for so long seemingly unaffected by his move to Forest and the repercussions of it – finally showed a degree of vulnerability. It seemed that he was suddenly gripped by anxiety and started to have second thoughts about the entire move.

'We were in a three-seater: I was on one side, Roy on the other and Tommy Dunne in the middle,' Purdy says. 'We were wishing him well for the season and saying goodbye. But he wasn't going to get off the plane. It was unbelievable. He was a bit nervous and he was saying that he was on so much at Cobh and so much on the FÁS course that there wasn't much difference to what he'd be getting at Forest. He was saying, "No, I don't want to do it. I'm happy enough." I think he knew it was a big step for him. He really was nervous to take the opportunity. Maybe there was a bit of homesickness too. But I'll never forget it. He wasn't going to get off that plane. He wasn't going to go.'

Keane admits in his autobiography that the Forest opportunity was 'laced with sadness' as it furthered the distance between him and his family.[7] And so much had changed in such a short space of time that it made sense for him to feel overwhelmed at the enormity of the Forest switch and what it signified.

***

Things had already started to move quickly when he was selected by Forest for the Haarlem Cup, an Under-21 competition in the Netherlands, earlier that summer. Forest played Sporting Lisbon, PSV Eindhoven and Barcelona before facing the host club, HFC Haarlem, in the decider. The game went to a penalty shoot-out, but it was the home side who claimed the trophy. Dutch defender Arthur Numan, who would go on to face Keane at the 1994 World Cup and again in the famous qualifier at Lansdowne Road in 2001, featured for Haarlem and, although he 'kicked his penalty out of the stadium' against Forest, he was still voted Most Valuable Player at the tournament. Numan doesn't remember Keane specifically, but he does recall that Forest had some promising young players on display. And more were on their way.

Set up in a Forest-owned three-bedroomed house on Colwick Road, nestled at the back of the Bridgford Stand end of the City Ground, Keane lived with two other young professionals, Gary Bowyer – son of Ian, who was part of Clough's Forest team that won the 1978 First Division title and back-to-back European Cups in 1979 and 1980 – and a defender from Sheffield named Steve Hodder. Another youngster was Ian Kilford, who had just signed pro terms and was preparing to make the switch from the youth side.

'Brian Clough came around one night and said, "There's going to be a young Irishman coming to stay with you so make him welcome,"' Kilford says. 'The next day Roy turned up with a black bag, a couple of tracksuits and a couple of pairs of trainers.'[8]

Keane was still settling in when another Irishman made a brief stop at Forest.

Dubliner Robert Bruton, who'd been a decent prospect at Drimnagh club St John Bosco, was working for the Irish Export Board in London (a precursor to Enterprise Ireland) when he was spotted playing Sunday League football and invited for a trial in Nottingham. Upon arrival, he joined up with Archie Gemmill's underage group.

'I was introduced to Roy as "the other Irish guy", but he wasn't paying any mind, heed or attention to me,' Bruton says. 'Then, when it got into the training session itself, I held my own in terms of fitness and stamina. And then it was fine. I was one of the group and subject to the same ridicule and encouragement and castigation that everyone else was. The players were well used to the Clough style of play, with everybody passing and moving. There was no individual dominating the team. Everyone was part of the machine. I'd come from non-league where it was every man for themselves. But these guys were well-drilled. We were doing morning sessions but the invitation from [Archie] Gemmill and the coaching team was to come back in the afternoon to do weights in the gym. And that was the routine. Some guys would head for something to eat, others would have a commute to get to their place and Roy would tell us he was going to his digs to watch George Best videos and that he'd see us later. It was him doing his thing. And he was always back later that day to do more.'[9]

Though the Manchester United maverick certainly carried little influence on Keane's playing style, he was impactful in other ways. Firstly, like Keane, many had doubted whether Best would ever make it as a player owing to his slight physique. Secondly, one of Keane's standout memories from growing up in Cork was meeting Best in December 1987, when he opened a Ladbrokes betting shop in Mayfield, so perhaps the videos offered a little taste of home, particularly given that Keane's entire family – with the exception of himself – were United supporters.[10]

'Football was everything to these young Forest guys,' says Bruton, who stayed for a few weeks before signing with Fulham. 'It was Roy's oxygen. His lifeblood. I was a twenty-one-year-old getting a look behind the curtain. The focus, hunger, intensity these guys had – even the bad players. It was fun for me. It was everything for these guys. Roy was a few years younger, so our points of reference back home would've been different. I had played Leinster Senior League but he'd got League of Ireland experience with Cobh. But he was curious and asking about life in London: "What are you doing there?" "Who do you play for?" "What level is that?" "How many goals have you got?" Stuff like that. I remember Clough asked me about it too, but he was more succinct. He said to me, "Are you the guy looking after the safe house in London?" He was well-versed in the politics of the time.

'But I'll always remember there was a laser-focus on Roy being as good as he could be. And if you weren't up to that mark ... We played one game and I was free on the wing. Afterwards I said to him, "Why didn't you pass to me?" And he goes, "Why the fuck would I pass to you? You weren't in a better position."'

Keane's transition to life in Nottingham was helped by the arrival of a familiar face in August 1990. On the opposite side of the street to where he lived was another Forest property specifically for young apprentices and it was there that Darren Barry, Keane's old midfield partner at Rockmount, arrived early in the month.

The similarities were a little eerie.

Seventeen-year-old Barry, along with teammate Anthony Buckley, had also been spotted by Noel McCabe while playing for Wilton United in a national cup final against Belvedere in Dublin. During the pair's subsequent trial in Nottingham, Buckley was injured in the opening match and was forced to return to Cork to have an operation for a hernia. Barry impressed, was quickly offered a contract and moved into his new digs.

'Forest owned these two terraced properties across from each other on Colwick Road and sometimes Roy would just come out his front door, go through a back gate and into the City Ground,' Barry says. 'The hostel where I was staying was for the youth team players. Across the road – where Roy lived – was a kind of a halfway house to independence. It was for the young pros who weren't youth players any more and it was semi-sheltered living to give them their own space. John Galley, who used to play for Forest, looked after us with his wife, Liz, but they oversaw the house where Roy was too and kept an eye on them, but only to a point. Those lads, including Roy, were adults and could do their own thing. But they'd still come over to our place for food because we had a cook and a cleaner.

'Now, the food wasn't as science-orientated as it is now. I remember having lasagne and chips, hotdogs, stuff like that. Sometimes you'd have your rice and potatoes but it certainly wasn't a menu set by a dietician and specifically put together for athletes. But there was a budget for the food and a lot of the players were complaining because there were cheaper brands of stuff like Corn Flakes. I remember one lad having a go because he'd come down every morning and there'd be no orange juice. He was told that if he came down earlier, he'd get his drink. But his retort was – and rightly so, "Well, somebody has to be first and someone has to be last – there should be food here for everyone." So, it was slightly different circumstances for us. For instance, we had a curfew and had to be back in by eleven o'clock on Saturday nights, so I didn't socialise with Roy on the town for that first season.'

Training with what was effectively Forest's third string, Keane waited for his first meaningful interaction with Brian Clough. It had been a busy summer for the senior team, who started off their pre-season in Sweden and played five games before flying to Italy, where the big news was centre-back Des Walker, fresh from an excellent World Cup for Bobby Robson's England side, openly expressing his desire to join Juventus.

Clough didn't link up with the Forest squad for the games against Avellino, Salernitana and Foggia, preferring instead to return to the UK and leaving Ron Fenton in charge of the group. With the start of the First Division season approaching, he wanted to check in on the wider pool of players at his disposal. Some of Forest's youngsters were included in an upcoming pre-season game in nearby Sutton-in-Ashfield and Clough was enthused.

'He said, "I'll see the Irish boy play today",' chief scout Alan Hill recalled years later. 'But I told him, "You won't because he's a sub."'[11]

The memory aligns with Barry's, who had tagged along to watch his friend in action. 'It was a bit surreal, a bit odd, arriving over to Nottingham and having someone I knew already there,' he says. 'He was playing for the third team when I arrived, so I went along to a Saturday game and he was on the bench. He came on in the second half, maybe for the last half an hour. I don't recall anything spectacular. He did well, but there was nobody really talking about him based on that performance.'

This game has taken on mythical status because of Clough reportedly instructing the team manager, Archie Gemmill, to replace his son, Scot, with Keane at half-time. Gemmill initially ignored the request and during the second half, Clough jumped the hoardings to reinforce his wish. Keane talks about this incident in his autobiography but mentions how he heard about it second-hand and, inevitably, there are various versions of the same story. Later, Hill even maintained that Clough stormed the pitch, told the referee to stop the game and instructed Gemmill to leave the field.

'They're interesting anecdotes, but I don't know how true they are,' Barry says. 'It's obviously been said in other places, but I don't recall hearing about it at the time and I was mixing with that age-group and those players. My vague memory is that Clough went to the dugout to see Archie.'

Liam O'Kane, who was the Forest coach, offered a softer version of the tale and outlined how it was during the next pre-season 'A' game, against local side Arnold Town a few days later, when Clough showed up and enquired about Keane.

'I said he was on the bench,' O'Kane recounted to *Bandy and Shinty* magazine. '"Well, tell Archie to put him on" [Clough said]. I went back to Archie and said, "The gaffer wants Keaney on." Archie says, "All right" but Archie's a funny little fucker. Stubborn, and he won't do it. "Come on, Arch," I said. "Get him on – our lives aren't gonna be worth living otherwise." I can see Cloughie staring daggers at us, with his arms folded. So, Keaney comes on and scores – a couple of headers.'[12]

But it seems like O'Kane has melded two memories together.

The game against Arnold Town took place on Tuesday evening, 21 August. But the following night, Clough's first team had a County Cup final against Mansfield Town. He was also dealing with potential new signings and preparing for the First Division season opener against Queens Park Rangers on the Saturday. He may have been at the reserve game at Arnold's venue on Gedling Road, but it seems unlikely, especially considering he was so detached from the day-to-day grind of club operations by that stage. Still, he was Clough and wholly unconventional. Earlier in the month, while the first team was still in Italy, he went along to Coronation Park in nearby Eastwood to watch a Forest XI beat the local side 8–3.

Keane started against Arnold Town and describes the game in great detail in his autobiography, mainly because Forest were 3–1 down to a team he likened to Cobh Ramblers: 'a mixture of part-time pros with great attitude but little ability – and guys with loads of ability but questionable temperament'. It was a pre-season reserve fixture, a game arranged to celebrate the opening of Arnold Town's new clubhouse, and Forest were without the usual collection of experienced figures, who were either involved the next evening against Mansfield or nursing knocks. But Keane was 'mortified' as the home side began to 'strut like fucking Real Madrid'. He 'raged' at his teammates to try and muster a response from them. The game ended 3–3, with Keane scoring twice. 'It got us out of there with a degree of self-respect,' he said.[13]

It's all a bit hyperbolic, reminiscent of his similar Kiplingesque take on Cobh Ramblers' youth game against Belvedere at Fairview Park back in February: 'Even when I knew the game was lost I kept going,' he wrote. 'I'd show those Dublin bastards that I could fucking play.'[14]

And here Keane was, in the middle of Nottinghamshire this time, an isolated warrior still raging against the amateurish everyman. It's overly romantic and, more importantly, a wildly unfair summation.

With the exception of Phil Starbuck and Brett Williams, not one Forest player involved that night had a single competitive first-team appearance to their names. Effectively, it was a group of raw, inexperienced youngsters trying hard not to get released. For the most part, it was the Forest team that competed in the Midlands Senior League, the third-string side made up of young pros in their late teens and early twenties.

The way Keane describes it in his book, Forest's reserve dressing room was full of whingers, moaners and bluffers who were 'looking for excuses to fail'.[15] But certainly, in the extremely short time Keane mixed in those circles, the majority were merely kids – the same as him – just looking for a break. In fact, two fringe players who didn't even see a second of action that night against Arnold Town were Keane's two housemates at Colwick Road: Gary Bowyer and Steve Hodder.

But that night, Keane definitely left an impression, and not just on the local press, who whipped together a brief report on the game for the following day's paper and mentioned Keane's double. Afterwards, word got around about his performance.

'I'd go along and watch quite a few reserve games, and I went to one against Arnold Town and there was this young lad playing,' says Brian Rice, who'd been with the club since 1985 and was a fixture in Clough's first-team squad. 'I didn't know who he was but he was playing outside-right and he was just sensational. I was transfixed. I couldn't take my eyes off him. He was strong, quick and something completely different to what I'd seen at Forest. This boy, a baby-faced, quite thin but wiry lad who could run for fun, who could jump and head the ball as high as you wanted. I just marvelled at him, how he could get up and down the pitch and how he could get stuck in for a winger. I remember thinking, "Wingers don't tackle like that" but he did. He played like an absolute beast.

'I was trying to find out if he was a trialist or a young lad coming in and it was the next day when I found out it was Roy Keane. I was chatting to the first-team players about him and saying, "You should've seen this kid who was playing last night, he was superb."'[16]

But as good as Keane had played, other youngsters were still ahead of him in the pecking order. The following night, Forest thumped five past Mansfield to claim the County Cup at the City Ground. Included on the bench – despite having played a full game the night before – were Starbuck and Tony Loughlan, with the latter even getting on for a brief cameo in the second half.

Still, Keane had made significant progress. And when he was named in the Forest squad for the first Pontins League reserve fixture of the season at home to Rotherham the following Monday, it represented a huge step. There were other young players included, with the likes of Stuart Cash, Craig Boardman, Loughlan and Starbuck all having featured against

Arnold Town. But Keane was now rubbing shoulders with established Forest first-team personnel too. Rice started the game, as did Toddy Örlygsson, Terry Wilson, goalkeeper Steve Sutton and Limerick native Tommy Gaynor. Defender Darren Wassall had played in the 1–1 First Division draw against QPR two days earlier, where Nigel Jemson's penalty ensured a point for an unimpressive Forest.

Keane was handed the number twelve shirt and took his place on the bench alongside Starbuck and Jason Fletcher. 'This was the reserves and at the time it was rare for a youth player to get a game,' says Darren Barry, who watched Keane that afternoon. 'They'd normally spend a season or two in the "A" team and then progress to the reserves. So, this was a promotion for him. Roy didn't get a full game but came on and played on the wing. Again, he did well but I wouldn't say he stood out. He was comfortable and looked like he fitted in. And, it's worth bearing in mind that playing for the reserves was a step up for him at the time.'

Recounting that experience seven years later in RTÉ's *Have Boots, Will Travel*, Keane admitted he was 'delighted just to get involved with the reserves', despite only getting minimal time on the pitch. Still, it was his first time playing at the City Ground and a special memory.

The game ended 3–3, with Rice scoring twice and Loughlan also finding the net. It got two lines on the back page of the 28 August edition of the *Nottingham Evening Post*, as the paper heavily previewed Forest's trip to Anfield later that night for their second game of the First Division season.

Stuart Pearce, Forest's talisman, missed the league-opening draw with QPR due to a hamstring strain and was still unavailable. But there were no other injury doubts and Clough wasn't expected to make wholesale changes.

Then, on the morning of the game, Steve Hodge began to feel unwell and was ruled out with flu while Wilson – another experienced face – was unable to shake off a knock. So Forest needed midfield reinforcements. Rice travelled with the team to Merseyside but had just played a full reserve game the day before, like fellow midfielders Örlygsson and young winger Ian Woan.

'We needed to bring another player up,' said Alan Hill. 'We only had Keaney and Phil Starbuck so Liam [O'Kane] said, "We'll take them both."'[17]

A weary, fuzzy-headed Keane was at the training ground. As was customary, he'd gone for a post-game booze-up and got back to Colwick Road in the small hours.

Ron Fenton told both him and Starbuck they were needed in Liverpool, so they jumped in the back of his car and headed for the A50, though there was a brief stop along the way.

It remains a mystery if Brian Clough already knew he would start Keane at Anfield that night and if the somewhat frenzied circumstances were completely inexplicable or something he had specifically orchestrated. The pair had met in Nottingham when Keane's deal was hammered out. Clough had seen him play, briefly, in a pre-season game. But it does seem like Keane's involvement wasn't as last-minute as many made out.

'I was an apprentice at the time, but Head Boy, if you like',' says Ian Kilford. 'I can remember the youth team manager coming in [after the reserves game against Rotherham] and saying to me, "Make sure Roy Keane's boots are in the skip tonight because he's going to Liverpool." And it was like Roy didn't know, that type of thing. I had to make sure all the pros' boots were sorted and when I was told to put his in with all of the other first-team players, I thought it was a bit unusual but nothing that Brian Clough wouldn't have done. And lo and behold, Roy went and made his debut at Anfield.'

Clough wanted to see Keane on the morning of the Liverpool game. As Fenton pulled up to Clough's house, he directed Keane – not the more experienced Starbuck who had already made over thirty first-team appearances – to go and fetch him. And when Clough answered the door, he greeted Keane like he was an old friend.

'Irishman, how are you doing?'

Then he made Keane down a bottle of milk on his doorstep.

It wasn't unusual for young players to be taken along to first-team games for experience. So, when Keane turned up at the hotel with Starbuck for the pre-match meal, he faded into the background so much that many of the players don't even remember him being there. On the team bus, he still seemed innocuous. In the dressing room, some players recognised him but didn't exactly dwell on his presence either.

'When we travelled down, Roy wasn't with us,' says Rice, who was named on the bench. 'We prepared for the game as usual and headed for a sleep in the afternoon at the hotel. When we got into the dressing room for the game, he was already there. I recognised him straightaway. We didn't know the team until the gaffer named it and Roy was playing. Some people looked around at him because they'd never even seen Roy before. I don't think he had even trained with the first team. We'd never met him. We didn't know him. And then he played. And once he was in, he wasn't coming out.'

Like so many seismic sports moments, the story of Keane's professional debut has taken on a mythical quality. Some raconteurs have coloured in their own memories and told the tale so often that even the factual inaccuracies have become seemingly unimportant.

When Hill recounted the story years afterwards, he fondly quoted a supportive, encouraging, off-the-cuff Clough: 'Irishman, put the number seven shirt on. You're playing.'

Keane used that same quote in his book, describing how he felt surplus to requirements in the dressing room and helped put the gear out to feel like he was contributing. It was then that Clough approached and told him he was starting, almost partly motivated to do so because of Keane's apparent humility.

It's a great story, but there is a pretty sizable and easily avoidable error. Keane didn't wear the number seven shirt that night. Gary Crosby did.

He's certainly not one to care about such details, but this was the biggest moment of Keane's life and you'd expect these poignant debut memories – taking that white shirt off the peg, pulling it on, fixing the collar – to have stayed with him even a little given the circumstances. But the incorrect shirt number has now become a crucial ingredient of many players' recollections.

Brian Laws, then the team's first-choice right-back, has subsequently described a somewhat comedic episode, where Clough used the Forest jersey as a prop to cajole Keane with in front of the rest of the squad.

'No one in the team had heard about him. We just thought he was this young kid pushing the skips and helping with the kit,' Laws recounted a decade later. 'And then Clough, just over an hour before kick-off, told Roy to put the number seven shirt on to see what he looked like. Roy put it on, and he [Clough] said, "You look a million dollars. In fact, you look that good, you're playing." We started laughing and thinking it was a bit of a wind-up but he went, "I'm serious. You're playing, and you're looking after him", and he pointed at me. Roy was playing on the right wing. I'm playing against John Barnes who's absolutely in tip-top form, so that's enough on my plate without having a young kid who I don't even know making his debut.'[18]

'It was bizarre,' admits Steve Chettle, a centre-back who'd come through the ranks at the club and was in his fourth season under Clough when Keane arrived. 'We knew the kid was Roy Keane and that he'd come over from Ireland, but he near enough had his boots in a carrier bag and gets named in the team.'[19]

Meanwhile, Rice knew all too well about making a debut at Anfield. Almost five years earlier to the day, Clough threw him in for what proved to be a 2–0 defeat. 'In my case, I went up on the morning of the game with the boys and I thought I was just there for experience,' he says. 'We went to bed, got up and when the manager named the team I was playing. And I was bamboozled. I was shocked. If Roy felt anything like me, you didn't have time to get stage fright. It happened that quickly. "Okay, let's get going." And that maybe helped a little bit. How could the gaffer get rid of that fear or anxiety in players? Well, don't tell them. Just spring it on them. Don't give them the time to have that fear-factor.

'But I do remember thinking about Roy at Anfield and saying, "This is going to be too much for this kid, maybe." And it wasn't at all. He just took to it like a duck to water. It was like he was saying, "This is what I was made for. This is my arena." Strong and quick. The player that was in front of me at Anfield was the same one I'd seen against Arnold Town. It didn't faze him one little bit. I was sitting there thinking, "This kid is as good as I think." He was just made for that game.'

Clough dropped a young player in the deep end every so often. To do it in such a high-profile fixture was certainly brave, but he was editorial and once he saw something in a player, he either really liked them or really didn't.

In 1972, when he won the First Division title as manager of Derby County, the final game of their season pitted them against Bill Shankly's Liverpool. It was a must-win situation at the Baseball Ground, but Clough was without experienced right-back Ron Webster. The visitors were in ominous form, without a defeat since the middle of January. But, despite the intensity of the occasion, Clough decided to hand a teenager his very first start. More than that, he would go on to refer to the decision to bring in local boy Steve Powell as one of his most 'vivid and satisfying memories of the championship season'.

'He was sixteen years old,' Clough later recalled in *Walking On Water*. 'We had to fill the gap somehow and [Peter] Taylor [Clough's then assistant] and I took no time at all in deciding the kid should play. "He's good enough, he's not inclined to freeze or to panic – gerrim in." That was our attitude and the youngster strolled through the match.'[20]

John McGovern scored the winner that night. Don Revie's Leeds – two days after beating Arsenal in the FA Cup final – failed to get the job done in their final league fixture against Wolves, and Liverpool were unable to take advantage. Derby were champions, Clough was vindicated and Powell would go on to make over 400 appearances for the club in a fourteen-year spell there.

And there were plenty of other examples too.

'The manager did it before with Mark Crossley, against Liverpool again,' Chettle says. 'You're not finding out until about an hour before kick-off that you're going to play so there's no real fear or worry about what's going to happen. But I don't think Roy worried about too much anyway and just took the bull by the horns in everything he did. And he was outstanding.

'The manager knew everything about everybody. He didn't miss a single, minute detail. He had an unbelievable memory and a super eye. It was the twilight of his career but he knew a player. From what he'd seen and heard from his backroom staff – which was very close-knit – regarding the reliability and ability that Roy had was something he implicitly trusted. And he was right.'

When it came to general team selection, Clough could always spring a surprise. But that night at Anfield, his line-up remained somewhat curious. Hodge's absence was enforced, but Clough also dropped Franz Carr, an electric right-winger, in favour of Keane. Perhaps acknowledging the combative and aggressive tendencies of the 'Irishman', it was Clough's way of trying to nullify Barnes and hand Laws some more protection. According to the full-back, it worked.

'I went to him and said, "What's your name, son?" "Roy." "Listen, Roy, I will try and help you as much as I can." But there was no fear in him,' Laws said. 'After ten minutes in that game, you just knew what Roy was about.

He kicked seven bells out of Barnes. He turned to Roy and said, "Who the hell do you think you are?" "Fuck off," said Keane. I said to myself, "Keane's going to be a star." That was the best game I played against John Barnes. It was an incredible debut. It was just so refreshing.'[21]

The plan worked for the first half, but Barnes still inflicted plenty of damage. Shortly after the restart, he evaded both Keane and Laws for long enough to set off on a dribble infield, darting past a couple of challenges before playing in Ian Rush with a delicate pass. The striker slotted beyond Crossley at his near post and Peter Beardsley added a second with seven minutes left.

Keane was solid, unspectacular and certainly nervous. It took him more than a year to admit to not knowing who some of the Forest players were. He probably should have been booked for a rash challenge on David Burrows midway through the opening period, while he showed some initiative with a long-range strike shortly before half-time that was blocked by Glenn Hysén. Nothing too fanciful. It was all very steady and assured. But that's exactly what had caught the eye of the Forest coaching staff in Keane's appearances for the reserves.

'He went from the third team to the first team in about a fortnight – it was amazing,' says Darren Barry. 'But for him to have been fast-tracked, you'd think he'd have needed to do something spectacular – beat lots of players, score lots of goals, something amazing. But he didn't do that. He played well and the coaching staff were raving about him to Clough, no doubt. They were watching what he was doing off the ball and could see he had something about him that maybe people with less experience – like myself – wouldn't have spotted, like his movement, his positioning, his decision-making.'

'He went white when Brian told him he was playing,' Hill said. 'But once he got out on the field, he was unbelievable. Like he'd been there years. After he came off he was drained, but what a performance.'[22]

A number of memories stood out for Keane that night. The first was Clough's brief pre-match chat, which reassured him. It wasn't tactical jargon. It was the fundamentals. And it established confidence rather than confusion. The message was clear: do the simple things right and you'll be okay.

'He asked could I control the ball, pass,' Keane said later. 'I said "Yeah, I can do that."'[23]

During the game, Keane was running alongside Liverpool's combative central midfielder Steve McMahon and, for a second, stepped out of the moment, suddenly realising the magnitude of everything. 'I remember thinking, "Is this really happening?"' he said years afterwards.

Another memory was less pleasurable, as Keane found himself on the receiving end of a Ronnie Whelan reducer early on.

'I discovered the limits of patriotism that night,' Keane later wrote.[24]

Whelan didn't remember much, just 'this Cork accent, ranting and cursing'.[25] But Keane would file the incident away and get his vengeance two years later.

Despite Forest having suffered a 2–0 defeat, the *Nottingham Evening Post* had a perfect splash for the next day's back page. Under the headline: 'Keane's Big Night', the accompanying match report referred to his motorway dash to Merseyside: 'Teenager Roy Keane was given a baptism of fire against champions Liverpool last night,' went Ian Edwards' opening line. 'Keane, only 19, answered the SOS from Nottingham Forest boss Brian Clough, forced to patch up his side because of injuries and illness. Irishman Keane found himself in the cauldron of Anfield only 24 hours after facing Rotherham reserves at a half-deserted City Ground. It was only an hour before kick-off that Keane knew he would make his League debut. Even without Hodge and with both Stuart Pearce and Terry Wilson unfit, Forest managed to produce a gritty display epitomised by Keane.'[26]

The national coverage was more muted.

'The 19-year-old debutant from Cork showed promise in midfield,' wrote Phil Shaw in *The Independent*.

Others were harsher, with *The Guardian* describing Keane as 'unequal to the task', adding it had been a case of 'into the lion's den' for him.

Clough, however, was glowing in his praise. 'I was thrilled to bits with him,' he told reporters afterwards. 'I know it's very difficult to judge a player on one performance. But he showed enough qualities in all aspects of his game to make me feel sure that I can't be wrong about him.'[27]

Afterwards, Keane understandably struggled to come to terms with what had happened. At 1 a.m. he got back to his digs and called Mossie and Marie in Mayfield.

'I'm not sure they believed me at first when I told them,' he said. 'Mind you, I didn't really believe it myself.'[28]

Finally, the opportunity he'd craved.

Now Keane was intent on not squandering it.

PART 2

5

THE STAGE DOOR

It was the day after Christmas in 1962 when Sunderland faced Bury in a Second Division game and Brian Clough's life changed forever.

There were concerns over whether the fixture should even have been played, owing to the piercing, frigid weather conditions. It had been a relentless winter and postponements were commonplace, but referee Kevin Howley inspected the Roker Park surface and deemed it playable. However, a hailstorm rolled in half an hour before kick-off and covered an already icy pitch with a fresh downpour. After twenty-seven minutes, Clough – an England international and prolific goalscorer who'd found the net 250 times in 269 games, a record that still stands – raced onto an angled, slightly overhit, through-ball from Len Ashurst.

Four decades later, the anger and bitterness still lingered, not only regarding the misfortune of what followed but the reaction of an opposing player to his plight.

'Bury goalkeeper Chris Harker's shoulder slammed into my knee as we challenged for the ball, my head hit the ground and everything went black,' Clough wrote. 'I came round soon enough and knew immediately that this was no minor injury, no simple sprain. Instinct demanded I get up but I could only crawl and I'll never forget the voice of Bury's centre-half, Bob Stokoe – who somehow managed to win the Cup as manager of the Sunderland side that beat Leeds against all odds in 1973. He moaned at the referee, telling him to get on with the game, accusing me of play-acting.

I'll never forgive Stokoe for that.'[1]

Clough had torn both his medial and cruciate ligaments.

After lengthy rehabilitation, he attempted a comeback at the beginning of the 1964/65 season, but it was ill-fated and inevitably brief. His career was over at twenty-nine years of age.

The incident fuelled a number of things in him, notably a lifelong hatred of Stokoe for suggesting he was faking an injury: 'I had a joke with my sons that if they got naughty I'd send them upstairs to their room to throw darts at Bob Stokoe's picture,' Clough said later.[2]

It wasn't the pain of the injury that he seemed to hold onto either, or the symbolic white sheet soaked with blood that he lay on in the dressing room afterwards. In Clough's various recollections of a traumatic life event, Stokoe's role in it is always the standout detail.

'I can hear him saying, "Get up you bastard, there's nowt wrong with you,"' he told Ron Atkinson in an ITV interview. 'Now, *that* was Bob Stokoe. And I never kicked a ball again.'[3]

Clough enjoyed scapegoats and apportioning blame when things went wrong, playing a perennial and exhausting game of word association.

'There are two key moments in his pre-managerial life,' says his biographer Jonathan Wilson, author of *Nobody Ever Says Thank You*. 'One is when he fails the eleven-plus exam and the other is the injury. He had this big family and everyone passed the eleven-plus so he's left as "the thick one". Whenever he told that story, he'd always talk about hearing his older brother saying, "Oh, our Brian's failed his eleven-plus" and that's what he focuses his anger on. It's the same with Bob Stokoe. He needed a person to blame for something that was either his own fault – like his exams – or a really unfortunate accident, like the injury.'[4]

Clough struggled to cope. And he was never the same again. There was an embittered view of the world and about football, especially when his relationship with Sunderland was so coldly and ruthlessly ended by the board, thus beginning another lifelong irritation with club executives whom he treated with contempt, deeming them nothing more than unremarkable, clueless charlatans.

'Sunderland got him a job as a youth coach and he did really well at that,' Wilson says. 'In 1964 they were in the First Division and Clough took on a greater coaching role under George Hardwick. But they were struggling against relegation and a decision was taken that Hardwick would be sacked at the end of the season. It was decided that Clough would go as well, partly because he was seen as Hardwick's man and partly because while he was still at the club Sunderland couldn't get the insurance payout they were due from his knee injury. So that disillusionment creeps in with life, with Sunderland and with football in general as being this horrendously cruel game. But Clough was also a difficult figure and became more difficult after the injury. It looks harsh to clear out an ex-player to get some insurance money, but if Clough is moping around corners, pissing people off and not being able to play, what's the benefit of keeping him on?'

The experience was scarring, but it shaped him. It fed an obsession with financial security, a desire for autonomy and it also ensured that through-out his subsequent management career, he had his principles. A correct way of doing things. The fundamentals he expected from his players. He was hard on many, soft on others. But always respected those in possession of a certain mindset, who carried a moral courage. Admitting a mistake, right-ing a wrong, not shirking responsibility during a bad game, taking risks, having a resoluteness in adversity.

When you attempt to dig down into why exactly he warmed to Roy Keane so much, that's certainly a decent starting point.

It was the wee small hours of Monday morning when Clough returned from Anfield to 'The Elms', the rural family residence in Quarndon, Derbyshire. Regardless, he did his usual and took his Labrador, Del Boy, for a walk. Alongside him was Craig Bromfield, who – like Keane – was another teenager with an inexplicable story. Clough met him initially, alongside his older brother, in late 1984 and the pair – who had a difficult family situation in Sunderland – ended up visiting countless times. In 1988, then aged fifteen, Craig moved in permanently and became Clough's shadow: part office boy, part personal assistant. He embedded himself in every facet of the football club and formed friendships with many of the players, even training with the first team on occasion.[5]

'Brian was absolutely blown away with him …' he says of Keane. 'We'd sometimes get home at one in the morning, half one … it didn't matter. We'd still take the dog out, we'd still have a chat on the Quarndon cricket ground or down the lane … And Brian was just – it was very rare that I saw him like that … all he could talk about was how amazed he was with Keaney and how, you know, he was a special talent.'

Bromfield said of the run-up to the Liverpool game: 'I remember Nige [Clough] coming out before the game to see Simon [Clough's oldest son, who'd driven to Anfield with Bromfield], maybe to give us a couple of tickets or whatever, and he said to Simon, "Listen, get your mortgage on Liverpool," he said, "we've got a young lad playing in midfield, a young Irish boy … none of us even know who he is."' But apparently Brian would say fairly often that if he was 'going to bed [in] a young player, he'd do it away from home … because then if the young lad has a stinker, he's only gonna get seen by three or four thousand … and not by twenty thousand at the City Ground.'[6]

Clough had clearly made his mind up about Keane following his Anfield performance and so acted quickly and immediately pulled him out of a pending youth tournament in France because of the upcoming First Division clash against Coventry.

'We might need him and if we do, I'd have no reservations about putting him in again,' he told the *Nottingham Evening Post*. 'For someone who's only just nineteen, he did incredibly well at Anfield.'[7]

The local press were caught cold by Keane's rapid emergence. When Duncan Hamilton – the *Post*'s long-time Forest correspondent – went to interview him about his debut, he had to ask Ron Fenton to fetch him from the dressing room because he didn't know what he looked like.

'We walked up to the Main Stand and sat there overlooking the pitch,' Hamilton says of their subsequent chat. 'He was so shy and so nervous and so reserved that he could barely make eye contact.'[8]

Others were also trying to play catch-up. The game hadn't been televised, so when Stuart Pearce, Forest's captain, continued his treatment with club physio Graham Lyas once the squad got back to Nottingham, he looked for a detailed breakdown of how things went at Anfield.

'Graham told me that Roy Keane had played on the right wing,' Pearce wrote in *Psycho*. 'I assumed he was a Liverpool youngster as I had never heard of him and asked why [Liverpool's] Ray Houghton hadn't played! Because I was injured, I had never even trained with him.'[9]

It took some time for news of Keane's ascent to filter back home.

The day after his debut, various outlets carried reports on Liverpool's victory. Some even offered an Irish angle, like the *Evening Herald*, who led with quotes from Houghton. But there was little mention of Keane, even in *The Cork Examiner*, which merely had skeleton round-ups on the five top-flight games that were played the night before. Instead, it went big on a preview of the local derby at Turner's Cross later that evening as Cork City hosted Cobh Ramblers in a League Cup clash. The big news was that Cobh were expected to hand a debut to Eric Hogan, Keane's former Rockmount teammate. Meanwhile, City would do likewise with Alan O'Sullivan, another of Keane's ex-allies, who had just been released by Luton Town. And there was an update too on goalkeeper John Donegan, one of Keane's travel companions on those weekly Monday morning Cork-to-Dublin train journeys, who was leaving City and joining Kilkenny in search of regular first-team football.

Unintentionally, it put Keane's remarkable week into context and reaffirmed just how far he'd strayed from the reality faced by so many young Irish footballers, though there was no chance Clough would let him get too carried away.

After reporting to the City Ground the morning after his debut, Keane was approached by Clough, who was fresh from a walk along the Trent with Del Boy. Clough asked him his name and when a confused Keane responded, Clough took off his muddied shoes and handed them to him.

'Give those a clean for me, will you, Roy?'

It was Clough's oft-repeated way of ensuring nobody developed an ego bigger than his own. And there are countless examples of how he reasserted his authority and influence on players he felt needed reminding of their place. Which was beneath him. This distinctive and idiosyncratic approach was also to keep those players grounded, humble and respectful: three pillars of any Clough squad.

Peter Shilton was once on the receiving end of a barrage, with Clough suddenly irritated by the goalkeeper's green jersey and, more importantly, what was on the back of it.

'There's only one number one around here and it's not you,' he told Shilton.[10]

Afterwards, he began to wear a green sweater to training and games, just to reiterate the point.

When nineteen-year-old Mark Crossley made a winning debut against Liverpool and kept his place for another victory at Newcastle a few days later, Clough summoned the goalkeeper to his house the following Sunday morning and told him to bring his boots and gloves. A bemused Crossley did what he was told and later that day, at Clough's behest, played as a ringer for AC Hunters, a team in the lower tiers of Derbyshire Sunday League football and managed by Clough's oldest son, Simon.

After Toddy Örlygsson played himself back into contention and then enjoyed a consistent run in the Forest first team, he paid the price for successive league defeats.

'We were at Highbury – the best dressing rooms in the country because they had heated floors – and he'd dropped me so I was on the bench,' he says. 'I went to clean my boots and he was taking a bath and he said to me, "Well, Toddy, I think you're very unlucky not to be picked today." But he told me I'd probably come on and then he said, "Can you just put some soap on my back?" So I went over to him and started to lather his back. I was bathing Cloughie just before kick-off at Highbury. We went out for the game, Terry Wilson got injured and I was on after about ten minutes.'[11] It certainly seems that, in the pantheon of Clough's man-management techniques, Keane got off lightly.

Back in Cork, Noel Spillane finally spoke to Keane forty-eight hours after his debut and the quotes featured in Friday 31 August's *Cork Examiner*, as attention turned to whether he would keep his place for the clash with Coventry.

'I was happy enough with my performance [at Anfield] but there was no room for pre-match nerves really as the manager only told me I was playing an hour beforehand,' Keane confirmed. 'All the other players helped to relax me, though, and they tried to bring me into the action as much as possible. I thought I did reasonably well and I was nearly booked too. I felt I should have been yellow carded but I got away with it.

'The manager told me I was on stand-by for the Coventry match but Steve Hodge didn't train, so I could be in the team again. Terry Wilson has recovered from injury and is back to match fitness so the boss may go for him instead. I just don't know yet but it's been in the papers here that I could be playing again.'

Asked about settling into the city and the club, Keane – with that dead-pan Cork droll – described it as 'dead handy, really'. He added, 'Darren Barry is just across the road from us so it's nice to have him close by.'

At Highfield Road, in spite of Wilson regaining fitness, Clough handed Keane another start, but brought back Franz Carr and Steve Hodge too. That meant Keane was pushed into a radically new role, but he seemed largely unaffected by it.

'He played on the left side of midfield that day and I just remember thinking how comfortable he looked,' Barry says. 'To go up so many levels so quickly, he didn't look out of place. He didn't look nervous or raw. And obviously Clough saw it immediately – all these things about him that made him this player. He didn't have to dribble and beat three guys, but Clough could see him tracking back when he didn't have the ball, making runs into the box. You might make those runs and not always get the ball so you think you don't look that good. But Clough saw it. Making the simple passes, the decision-making, the tackling, the heading. I wouldn't say Roy was exceptional at any particular aspect, but he seemed to excel at all the things a midfielder needs, particularly a midfielder playing in the English First Division.'

Forest seemed set to take a 2–1 victory, thanks to a brace from Jemson, but conceded their third penalty of the game with just two minutes left. Brian Burrows stepped up, scored and Forest were still winless after three.

Keane remained on the left wing for Southampton's visit to the City Ground a week later, a special occasion for a number of reasons. It was his home debut, but also, more importantly, his family travelled from Mayfield to watch him. And he didn't disappoint as an intrigued English press pack began to take notice.

The guests went ahead courtesy of a fine goal from Rodney Wallace midway through the first half, the winger jinking away from Keane in the corner of the area, then speeding past the fit-again Stuart Pearce on the outside before driving a low strike to the far corner.

But Keane was a delight and attacked the unfamiliarity of the number eleven on his back with an abundance of energy and industry and was a constant source of irritation for the Saints' full-back Alex Cherednik. Terry Wilson equalised for Forest with a header before Jemson continued his excellent start to the campaign with a deft chip over Tim Flowers shortly after the restart to put Forest in front. A minute later, Keane almost had his first Forest goal.

Franz Carr's deflected cross bounced into his path at the far post but his first touch was heavy. Flowers flung himself wildly, getting plenty of Keane but enough of the ball too and it squirmed clear. In the ensuing scramble, Jemson acrobatically hooked to the net via the inside of the upright and the win was secure.

Writing in *The Independent* the following Monday, 10 September, Paddy Barclay described Keane as one of Southampton's 'chief tormentors', before delivering some gushing praise: 'Keane consistently troubled the Soviet defender Alex Cherednik with a willingness to change direction and dribble that one hopes will not be knocked out of him. The youngster made his first appearance at Anfield thirteen days ago and, by all accounts, played there as if totally undaunted by the occasion. On Saturday he began with a couple of attempts at shots that were more like misdirected pass-backs, but went on to delight the Forest fans, making them forget all about the absence of Gary Crosby and Steve Hodge. His confidence was infectious.'

The *Times* offered a similar, if more muted, sentiment while also presenting a prescient insight. Focusing on Pearce's return and the effect it had on the Forest crowd, Vince Wright remarked that the captain was 'rivalled in popularity' by the new arrival. 'Keane has not looked back since his debut at Anfield two weeks ago and his impact was such that the injured Hodge was hardly missed.'

Again, Darren Barry was watching. And again, there was an element of disbelief to everything he witnessed, particularly when Clough replaced Keane with ten minutes to go.

'It was another standout performance,' he says. 'He was substituted late on and got a standing ovation from the crowd. The whole stadium. The performance had been that good. I remember watching him and thinking, "Wow, I can't believe this. He's three matches into his Forest career and this is the reaction." And obviously it was lovely for his family to see that as well.'

Keane treasured that moment, and when recalling it in his book, launched into a heartfelt tribute to Clough. 'I've never forgotten what he did for me – and how he did it. On the day of the Southampton game, Clough was particularly courteous to my family. For all his success, Clough could be touchingly human, which is not too frequently the case with living legends.'[12]

The following morning, a Keane family excursion was planned. The brood – perhaps still overwhelmed by the modern miracle they'd witnessed at the City Ground the previous day – were hell-bent on seeking some divine guidance, clarity and counsel.

'Roy's parents would've been under the impression that we were going to Mass every weekend and obviously we weren't,' says Barry. 'But on the Sunday, we had to bring them. It shouldn't have been a problem because we went "all the time", so it was quite funny because we couldn't find the church. Supposedly, we were bringing them to a place we went to every week and we were lost. But we managed to get there in the end.'

Back in Dublin, Larry Mahony watched Keane's breakthrough and not much surprised him. Like in Palmerstown, he stepped up and remained completely unaffected. He was playing in an unfamiliar position but that didn't seem to faze him either.

'I wouldn't have said it was a different player,' Mahony begins. 'I would've said he was doing the job he was being asked to do. And the difference was Clough, telling Roy what to do. And telling him he could do it. And knowing Roy then, I'd imagine he was saying to himself, "Jesus, this isn't that hard. This is fucking easy." He brought his game down to the bare bones. And the force of personality, strength and tackling made him stand out. I never coached in England, but I did in the League of Ireland and one of the problems you have with players who get to that level is that they fucking complicate everything and ruin their game by doing so. Managers and coaches appreciate players – especially in the centre of midfield – who will get it and link up, get it and move the ball. So I could see why Clough wanted him in the team, even though Roy may not have been sticking out to the punters and even to his fellow players. They don't think that way. They want to see the passes with the outside of the foot played in behind the defence. But if you look at Roy's stats, I'd imagine he would've been at around ninety-five per cent pass completion or higher. He was always responsible to the team in that way. But he also didn't want "Roy Keane" to be seen giving the ball away.'

Clough extolling the virtues of simplicity appealed to Keane, who'd seen the perils of the other side. At Rockmount, the standout player was Alan O'Sullivan, a skilful winger who failed to make the grade at Luton. At Cobh, Keane's older brother, Denis, was another flashy wide player with innate talent, but one who lacked the fundamental principles to carve out a career. And that fateful afternoon at Fairview Park should have been Jamie Cullimore's moment to shine. But he was quietened by full-back Graham Brereton and didn't have enough to his game to find a way back in. Keane prided himself on the consistency of various attributes. Later, when his younger brother, Pat, was trialling at Birmingham, Keane told him to focus on getting the basics right – control, passing, tackling – because that's what scouts were looking for.[13]

Clough had taken an immediate liking to Keane. He knew the City Ground faithful would grant him a rousing reception upon leaving the field that Saturday afternoon and also knew the significance it would forever carry for Keane's family. With only a few minutes left in the game, Keane had headed for the dressing rooms and an early bath, but was fetched by

Archie Gemmill, who said Clough wanted him in the dugout. When he made his way to the bench, Clough planted a kiss on his cheek.

It seemed another turning point, another test Keane had passed. Clough's gut feeling had been correct and he was definitely enjoying revelling in that too.

'Roy brought something different,' Brian Rice says, aphoristically echoing his former boss. 'He brought youthfulness, energy, fearlessness, toughness. He'd go and tackle anybody, Stuart Pearce – anyone, it didn't matter to him. It was just the way Roy was. "This is what I do. This is how I play football." For a kid to come into an environment like ours – as one of the top teams in England at the time – from a team in Ireland that nobody had heard of, and make it seem like he'd been there for years … it was like he was outside playing with his mates.

'I think the gaffer knew when he had something special. He'd dealt with special players before and he'd had very, very special players at Forest. But I think he saw that Roy had something different. Something really different. So, in terms of the dynamic, the manager knew what he had and Roy knew he had a manager who trusted him and loved him.'

It had been a decade since Forest were crowned European Cup winners for the second straight year. It was twelve years since they'd won a championship. These achievements were astonishing for a provincial club so bereft of any type of winning culture and lacking in economic heft. Afterwards, there seemed a weary acceptance that the trick would never be repeated. Forest reverted to the mean and were lost in the haze of both Merseyside clubs dominating the 1980s, though Clough did oversee three third-place finishes and two League Cup victories. Occasionally, there was a reminder of how things could be, but all too regularly Forest seemed to lack spark.

Writing in *The Observer*, Mike Rowbottom put it succinctly. 'There are times when Forest, overflowing with wit and invention, resemble brilliant conversationalists. But they do have this horrible habit of losing their thread.'[14]

'Forest were not a rich club so finishing fifth or sixth repeatedly was a great achievement,' says Jonathan Wilson. 'They were restricted in what they could do. But they had no money when they won the league in 1978 too. So did Clough lose the drive and hunger? He certainly had changed what he expected from players. In the late 1970s, he was quite prepared to take on difficult people and have tough players in the side. But as time went by, he seemed increasingly content not to win things but to just play nice football with nice kids. There was a template of a Forest player: Gary Crosby, Lee Glover, Nigel Clough. They all looked the same, they all acted the same: very clean-cut, very neat, very technical players but without the hard edge of a Kenny Burns or a John Robertson [key players in Forest's successful late 1970s period]. So I wonder if that became an easy excuse for Clough? That Forest would do things "the right way", which removes the burden to win. Keane gave aggression to a side that had become very nice and was a throwback to the late-seventies era.'

Duncan Hamilton, who covered Clough's tenure at Forest in-depth for the *Nottingham Evening Post*, maintains that by that stage of his career, Clough did not want to deal with any 'shithouses' in the dressing room. 'The days of him having to put up with Kenny Burns, or maybe even Robbo [John Robertson] were over. What he wanted was people who wouldn't give him any trouble. Keane came in and just played. Even if you take Martin O'Neill's time at Forest [1971–81], he was too much of a handful. Clough never knew what to make of him. He was always impressed with those who had an academic background [O'Neill studied law at Queen's University but dropped out to pursue professional football] because he didn't. But he also didn't particularly want people to use it and Martin was formidably bright.'

Because of O'Neill's apparent penchant for using an extensive vocabulary,

Clough likened him to James Joyce, dismissing both as two Irishmen nobody could understand. He didn't have the same issue with Keane, though the accent did make it tough occasionally.

'His Irish brogue was so pronounced that we considered employing an interpreter in the early days,' Clough would later write.[15]

'He was the butt of some jokes because it was something new for us,' Rice says. 'We'd had Gary Fleming who was from Northern Ireland but his accent was nowhere near Roy's. Trying to have a conversation, you'd ask him three or four times to repeat himself. And he'd give you one of those "Roy Keane stares".'

Of course, Keane may also have found some irony in Rice, a hardcore Glaswegian from Belshill, offering him elocution tips.

Very quickly, Clough had earmarked his teenage midfielder as a new favourite. Keane was talented, certainly, but also agreeable. Perhaps offering him that bottle of milk to drink on the morning of the Anfield debut was more than just an innocuous display of Clough's eccentric ways. Keane told Clough he didn't like milk, but once encouraged by his manager, he knocked it back anyway.

In three games, he'd already played in two different positions. There was no dissent. There was no irritation. Just acceptance. And that didn't happen with every young player at Forest. In his autobiography, Pearce recalled walking into Clough's office where a teenage Lee Glover was telling his manager that he didn't want to play for the youth team any more.

Before Keane's fourth appearance – a 2–2 draw away to Crystal Palace – Clough was already encouraging Jack Charlton to cap him at senior level. 'He might only be nineteen and a total stranger to the First Division, but you would think he had been playing there all his life,' Clough declared. 'He has made Stuart Pearce's job so easy for him. I bet Pearcey was wishing he could have put him in his bag and taken him down to Wembley with him for England's match against Hungary.'[16]

In one memorable dressing room incident, Clough rounded on every member of the squad except Keane.

'[He] came in in one of his for-no-reason bad moods … and had a go at all of us, one by one,' Hodge remembered, 'off the cuff. It was brilliant to watch.'[17]

Clough raged at the group, telling Pearce he'd been 'crap' since he signed a new contract. 'Get a house in Nottingham or go and play for Barnsley,' he told Crossley. For Hodge, there was a quip about his injuries. Clough went through every player and finally came to Keane. '

'I love you, Irishman.'[18]

There was a special smugness to Clough's continued praise of Keane. After all, his emergence had been down to him. Owing to his patchy acquisitions and general squad management in the previous few years, his judgement of players was being questioned. Keane seemed to be an overdue reminder that he could still spot talent.

'At the end of the game, Clough would normally be on his knees, offering to untie Keane's boots for him, because he idolised Keane,' according to Scot Gemmill. 'He'd tell him: "Run hard on the pitch and if you can't run any more I'll come on and carry you off myself." Basically: give everything.'[19] It never got over-complicated.

'Under Cloughie, when a player had the ability, there was a simplicity to how he'd teach you,' says Toddy Örlygsson. 'Stop the ball, turn with the ball, pass the ball. Every player that played under him knew what he meant. But if you give that instruction to players today, I'm not sure they'd know what it means. I think Roy learned a lot from those simple things.'

Clough repeatedly leaned on instinct when gauging a player's ability, but the system occasionally backfired. The year before Keane arrived, John Sheridan was signed from Leeds as a replacement for Manchester United-bound Neil Webb at a cost of £650,000. While at Elland Road, the midfielder had racked up over 200 appearances and a senior debut for the Republic of Ireland. But Clough made his mind up after watching him play for the Forest reserves against Coventry. According to Steve Hodge, who'd come off early and was getting showered in the dressing room, Clough stormed in with Ron Fenton and furiously vented at Sheridan's performance.

'What have I signed him for?! He can't head! He can't tackle! He can't run! What the fuck have I signed him for?!'[20]

Clough did hand Sheridan a debut in a League Cup clash with Huddersfield, where he set up Gary Crosby for the game's opening goal. But Clough wasn't one for second chances. Sheridan, remarkably, would never play another minute for Forest. By the end of the year he was at Sheffield Wednesday, where he'd go on to score a Wembley winner in the 1991 League Cup final against Manchester United, ironically getting the better of Webb in the process. With Wednesday, there was a third-place First Division finish in 1992, appearances in both domestic cup deciders the following year and starts in all four games for the Republic of Ireland at Sheridan's second World Cup in 1994.

His name regularly cropped up at the City Ground well after his departure as Clough's trend of treating some other expensive signings with contempt continued. When he splashed £750,000 on Dundee United's Ray McKinnon in the summer of 1992 and then effectively ignored him, Phil Shaw memorably suggested in *The Independent* that the Scot was already vying for the 'Gary Megson Invisible Award', named after the player Clough signed in 1984 and then sold months afterwards without ever having started him. Shaw mentioned how the accolade was also held by Sheridan and Asa Hartford, who at least managed three appearances in 1979 after Clough spent £500,000 on him to replace Archie Gemmill.

And at the beginning of the 1990/91 season, just as Keane settled in to life at Forest, there was another reminder of Clough's treatment of certain acquisitions.

Striker David Currie had been signed from Barnsley for £700,000 in

January, but Clough had doubts immediately and favoured Nigel Jemson up front instead. By mid-August Currie had been sold to Oldham at a loss of a quarter of a million pounds and it surprised nobody.

'Certainly players who stepped out of line or who didn't fit the bill were out on their ears no matter how much they cost or what their potential was,' Pearce noted. 'Gary Megson arrived with a fanfare but lasted just a couple of weeks because Clough was forever in his face. He couldn't stand it and had to leave. I saw it first-hand when he signed Dave Currie from Barnsley. I knew what was coming the day I was in an away dressing room with Currie, Clough and a handful of others. Clough turned to Currie and said, "Ey, son, have you got yourself a house yet?" Currie said, "Not yet, boss." Clough gave him the all-time put down. "Don't bother," he said. It made Currie laugh because he thought Clough was joking, but the lads who had been around a long time knew differently. I looked across the dressing-room at Des Walker and we both knew he meant it. Sure enough, Currie was soon on his bike.'[21]

But Clough still carried that aura. He remained a radical, an iconoclast, a contrarian. And, for the time being at least, there was more good than bad.

'Clough has made his mistakes,' wrote David Lacey in *The Guardian*, just after Clough signed a new three-year contract in September 1990. 'The biggest cost Forest £1 million in 1981 and went by the name of Justin Fashanu. But the lapses are far outweighed by the number of footballers whose playing careers have been transformed once they have passed through the hands of Clough and his coaching staff.'[22]

Lacey pointed to Jemson, who had already tallied five league goals, as the latest of those. However, it was apparent Keane equally fitted the bill and he rounded out a spectacular debut month with a number of important displays.

Against Arsenal, Forest's mixed league start continued with a 2–0 home loss, but Keane again was singled out for praise. Unmoved by the presence of David Rocastle, Paul Davis and Michael Thomas in the guests' midfield, he offered flashes of brightness in another colourless Forest performance.

'The 19-year-old from Cobh Ramblers will be a match-winner when his rambling runs can be harnessed to the team's needs,' opined *The Independent* on 24 September. Meanwhile, the *Nottingham Evening Post* voted Keane as Forest's best player, describing him as the team's 'driving force'. Also impressed was Arsenal manager George Graham, who made a note of Keane's impact.

With Clough bemoaning the side's defensive lapses, there seemed a perfect antidote when Argentine international centre-half Néstor Lorenzo arrived at the club for a trial. In typical Clough fashion, he wasn't afforded any red carpet treatment and instead was given a run-out in a Midlands Senior League win over Darlington's reserves in front of a hundred people at the City Ground. Given Lorenzo's previous outing was the World Cup final against West Germany at the Stadio Olimpico, you'd have forgiven him for being a little aggrieved. But it said much about Clough's continued cachet that the stopper merely shrugged off the arrangement as being 'part of the game'.

'Clough is stranger than fiction,' Phil Shaw outlined in *The Independent*'s post-game coverage of the Arsenal defeat. 'Who else could persuade someone who played in the World Cup final to undergo a month's trial?'

Midweek, Clough handed Keane a central midfield role alongside Garry Parker for a League Cup first leg at home to Division Four side Burnley. Taking no prisoners, the visitors attempted to lay down a marker early on and when Keane cleverly slipped away from John Deary, retribution was immediate and painful.

It was a tetchy game throughout and Forest took a while to get going. Chettle opened the scoring, but they were pegged back early in the second half and it wasn't until Jemson made it 3–1 that the result truly seemed safe.

Keane had bagged the second goal, rising unmarked to powerfully head home Laws' right-wing cross. He knew as soon as he made contact that it was going in, the momentum of his jump immediately carrying him into a brief but ebullient celebration. A wide-mouthed roar to the Forest fans behind the goal, accompanied by a raised right fist.

He played a crucial role in the third too, stretching to perfectly knock down Parker's searching cross for Gaynor, who teed-up the in-form Jemson to drive home. Pearce – who'd hit a superb brace in the league game against Palace – got the fourth with a venomous strike.

In truth, Keane should have scored at least twice. During the opening half, Clough pushed him to the right of midfield and from that position he wasted three decent chances. But he seemed more at ease after the restart when he swapped with Crosby and reverted to the centre. The switch also ensured it was a little easier to seek some retaliation. As Deary attempted to break and launch an attack from midfield late on, Keane dived in and sent him tumbling.

In a symbolic foreshadowing, the match referee – David Elleray – pulled Keane aside for a quick word and asked for some restraint.

'I was absolutely delighted to score. It was a fantastic feeling,' he told the *Nottingham Evening Post* afterwards. 'When I jumped to meet the cross, I was worried I would miss, especially as we needed a goal at the time. But it was great when the ball hit the net because I wasn't really having a good game until then. I thought I had scored in the first half when I played a one–two with Nigel Clough, but the keeper made a good stop. I just hope I get a few more goals if I get picked.'

Keane's moment was perfectly captured by *Post* photographer Trevor Bartlett, the image an obvious choice for the following day's back page. He's mid-jump, eyes wide open and has just sent a powerful downward finish towards goal. The ball remains in the edge of the frame, Keane still unaware of what's to come. It's a striking photograph for a few reasons. In that frozen second, he appears so physically commanding, in spite of a compact upper body and skinny frame. Arms are locked in front to aid his leap, thighs are bulging, torso is tight. He's determined but controlled. As an opposing boot tries to make a frenzied, desperate intervention, Keane floats above.

'His physical prowess in that first season … he seemed to evolve into this athlete that he hadn't been previously,' Barry says. 'He had this engine and seemed to have an extra injection of pace now too. But his legs seemed to get much stronger all of a sudden and his thighs seemed to get big. He had these muscular quads but his upper body wasn't that big. I have a picture of us at Under–15 level with Rockmount and I'm standing next to Len Downey. I come up to below his shoulders. Roy is about the same size as me but he would've been a year-and-a-half older. I know he gives a lot of credit to the FÁS course for his physical conditioning, but I think it was partly biology too, that it just happened for him at the time.'

When Noel Spillane visited Keane in Nottingham, he also noticed a substantial physical change.

'Everyone had said he wouldn't make it because of his physique,' he says. 'And you'd want to see the size of the fella that met us at the train station. You'd have been blown away. The legs. The strong upper body too. I was saying, "My God, look at him." That was after just a few months of training.'

That night against Burnley, Keane was named Man of the Match and earned himself a colour television courtesy of the sponsors, Midland Commercial Pressings.

The glamour was upped a notch for his next outing: a trip to Old Trafford to face Alex Ferguson's Manchester United. He remained undaunted by the high-profile nature of the fixture. 'I wasn't frightened at the prospect of playing Liverpool at Anfield so why should I worry too much about playing United at Old Trafford?' he told reporters.[23]

Still, the calibre of the game ensured plenty of hubbub and a profile appeared in the *Irish Independent*, accompanied by the queasy headline of

'Roy's oh so keen'. It carried the usual fairytale and meteoric rise tropes but also a significant admission from him.

'Everything has happened so quickly that I'm having trouble taking it all in,' Keane said. 'I'm just delighted to be playing football at such a high level so soon after coming over from Ireland. It just carried on after making my debut – and I still can't quite believe that. When I was told I was going to Anfield with the first team, I thought I was there for a little bit of experience. The fortunate thing is I didn't have time to be nervous.'[24]

Circumstances were different in Manchester, however. He now went there as a routinely praised, first-choice player, no longer an unknown quantity. Ferguson was especially aware of him because his chief scout, Les Kershaw, had been at Anfield that fateful August evening when Keane made his debut, to research both Liverpool and Forest.

'He phoned me on the way back from the game and said, "I've seen a player,"' Ferguson recalled years afterwards.[25]

At Old Trafford, Keane retained the number six shirt and continued alongside Parker in what proved a resilient Forest display, one of those that effortlessly silenced Clough's critics. Though he carried a poker face at the final whistle, the kiss he landed on the cheek of eighty-four-year-old United steward Charlie Tyake spoke volumes. The 1–0 Forest victory – thanks to another magnificent Pearce free kick – was a sweet one.

When Ferguson later recounted his memory of the game in the RTÉ documentary *Have Boots, Will Travel*, he conjured another Keane myth in the process. 'I always remember the kick-off, the ball went back to [Man United legend Bryan] Robson and Roy absolutely cemented him. And I said, "The bloody cheek of him – coming here and tackling like that."'

Again, a terrific anecdote. Except it didn't happen. Robson was still nursing an Achilles tendon issue and missed out. But though the memories are muddled, Ferguson most certainly was impressed by Keane that afternoon. Because everyone was.

'Forest are, quite simply, an accomplished footballing side,' declared *The Sunday Times*. 'They pass cleanly and run well for one another, and although they are still without Hodge, who got as far as the substitutes' bench yesterday, they may have found another midfielder of quality. He is Keane, a nineteen-year-old Irishman who belied his slight build with some determined ball-winning and foraging.'[26]

He should really have got on the scoresheet too, slipped through by Jemson just after the restart, but United's goalkeeper, Les Sealey, blocked well with his legs.

'It was Parker, Keane and Clough who continually unhinged United, Keane out-Hodging Hodge with his decisive forward runs from deep positions,' read *The Guardian*'s match report. 'Home supporters must have been mortified to learn that Forest snapped up Keane last summer from Cobh Ramblers in the League of Ireland, once the backyard of United's scouts, for all of £15,000.'[27]

The figure was off, but the point still stood. Ferguson *was* irritated, especially because three of his midfielders – Ince, Webb and Phelan – cost £3.25 million cumulatively. Keane had outshone them all.

'Throughout the match, his persistence and courage [was] just phenomenal. And I said, "Pfff, this is a player." Even though he annoyed me,' Ferguson later said.[28]

It wasn't only the opposition left frustrated by Keane's development.

Hodge, an established England international, a member of two World Cup squads and who had made the PFA Team of the Year at the end of the previous season, was attempting to recover from a persistent calf injury.

'I watched Keane score his first goal against Burnley,' he wrote in his autobiography. 'I also watched as he played at Old Trafford, he had a good engine on him and was completely unfazed by Paul Ince. I was starting to have doubts in my mind about my contract coming to an end, my calf problems and realising that Keane was good.'[29]

6

CIRCUS ACT

The irony was that when both Roy Keane and Steve Hodge played alongside each other in Nottingham Forest's midfield, the team tended to do quite well. For example, against Everton at the City Ground in early October, when Hodge returned from injury with a brace as Keane was pushed to the left of midfield.

The game proved another example of Clough's handling of Keane. Shortly before kick-off, he told him he was dropped from the squad entirely. Keane called his parents to tell them the news, but when he returned to the dressing room, he saw that Clough had changed the line-up and that he was now starting.

'He came across and asked if I had got a fright when I found that I was out of the team,' Keane said a few days later. 'I didn't know what to say at the time but after a moment or two he just took my arm and whispered, "Don't be stupid, lad. You are playing too bloody good to be out of my team. Get your gear on quick."'[1]

Like the milk bottle on the doorstep, it was another test from Clough to gauge Keane's reaction. The youngster had lived out a collection of fantasy moments throughout the previous weeks. How would he deal with disappointment? Would he show the same level of emotional maturity? It was straight out of the Willy Wonka playbook, but Clough got the answer he was looking for. And Keane got the chocolate factory.

In an absorbing game at home to Tottenham a few weeks later, where

Keane and Hodge both played, Clough – just as he did at Anfield – earmarked Keane for a specific role.

Paul Gascoigne, fresh from a career-defining World Cup, had started the season with a flourish and even managed four goals in a League Cup demolition of Hartlepool at White Hart Lane. Given Keane's aggression, energy and ability to cover so much ground, Clough knew he was ideal to disrupt Gascoigne's contribution to the game, while also taking advantage of his defensive shortcomings.

And, as Hodge later pointed out in his autobiography, Keane set about the task with gusto. 'Keane took it all in his stride and got stuck in,' he wrote in *The Man With Maradona's Shirt*. '"You fat bastard," he called in his Irish accent. "The only thing fat about me is me fucking wad," replied Gazza. It was real, harsh banter, they weren't smiling.'[2]

'I think Paul would've instigated that, rather than Roy,' says Paul Stewart, who was part of the Tottenham midfield that afternoon. 'Paul did that in every game and to whoever he was facing. Because I never found Roy that verbal on the pitch, in terms of getting involved in spats. He'd tell you to fuck off and he'd call you a "fucking this, that and the other", but not in the same way that Gazza would. He'd go above and beyond when it came to taking the mick. As much as Roy would tell people where to go, he never really got involved in that sort of stuff.'[3]

There was one mesmerising dribble early on when Gascoigne slipped by Keane's challenge close to the halfway line and shimmied past a litany of splayed red shirts, with only an impeccably timed intervention from Walker preventing a spectacular goal. But other than that, Keane rendered Gascoigne largely ineffective, the verbal jousts and his technical proficiency proving a potent cocktail. It motivated Forest too and after they went ahead through Nigel Clough's neatly crafted strike, Keane came agonisingly close to doubling the lead as the midfield strategy worked to a tee. Parker, who started on the left, spotted his unchecked run from deep and swept a superb pass over the top and into his path. Keane stretched and got there before Spurs goalkeeper Erik Thorstvedt, but the looping effort crashed back off the crossbar. As Spurs attempted to break quickly down their left flank, Keane immediately raced forty yards, closed down Mitchell Thomas and forced the ball out for a throw-in. 'Everything but the goal' is how Martin Tyler described it in his TV commentary, dropping a delicious indie-pop reference in the process.

When Keane won another tussle with Gascoigne later in the half, rousing a passionate response from the home crowd, Clough was undoubtedly pleased. But, despite Forest being the better side and despite Keane having such a handle on Spurs' key player, David Howells supplied an unlikely double – the second of which came in injury time – to hand the visitors the win.

But Keane's contribution was afforded some fine recognition.

'Memory can play tricks with the passage of time, but the sight of Keane took my mind back to Bill Whelan, that marvellous inside forward from the Republic who perished in the Munich air crash and had been such an architect in that team of the Babes,' wrote David Miller in *The Times*, under a headline of 'Keane revives the golden memory of a Busby babe'. 'Keane has the true midfield player's nose for the opposition's momentary point of weakness, and he could become a jewel for Forest and for Jack Charlton.' Miller added that Keane, 'bought for a song from southern Irish obscurity, at times lacerated Tottenham's defence from midfield'.[4]

Afterwards, Keane spoke to the *Post*'s Ian Edwards about his battle with Gascoigne, and some of his quotes subsequently became headline fodder in the UK tabloids. *The Sun* went with 'You're Soccer's Supergob' as their headline of choice, while the *Daily Mirror* and the *Daily Express* ran the story too.

'The lads had warned me beforehand that Gazza would be trying to wind me up and they were right. I couldn't believe it,' Keane said. 'He was at it all through the game and never stopped. He kept telling me I was rubbish – and that was one of the compliments. Most of the things he said were unbelievable and unrepeatable. I tried to ignore him and get on with my own game.'[5] Gascoigne later referred to Keane as a 'spoilt kid' for having whined to reporters. 'He just couldn't handle it, that's all,' he said.[6]

Keane's version of events led to some jokes in the Forest dressing room. The shrinking violet argument didn't exactly tally with his persona.

'He was a horrible bugger to play against in training,' Steve Chettle says. 'We had an aggressive player and captain in Stuart Pearce and they used to fight tooth and nail in the five-a-sides just because they both wanted to win. They were competitive games and nobody wanted to lose, but you'd have stand-up rows. They were all done in good spirit and those two were just natural-born winners, but I would have hated to play against him.

'Roy wasn't afraid of anybody. That's one of the reasons why he did what he did. Even at nineteen, he was full-blooded in everything and just wanted to win, however it had to be done.'

Keane was annoyed with the press coverage for a few reasons. Firstly, that he'd allowed himself be dragged into the English red-top hysteria relating to Gascoigne's every move and, more importantly, that the quotes made him out to be a soft, sensitive, whingeing type who couldn't look after himself.

'It got out of hand and the papers over here made a meal of it,' he told Noel Spillane in *The Cork Examiner* the following month. 'They blew it out of all proportion and got it wrong again. I think Gazza was just trying to have a go at me because I was so young and settling into the team. It had nothing to do at all with the fact that I am Irish. He was just trying to unnerve me but I didn't listen to him. I was too involved in the match and what was going on around me.'[7]

Spillane had nabbed another interview with Keane when he returned to Cork ahead of an Ireland Under–21 qualifier with Turkey at Dalymount Park in mid-October. It was a well-deserved weekend break and a chance for him to take a breath, but when he arrived into Cork Airport, he got a taste of his newfound celebrity as, along with his parents and uncle Pat Lynch, there was Spillane and a *Cork Examiner* photographer greeting him at the arrivals hall.

There was plenty to catch up on, but mainly what life was like under his charismatic but controversial boss. 'I have to be careful what I say about Clough because everything gets back to him – you'd be amazed,' said Keane, who was described as 'well-groomed and unassuming' by Spillane. 'He's fairly down to earth and basically a very nice man. He's a great manager and a great motivator. He's brilliant at his job – it's as simple as that. He took a chance by throwing me in at the deep-end at Anfield. Forest play the ball to your feet most of the time and that suits me. I remember with Cobh Ramblers and the ball was in the air most of the time.'[8]

Ironically, the direct approach was still preferred at international level too, but in spite of that, Keane had an impact on proceedings against the Turks and set up Tony Cousins for one of Ireland's three goals that night.

Such was his contribution to the group across 1990, Keane was voted Youths Player of the Year at the annual FAI/Opel International Awards in Dublin in early November. It was quite the turnaround. Twelve months prior, Maurice Setters hadn't even deemed him good enough to make a sixteen-man, match-day squad.

Still, when Setters was quizzed on Keane's rise at Forest and him possibly stepping up to Jack Charlton's senior team, he warned of people getting too carried away.

'I had Roy in the youths squads with me and I always felt he would make it at a higher grade of football,' he began, seemingly reworking history a little. 'Now that he's made the breakthrough at Forest, we will be keeping a very close watch on his performances. All the publicity that he has been getting since taking over from English international Steve Hodge has made us all more aware of him. People must remember he is still learning his business at Forest. There is always the inclination to jump on the bandwagon.'[9]

Keane wasn't an untested youngster any more. He was regularly facing and besting some of the elite players in England's top division. But Charlton seemed to have little interest in promoting him so quickly, preferring to keep faith with Ronnie Whelan, who hadn't played for Liverpool in a month, and bulk out his midfield options with John Sheridan and Alan McLoughlin – both plying their trade in the Second Division – as the senior side hosted England at Lansdowne Road. Still, it wasn't surprising that Charlton seemed ignorant of Keane's progress, considering a previous lack of knowledge regarding another Forest player.

After Limerick native Tommy Gaynor joined from Doncaster, became a consistent part of Clough's first-team squad for the 1988/89 season and was chipping in with some goals, Charlton was asked about the possibility of calling him up.

'Is Tommy Gaynor Irish?' he asked. 'If he is then we'll have to consider him.'[10]

Setters had been to watch Gaynor twice.

While the senior side prepared for the high-profile clash with Graham Taylor's England in Dublin, Keane was back in Cork for what proved a miserable Under–21 encounter at Turner's Cross. He and his teammates were on the receiving end of a battering from their neighbours as Southampton's Alan Shearer netted a double on his English debut. It seemed like the relentless run of games had finally caught up with him.

'I think people were expecting a lot from me and the Irish team that day but it just didn't happen for us,' Keane said later. 'The game passed me by. The ball was in the air a lot of the time and it tended to by-pass midfield. I was a little dejected afterwards. I never seem to play well at Turner's Cross. Even when I was with Rockmount and Cobh Ramblers, I can't recall a good match [there].'[11]

November saw Forest win just once in five games and bow out of the League Cup in spectacular circumstances as Coventry became the first team to beat them in the competition since Manchester City three years earlier – breaking a twenty-two-game run. 4–0 down at Highfield Road after thirty-four minutes, it was 4–3 at half-time thanks to a Nigel Clough hat-trick. Shortly after the restart, Parker scored to make it 4–4, but Steve Livingstone forced home a header from close range to win it for the home side.

That proved to be Hodge's last appearance for a month as his long-running calf problem flared up again. Clough had attempted to accommodate both him and Keane in the line-up but found it difficult. His preference was for a midfield four and Keane's flexibility and agreeable demeanour ensured he was usually pushed to the left wing. Tactically, Clough was a minimalist, and even when opposing teams had an edge based on their set-up, he seemed disinterested in altering his team's shape.

At half-time on the opening day of the season, Hodge had commented to Clough that because of QPR's system, he and Parker were outnumbered in the middle and needed help.

'Okay, darling. Thanks for telling me that,' was Clough's response before he added, 'Do your best.'

'What he actually meant was, "I don't give a fuck what you think. We play 4–4–2, get on with it,"' Hodge later wrote.[12]

It didn't help that Clough's relationship with Hodge had started to disintegrate long before that.

At the end of the 1989/90 campaign in May, Hodge had accumulated fourteen goals and finished as Forest's top scorer. It was the best season of his career and he was rewarded with a place in Bobby Robson's World Cup squad. But he didn't play a single second and there was speculation about his Forest future during the tournament.

Clough also increasingly seemed to question the legitimacy of Hodge's fitness issues, which began with the bug he picked up in Liverpool that had led to Keane's debut. It made him a doubt for the following fixture against Coventry, which Clough could scarcely believe. 'He must have Tibetan flu,' he remarked cuttingly at the time. 'The last bloke who got flu in August was a Tibetan monk in 1874. But I've got good news for Harry [Clough's nickname for Hodge]. The fella lived until he was 114, so he's assured of a long life.'[13]

During Hodge's absence, Keane began to exert more influence on games from central midfield and enjoyed an excellent December. He was close to scoring in a 2–2 draw with Luton and set up Nigel Clough's opener in a win away to QPR. As Christmas approached, everything seemed to click for Keane against Sheffield United at Bramall Lane, though the team's continued defensive woes tainted a memorable afternoon for him.

Already 1–0 behind to the league's basement club, Forest responded straight from the restart with Clough cleverly dummying Franz Carr's through-ball, allowing Keane to race through, take two touches to set himself up and calmly push the finish inside Simon Tracey's near post for his very first top-flight strike. Instinctively, he sprinted towards the Forest fans behind the goal, scaled the advertising hoardings and raised his right fist in celebration. A handful of supporters evaded the stewards and jumped on top of him.

Six minutes later, Keane turned provider for Pearce to sprint through in the left channel and bend a wonderful finish to the bottom corner via the outside of his boot. But Forest shipped two goals in the space of nine minutes midway through the half and United had their first win of the league season at the seventeenth attempt.

On Boxing Day, Forest hosted Wimbledon, a team – along with Palace – Clough always enjoyed beating, owing to the brand of direct, physical football they were noted for. But despite taking a fortunate early lead when Hans Segers' attempted clearance struck Pearce and rebounded into the net, they were constantly on the ropes. When John Fashanu equalised from a set piece, the guests were good value for it. But when Franz Carr's cross was flicked on by Chettle and hung in the air, it was Keane who arrived at the far post, sending a thumping header to the net, leaving Segers in a crumpled heap on the ground. Keane saluted the Forest fans with the increasingly familiar celebration. At full-time, Clough knowingly embraced opposing boss Ray Harford and offered him a peck on the cheek. Wimbledon's Paul McGee had hit the woodwork, John Scales had an effort cleared off the line and Wimbledon squandered a litany of other chances. Clough was highly aware his side had deserved to lose, even though every facet of Wimbledon's approach had been so predictable.

At the end of December, Forest faced something similar at home to Manchester City. In Niall Quinn, they possessed a limited target man, described by Ronald Atkin in *The Observer* as a 'floodlight pylon that masquerades as a striker', but who was a relentless threat in the air.[14] Nevertheless, because of Clough's disinterest in practising set pieces and defensive shape, and his belief in individual rather than collective responsibility, Forest kept conceding the same type of goals, including Quinn's headed opener after just ten minutes. He tapped in his second later in the half after an unmarked David White saw his header come back off the bar, while Wayne Clarke made it 3–1 with another simple aerial finish.

After Quinn had secured his brace, Clough stepped from the dugout and yelled a textbook instruction at his players: 'Get hold of the ball,' he told them, though that couldn't hide the defensive fragility.

There was a simplicity to Forest's approach under Clough, but also a wider suspicion of change that possibly reflected a lingering self-doubt, though it was well hidden by his expertly crafted public persona.

'He was a very simple manager and a coach, but you can't be that simple unless you're complicated,' says Toddy Örlygsson. 'I made my debut against Southampton and I went up to Liam O'Kane, our coach, in the dressing room and said, "Sorry, Liam, but where do I play?" And he said, "Well, you're number eight." And I said, "Yeah, but where do I play?" And he just repeated himself. "You're number eight." I was changing next to Lee Chapman and I said to him, "Excuse me but I don't know where I'm supposed to play. Do you know?" And he said, "You're number eight so you're in midfield.'"

'There was no real coaching, but the message was clear in regards of keeping the ball,' Scot Gemmill remarked later. 'Most of Clough's team talks involved a towel in the middle of the dressing-room floor with the ball on it, the referee banging on the door, demanding the teams go into the tunnel, but nobody was allowed to move or speak until Clough said "Get the ball and when we get it, we keep it and pass it to 'our Nige'."'[15]

Clough could always point to the tried and tested system having been a success. But the game was changing. Some sides played three at the back, some toyed with a sweeper, some started to pack midfield. Forest remained the same.

'We play to a system here,' Keane said at the time. 'Everyone in the team knows what's expected of him on match day. It makes it a lot easier for everyone to go out like that. Cloughie tells me to just get it and give it. That's my role in the team. Give it to the nearest man and keep it simple.'[16]

But while Keane stuck to Clough's steadfast orders, he was also beginning to inject some much-needed individuality, particularly in the team's first game of 1991. On a difficult Carrow Road pitch, he scored twice as Forest's helter-skelter season continued with a 6–2 win over Norwich City. The first goal was a solid drive from the edge of the area, Keane hanging back in the pocket and waiting for Nigel Clough to tee him up before arrowing the low shot past Bryan Gunn. Ten minutes later, he ran onto a breaking ball twenty-five yards out and thumped a superb strike to the top corner. He had struggled with his finishing in the early part of the campaign but now had four goals in four games. 'I've been having a crack all season and the lads were slagging me because I kept missing,' he said afterwards. 'Now things are going for me.'[17]

The brace was especially impressive considering he was complaining of double vision at half-time because of an earlier knock and Clough considered replacing him. 'I can never understand what Roy is saying, his accent is so strong,' he told reporters post-game. 'But I don't mind that one bit. He's talking with his feet these days. Everyone knows our recent record for buying players at this club is not too clever but I'd like to make it clear that I signed Roy. I only sign the good players. Someone else gets the credit for those who can't play. I just wish we could sign one or two like him because he has been like a breath of fresh air since he joined us.'[18]

Keane was now indispensable, regardless of Hodge's availability, and others were beginning to see it too.

'Pretty soon the contract changed and the car changed and it wasn't long before he'd moved on to the Mercedes,' Ian Kilford says. 'He used to always buy his Diesel jeans and T-shirts in a boutique called The Birdcage. And there used to be a little designer clothes shop in town too and within six months, he was going in and buying what he wanted. For me, I'd save up my month's wages and maybe buy a Ralph Lauren shirt. But whatever Roy used to get, it would have the logo plastered across it. He'd have a Hugo Boss T-shirt or something and it would have the name in big letters so everyone knew. We'd give him stick about that. "Roy, a bit more subtle." It was an unbelievable rise to stardom and he had a lot of things to deal with, but he handled everything the best he could.'

Before their televised FA Cup third round game at Selhurst Park in early January, Palace boss Steve Coppell was asked about Forest's thrashing of Norwich and, in particular, Keane's contribution. 'I think it was the best league performance I have seen this season, in very trying conditions,' he said. 'Forest were irresistible, a delight. I looked and thought "Where can we get at them?", but there weren't many lights at the end of the tunnel. They were magnificent strikes [from Keane]. He has come from nowhere, but what a revelation. Whoever spotted him has got to be the scout of the year.'[19]

Keane was subdued in the subsequent scoreless draw, but the acclaim continued regardless.

The double at Carrow Road certainly proved a calling card. In the middle of January, Keane was voted Barclays Young Eagle of the Month. The judging panel was a who's who of heavyweight football figures – both past and present – including then England manager Graham Taylor and Jack Charlton.

'This lad has done exceptionally well,' Taylor said when making the announcement. 'It looks like he's so easily picked up the Forest style of play. In fact, it looks like he's been at the club for two or three years and come through their youth set-up. He seems to be maturing and improving all the time: breaking from midfield, he can score goals – like his two against Norwich last week – and he has a good engine. At the moment, he's the find of the season and I just wish he was an English laddie.'[20]

The high praise continued from other judges.

'This is one of the best young players I have seen this season,' declared the esteemed former Wolves manager Stan Cullis. 'Coming from a practically unknown team in Ireland, he has shown no sign of difficulty in establishing a place in Forest's first team. A player with good ball control and composure in possession of the ball. It's reported that Forest paid £20,000 for his transfer. It must be one of the best bargains of the season.'

According to another member of the panel, former England manager Ron Greenwood, Keane showed 'a lot of mature confidence'. He added, 'He makes some good, telling runs, *à la* [Bryan] Robson.'

The legendary ex-Leeds United and England defender Trevor Cherry described Keane as a 'very good prospect and very fit, mature for his age', while 1966 World Cup winner Jimmy Armfield wondered whether 'Cloughie might have uncovered a real find here'.[21]

Keane was the first choice of four judges but, strangely, not Charlton.

For his trouble, Keane received a Silver Eagle trophy and a £250 cheque to his charity of choice.

However, the goodwill came to an abrupt halt. A fortnight later, in the replay against Crystal Palace back at the City Ground, which finally got underway after two postponements due to adverse weather, Keane suffered his first major misstep and incurred the wrath of Clough.

With Forest leading 2–1 and just a minute left in extra time, after an exhaustive battle Keane tried to wind the clock down and played the ball back to his goalkeeper Crossley from close to the halfway line. It was under hit, but Crossley still got there ahead of Mark Bright, though he skewed the attempted clearance. John Salako picked it up, settled himself and despite Keane's desperate attempt to block, measured a lofted forty-five-yard finish to the net.

Afterwards, Clough told reporters Keane was 'devastated' by his mistake: 'He's only a young boy and he'll learn that you have to overcome things like this in football. But knowing him, he'll go out and score the winner for us in the second replay.'[22]

But he was less understanding in the dressing room. As Keane walked in, Clough confronted him about the error and punched him.

'I came in after the game and he said, "What were you doing with the back-pass?"' Keane said over two decades later, describing the incident in detail at a Train 2B Smart charity event in Portadown in February 2016.[23] 'And really it was the goalkeeper's fault, Mark Crossley, … but obviously I'm a team player, I took the rap for him. And so he [Clough] punched me in the chest. I'll always remember it, the shock. It was a Wednesday night and I was that shocked I stayed in after the game. I'd always go out after a game to Ritzy [a Nottingham nightclub] … But I didn't feel bad about it. I trained the next day, I never felt angry towards him or that it was out of order. I just thought, he was angry, he hit me … deal with it.'

Phil Starbuck later painted a different picture and recalled that Keane was greatly affected by the incident. He claimed he cut an emotional figure immediately afterwards and wallowed in having let his manager down. 'He had tears in his eyes,' Starbuck said. 'It really hurt Roy. He was very dejected. Head down and just gutted.'[24]

But Keane's own response to the incident aligns with the spell Clough seemed to cast over so many people. Even when he was blatantly in the wrong, those on the receiving end still found it extremely difficult to offer any form of condemnation.

After a League Cup win over QPR at the City Ground in January 1989, jubilant Forest fans invaded the pitch at full-time. On his way to the tunnel, an angry and irritated Clough suddenly turned and stepped out onto the turf. He slapped one supporter – who was draped around striker Lee Chapman – across the head, landed a powerful left hook on another and dragged a third to one side. The incident sparked a storm and Clough, after a public apology, was handed a three-month touchline ban and a £5,000 fine. But when two of the fans were tapped up by the tabloids and offered payment in return for their exclusive stories, they both refused. They also refused to sue Clough. And before Forest played Aston Villa, they appeared on TV alongside him and made grovelling apologies. At one stage, like an encouraging priest in a confessional booth, Clough told them, 'Now, apologise to your mum and dad as well.' Then, as the pair were interviewed on camera, Clough appeared again and told them both to give him a kiss. They did as they were told.

Keane wasn't the first player Clough had punched. He'd done it before, but to Nigel Jemson, a player he had a difficult dynamic with.

'He had a love–hate relationship with Jemmo,' according to Steve Chettle. 'Cloughie said he was the only person who had a bigger head than he did. Before we played Derby away, we were just about to head out and he said to Jemmo, "Son, have you ever been hit?" And Jemmo just said,

"No, gaffer" and he gave him a dig in the stomach. I really don't know why. I think it's one of those cult stories. If you were there, you thought it was really funny. If you weren't, you wondered what the hell was going on.

'The manager was a sports psychologist before we had them. As soon as he saw a chink, where people might go too far thinking they'd arrived, he'd come down on them like a ton of bricks and make you feel really small again. But on the other side, if you were having a tough time, he'd make you feel great because he realised he was part of your growing up process too.'

Forest finally wriggled past Palace in the second replay on 28 January, with three well-constructed goals across a devastating eleven-minute spell in the second half as Crosby added to Parker's brace. But there was a weird and damning development with six minutes still to play.

With Clough already having made his two substitutions, he motioned for Hodge – who'd returned to the team earlier that month in a 1–1 draw with Southampton – to come off. As he trotted to the touchline, he realised there was no player coming on in his place. Instead, Clough would play the remainder of the game with ten men.

Even by Clough's standards, it seemed particularly vindictive. A few days later, he told Hodge it wasn't anything personal and that he just wanted to 'take the piss' and 'have some fun' with Palace, a team whose directness and aggression he disliked. Clough had also claimed he wanted to protect Hodge's calf injury, though that was certainly an empty excuse as Hodge had played 120 minutes in the first game against Palace.

There seemed to be a perverse satisfaction in how Clough toyed with Hodge around this time, taking the form of a type of emotional abuse. On one occasion, he told him Everton, Coventry and Manchester City were interested in signing him. But then, a few days later, he was telling him to agree a new deal. After a Zenith Data Systems Cup exit at the hands of Barnsley on 30 January 1991, Clough rounded on him. 'Harry, for an

England player, you were a fucking disgrace. If you're ready, get out of my fucking dressing room.'[25]

Keane missed that game after picking up a hamstring strain against Palace but still made the back pages in Ireland as Jack Charlton named his squad for the upcoming senior friendly against Wales and decided against including him. It was a curious development. Considering Keane's Young Eagle of the Month accolade, the buzz surrounding his performances and the level of praise he was receiving from so many of Charlton's peers, it seemed a perfect opportunity for the Ireland boss to see what all the fuss was about. Instead, he recalled midfielder Gary Waddock, then at Second Division Millwall, whom he'd dropped from the twenty-two-man World Cup squad hours before submitting the official list to FIFA the previous May.

'Roy Keane has just made the breakthrough into first team football and you have to remember he's only nineteen,' Charlton said. 'He's got a lot of time to play for the Republic of Ireland. When he's a more mature player and there's an opportunity to have a look at him without putting too much pressure on the boy, then we will give him a run. Every time a player of Irish origin appears, some members of the media assume that we don't know of him and they are telling us something new. Keane has been with us for the last two years, through the youths and Under–21s and his time will come.'[26]

The wording was strange.

Keane had been widely praised for how unaffected he had seemed in his debut at Anfield, facing the best team in the country in their own backyard. He remained unruffled when he shone at Old Trafford. He had quietened Paul Gascoigne. He'd already scored six times for Nottingham Forest. And in declaring Keane a Young Eagle of the Month winner, Graham Taylor, Trevor Cherry and Ron Greenwood had all alluded to his maturity as a crucial reason for his ascent. Charlton's concerns about whether Keane could handle the pressure of a meaningless friendly against Wales seemed misguided. And based on the comments, it was as if Charlton had never actually seen him play.

Instead, Keane was subsequently named in the Irish youth squad for a forthcoming friendly against Portugal set for a Tuesday evening at Dalymount Park. But by that stage, Forest were playing twice a week owing to a continued FA Cup run, so Keane, along with four other notable players, had to drop out because of the intensity of their club commitments.

But the pattern remained intact. For a long time, there seemed a tension when it came to Keane and Ireland, and it wouldn't be long before he was caught between club and country again, with plenty of finger-pointing and recrimination.

**

It had been clear for a while that Forest's best chance of success came in the competition Clough had never won, but their route was proving a relentless slog.

After the three-game saga against Palace, they needed another replay to slip past Newcastle, and it was only an equaliser from Hodge, assisted by the quick-minded Keane, ten minutes from time, that prevented elimination against Southampton at The Dell – his third goal in successive games. But, in keeping with his season, Hodge damaged knee ligaments that night and was ruled out for a month. In the replay, Jemson conjured a hat-trick to set up a quarter-final clash against Norwich.

At Carrow Road, the home side – still carrying the scars of the hiding they'd taken two months earlier with Keane helping himself to a brace – elected to play five across midfield. Forest responded by dropping Nigel Clough deeper than usual and using Jemson as a lone striker. Inevitably, it proved a much tighter affair and despite being largely anonymous as Norwich's system restricted his attacking contribution, Keane delivered when it mattered. Under a dropping ball, Jemson shielded well on the edge of the box before laying off to Keane, who struck a low shot beyond Bryan

Gunn and into the bottom corner. Running to celebrate, he glanced around twice in quick succession – possibly in the direction of the Forest bench to see whether they were watching – before propelling himself into an acrobatic forward tumble. The moment was slightly ruined, though, as the referee, Allan Gunn, yelled at Keane to get on with it and quickly escorted the players back to the halfway line.

It was out of character for Keane, who seemed unsure whether he should do it or not, and he received plenty of stick from his teammates for what Chettle described as a 'horrendous celebration'. Naturally, Clough wasn't impressed either. 'If he wants to do somersaults, I'll get him fixed up with a job in a circus,' he said afterwards.[27]

But with Hodge back in the treatment room, Keane seemed more relaxed. The previous month, when Hodge had returned to full fitness, Keane wondered if Clough might drop him. Ultimately, both players were selected, but Keane admitted later that he had shouldered a slight degree of anxiety: 'I felt there was a little uncertainty about places when it transpired that Steve Hodge was fit again, but I find I have adapted to his style. He is a great player to play with,' he said.[28]

Keane was now a 'cup hero' and the magnitude of his debut season was properly coming into focus. His performance against Norwich caught the eye of Hugh McIlvanney, doyen of British football writing, who waxed lyrical on the front page of *The Observer*'s sport section: 'There is nothing freakish about the significance the Republic of Ireland Under–21 international has assumed for the club that bought him so cheaply,' he wrote. 'Since being brought into the first team against Liverpool early in the season, he has resolutely refused to be displaced. His spiriting foraging from the midfield has disrupted opponents sufficiently to make openings for those around him and he has finished so effectively himself that yesterday's goal was his seventh of the season.'[29]

There was plenty more to come.

7

A CHARMING YOUNG MAN

After a 1–1 draw at home to Manchester United in mid-March, his peers shortlisted Keane as one of the six nominees for PFA Young Player of the Year, with him eventually finishing third behind Manchester United's Lee Sharpe and David Batty of Leeds. Twelve months earlier, he had been facing Newcastle West in a League of Ireland First Division game. It was an astonishing development.

And still, when Jack Charlton named his Republic of Ireland squad for the Euro qualifier against England at Wembley at the end of the month, Keane remained a notable absentee.

'Right now, midfield is the one area of the field where I'm not short of options,' he said, even though Ronnie Whelan was already ruled out. 'Roy is a very exciting player, a cool head on young shoulders,' he continued, changing his opinion from a month earlier when he said Keane needed to mature as a player. 'But right now, he's not experienced enough for a competitive game at Wembley.'[1]

However, such a sentiment was quickly rubbished when Forest visited title contenders and league leaders Arsenal at Highbury. George Graham, impressed when the teams met back in September, was so concerned with Keane's game-changing abilities that he pushed Lee Dixon into midfield to man-mark him. It worked too, as Keane – no doubt surprised by the close attention – was sufficiently kept under wraps in a 1–1 draw.

Ignored by Charlton, Keane did captain the Under–21 team in their qualifier against England in Brentford, but despite impressing – Setters described him post-game as 'a bit of a diamond' – in front of over 9,000 fans, the side suffered another 3–0 loss.

Clough turned up to watch the game, primarily to catch Barnsley defender Carl Tiler – a long-time target – in action. He later expressed both surprise at Keane's new role as skipper and confusion at Setters' decision to start him on the wing: 'I just couldn't believe it when I saw him come out of the tunnel carrying the ball,' Clough said. 'I was a little bit unsure what to make of it at first. But I need not have worried. Roy is a very level-headed young man and he took to the job as though he'd been doing it for years. He played outside right for the first fifteen minutes and looked as cold as I was in the stand. He stood there like a traffic policeman in Trafalgar Square but after a while decided to move in-field and played superbly. I was delighted for him … and Jack Charlton for that matter.'[2]

The following night at Wembley, as Keane's Forest teammates Stuart Pearce and Des Walker both started for Graham Taylor's side, a typically resilient Irish performance saw Niall Quinn cancel out Dixon's opener. On RTÉ's television coverage, an optimistic Eamon Dunphy predicted Ireland would top the group and qualify for the 1992 European Championships with them having accumulated four points from their opening three fixtures.

'I don't see us losing games at all, anywhere,' he told presenter Bill O'Herlihy.

He was right. It was winning games that would prove the issue.

Forest had a similar problem, with their cup run distracting from some exceptionally poor league form. A 2–0 victory over Sheffield United on April Fool's Day was their first win in the league since the middle of January, but Keane was central to the momentum they built up later in the month.

He was superb in a narrow win over Derby at the City Ground, an opposition he'd gamely irritated from the left wing the previous November but with perseverance and spirit more than anything else. Here, he was assured in the centre, effortless in possession and guiding the inexperienced figures of Scot Gemmill and Ian Woan. He should have beaten forty-one-year-old Derby goalkeeper Peter Shilton in the first half after running onto Clough's header, but the strike was straight at the veteran, who easily smothered. After the break, following a period of Derby pressure, Keane dispossessed full-back Steve Cross forty yards from his own goal and, whippet-like, opened his legs up and sprinted clear. As he neared the Derby area, he slipped in Lee Glover whose shot fizzed wide of Shilton's far post.

'I was amazed at how quick he looked on the pitch,' says Darren Barry. 'He was never slow, but you wouldn't ever have described him as a speed merchant when we were younger. And then I was watching him against these top-class players and he was a lot quicker. That surprised me. When you're back in Ireland, you have this perception that players must be so much better than you across the water. And then you see someone you know and the gap isn't as big as you think.'

Midway through the half, Woan sent in a cross from the left, hanging it up to the far post. Steve Cross watched the dropping ball and steadied himself to head clear. But Keane arrived from nowhere, leaping spectacularly to get there first and finish past Shilton in what was a similar goal to the winner he'd managed against Wimbledon on Boxing Day.

'It had to be the man whose skills have shone throughout this game who broke the deadlock,' said match commentator Alan Parry on ITV. 'How well the Irishman got up to head his eighth goal of the season. A superb goal by a magnificent player, Roy Keane, man of the match by head and shoulders. A real virtuoso display by the nineteen-year-old.'

It proved the only goal and *The Independent*, describing Keane as 'the game's outstanding outfield performer', detailed how he had 'lit up a scrappy contest with sublime passes and surges from midfield'.[3]

Four days later, there was the small matter of a cup semi-final against second-tier West Ham at Villa Park. Ever since eventually getting past Crystal Palace in the third round, the focus was on Clough and whether he could finally bury the hoodoo. He'd never made it to an FA Cup decider, either as a player or manager, and despite having reached this semi-final stage twice in the previous three years, Forest had fallen short on each occasion. Ahead of the game, he gladly deflected from that well-worn narrative and reflected on Keane's season instead.

'He's a charming young man and has a wonderful Irish smile,' he told reporters. 'He's only nineteen and he doesn't know where his talent comes from – nobody does, it's just there. That's been the lucky break I have had this season and it's all been a bit of a fairy tale. I didn't know anything about his ability and he'd only had twenty minutes in the reserves when I played him at Anfield. I stuck him in and it's just gone on from there.'[4]

Keane didn't believe he'd made much progress, but others thought differently.

Former Manchester United manager Tommy Docherty described him as 'one of the most remarkable finds ever in English football'. He added, 'Keane has everything – poise, skill and an exceptionally sharp football brain. Don't be surprised if he puts in a man of the match performance.'[5]

West Ham lined up five across midfield so Keane found it difficult to find space to exploit, but when West Ham's Tony Gale was controversially sent off after just twenty-six minutes, Forest began to dictate, before finally pulling away shortly after the break.

Somewhat ironically, given his older brother's well-documented concerns regarding Keane, during BBC's match coverage the Manchester United legend Bobby Charlton stressed how impressed he was with 'the young lad from Southern Ireland'. He told commentator John Motson, 'I find he's the most effective player that Forest have at the moment, both defensively and offensively. If Forest are going to score, he's one of the most likely. A very young, fresh, eager, enthusiastic player.'

It was a pretty accurate prediction, though it turned out Keane was the provider for the opening goal. After a good run, he latched onto a pass from Clough twenty-five yards out and evaded one challenge before slipping it to the advancing Crosby, who fired across Luděk Mikloško.

'Roy Keane picking the ball up and actually being positive,' Charlton commented, clearly enamoured of him. '[It's] really good play because it was a situation where he had to have a good engine to get there and he was always thinking about his positioning and where the rest of the players were.'

Just shy of the hour, Keane did find the net after a neat build-up. Parker played him in and he quickly angled the ball through for Lee Glover before instantly moving inside to pick up the return pass. The ball was slightly behind him so his first touch kept it unhelpfully close to his body, the proximity of Steve Potts unnerving him further and forcing him to take a decisive second touch very quickly. He stretched to shoot, losing his balance in the process but still getting enough power behind the shot to beat Mikloško at his near post.

'The nineteen-year-old Irish lad, who's made his name this season, has now written it across the FA Cup semi-final,' Motson declared.

Gesturing to the Forest supporters behind the goal, he stretched his arms out wide. They responded with a passionate chorus of 'Keaney, Keaney, Keaney', which was – given the season he was having – already a common refrain.

Later, Pearce and young full-back Gary Charles added further goals and Forest had breezed to a Wembley decider against Tottenham.

'When I joined, my folks at home were hoping that after three years I might get a chance as substitute,' Keane said afterwards, looking back on a staggering debut season.[6]

And yet, despite another two-goal contribution in a 7–0 thumping of Chelsea the following weekend – taking his tally to four in three games

– Keane was again left out by Jack Charlton for the Republic of Ireland's crucial upcoming home qualifier with Poland.

Increasingly fielding questions regarding Keane's continued absence from the squad, Charlton was now struggling to explain himself, especially as he'd been part of the judging panel for the Barclays Young Eagle of the Year award which voted Keane as the second-best underage talent in England, just behind another nineteen-year-old in Manchester United's Lee Sharpe – to whom Graham Taylor had handed a senior debut during the Wembley clash with Ireland in March.

Announcing the decision, Charlton was asked to describe what he liked about the Manchester United wide-man and inadvertently helped explain Keane's omission from the Ireland squad in the process.

'He's an old-fashioned type of winger who gets to the dead-ball line and crosses the ball well – and crosses from there are very hard to deal with.'

Essentially, Keane didn't conform to the directness Charlton wanted in his Irish team.

'He's only a kid and I don't need him yet,' Charlton said bluntly. 'It's always a bonus when someone comes through who captures the imagination like he does and I'm delighted he's developing so well. But it's a bit early to be pushing him into the senior squad. If I did that, I'd have to leave someone else out, and we have two or three who can't get in the side at the moment as it is.'[7]

There weren't many dissenting voices. Charlton had accumulated remarkable success with a tried and tested method. The system worked. Until it didn't.

After a brief stop in Cork to watch older brothers Denis and Johnson play for Temple United in the AUL Senior Shield at Turner's Cross, Keane captained the Under–21s again as they suffered a 2–1 loss to Poland at Dundalk's Oriel Park. He was highly praised for his performance but chastised for not stopping to speak to reporters afterwards, with rumours circling he'd set himself up with an unnamed London-based agent who was reportedly charging a fee for anyone wishing to speak with his client.

'It seems Roy's musings now carry a certain price tag,' wrote Vincent Hogan in the *Irish Independent*, bemoaning Keane's lack of post-game etiquette. 'The last thing he needs at this juncture is accountability to the bottom line of an agent's ledger. But that is the course young Roy has taken.'[8]

The following day, Charlton's senior side were held to a scoreless draw, a big blow to their hopes for qualification.

'What a Lansdowner', ran one newspaper headline, while the *Evening Herald* pondered whether it was the end of the 'golden era' under a simple banner of 'Shambles'.

Charlton criticised the condition of the Lansdowne Road surface and how it had ruined the strategy.

'I felt very sorry for Denis Irwin and Steve Staunton out there,' he told reporters at the post-game press conference. 'They had so much space and yet it took them so long to get the ball under control that many chances were lost and even then they delivered bad crosses. That had a huge effect on our game plan.'[9]

Recognising the tactics weren't working, he had changed things early in the second half. He brought off his penalty area poacher John Aldridge and replaced him with another in Bernie Slaven. Ten minutes later, he replaced his target-man Niall Quinn with another in Tony Cascarino.

The Irish Press wondered whether Charlton 'might have done better to have brought the perceptive passing of John Sheridan to bear on the occasion, especially when neither Ray Houghton or Kevin Sheedy were on their game on the day'.[10]

It was the first time in over four years that Ireland failed to score at Lansdowne Road. The result, coupled with England's win away to Turkey, meant topping the group and reaching Sweden was now out of their hands.

Within days, Keane had bigger things to worry about. Having damaged ankle ligaments in a cup final dress rehearsal against Tottenham at the start of May, a league game that ended 1–1, he had a fortnight to get himself fit for Wembley. And in between, a familiar face had played himself back into contention.

Hodge had been left out of the Forest squad altogether for the Spurs league clash, despite having played for England against the Turks three days earlier. With no sign of a new contract and his current deal up at the end of the season, he had been completely frozen out. But, owing to Keane's injury, Clough needed him and he started his first game in more than two months at, ironically enough, Anfield. Liverpool had to win to keep their paper-thin championship hopes alive, but Nigel Clough and Woan scored in a 2–1 victory that handed Arsenal their second title in three seasons.

The following Saturday, Hodge retained his place as Forest wrapped up the campaign with a 4–3 win over Leeds, ensuring an eighth-place finish. 'I thought, well, "I've had a bit of luck there. I've hung in all season, I've got myself fit and it's the cup final. [And] Keaney's injured,"' Hodge said.[11]

Still, Keane maintained his ankle was responding well to treatment and was earmarking a testimonial against Notts County – set for five days before the cup final – as his comeback target. And he seemed in good spirits when he posed for a Robin Hood-themed media day photoshoot at the City Ground wearing a green and red bycocket hat and carrying a sword.

But the injury was niggling and he didn't appear at Meadow Lane. Instead, he was given an extra twenty-four hours to work on the ankle and Clough would then watch him in a reserve game against Leeds on Tuesday evening.

'If I get through this okay I'll be very happy,' he told the *Evening Herald*. 'It's my last chance to try the injury out. I was jogging yesterday and there is a lot to do. The test will be when I have to strike the ball, when I twist, turn and get tackled. At this stage, I suppose it is a bit touch and go whether I make it or not.'[12]

Keane scored the opening goal in a 4–0 win and played the full ninety minutes.

Hodge went to watch, knowing any setback would guarantee him a starting role at Wembley. 'Keaney hobbled through it …' he said. 'I knew he wasn't totally fit.'[13]

Trying to second-guess Clough's mindset was always an impossible task but Hodge had reason to feel tentatively optimistic. Clough had an unofficial selection policy: if you have the shirt and we're playing well, you stay in the team. Since Hodge's return to the side, Forest had beaten Liverpool and Leeds. But Clough's behaviour ahead of the final was unusual, even by his own lofty standards. He was extremely nervous, telling Hamilton ahead of the game: 'I want to win the FA Cup very badly – but don't say that unless we do win it.'[14]

He began to create concerns, possibly trying to justify his anxiety regarding the magnitude of the occasion. After the reserve side had finished the season with three defeats from their final four games, Clough temporarily suspended the team manager, Archie Gemmill, one of his trusted coaches for over ten years. According to Hamilton, he was also convinced Forest had peaked too early and that it would affect their Wembley performance. Unbeaten in their last seven games, they'd won six of them and scored twenty-four times in the process, with Clough picking up a record twenty-third Manager of the Month award for April. If anything, it seemed they were peaking just at the right time, especially considering how mixed their season had been. But Clough was intent on magnifying any potential negative that could be squeezed from a situation. When full-back Gary Charles was involved in a traffic accident earlier in the week that resulted in the tragic death of a seventeen-year-old, Clough certainly would have felt it was an omen.

Despite the build-up being dominated by the 'Keane or Hodge' storyline, Clough – for the first time ever – made them share a room at the team hotel. Hodge, writing in his diary, wondered if the manager was 'taking the mickey'.[15]

'Both of us felt distinctly uneasy,' Keane said later. 'This arrangement led to a fraught couple of days. Neither of us felt inclined to mention the thing uppermost in our minds.'[16]

While Hodge's relationship with Clough was highly strained, the irony of the entire cup-final situation was that he got on well with Keane and they occasionally socialised together in Nottingham. In his late twenties, Hodge wasn't married and didn't have a steady partner, and his sexuality was a source of quiet chatter in the Forest dressing room. One night, when the pair were out for a few drinks, Keane brought up the topic and Hodge recounted the episode in his autobiography.

'He just asked me outright, "Hodgey, are you gay?" I told him that I wasn't and he left it at that. But that was the kind of person Roy is. He wouldn't talk behind your back, he'd say it straight to your face and I respected him for that.'[17]

The day before the final, the Forest side were returning to their hotel after training when Clough walked to the back of the team bus and threw a crumpled-up piece of paper at Pearce, telling him it was the line-up. Part of a four-man card school, Hodge was sitting alongside Nigel Clough and across from Pearce and Steve Sutton. As Pearce peeled back the corners of the page and studied the names, Hodge – desperate to find out if he was playing – caught Sutton's attention and gestured to him. Sutton shook his head. Keane was starting; Hodge was a substitute.

'The rules had changed, the kid was in ... but that hurt,' he said.[18]

Despite Gary Charles' harrowing week, he was selected ahead of Brian Laws at right-back. Ian Woan, the left-winger who'd been working as a quantity surveyor just fourteen months earlier, was in from the start too. And

Nigel Jemson, who had scored thirteen times in all competitions, including a hat-trick against Norwich the previous month, was left out completely. Visibly upset, he headed straight for his room once the players returned to the hotel. But while he waited for the lift, Clough called him back. An apology? An explanation? Neither. A Forest fan wanted a photograph.

For Keane, the final proved – in a season of inexplicably wonderful occurrences – a frustrating conclusion. The injury issue was two-pronged: it prohibited a proper influence on proceedings, but the two-week lay-off also severely affected his sharpness. With Spurs spreading five across midfield, he would have less time and space in which to work. And having been selected ahead of Hodge and winning that internal duel, there was even more of a spotlight on him. Of course, there was also his own journey to comprehend too.

Twelve months earlier, he'd watched the cup final with some of the FÁS group in a living room in Leixlip.

'Everything seemed to happen really quickly for me,' he said in a local TV interview ahead of the game. 'I didn't get much chance to think about it because one minute I was on trial and the next they're offering me a contract. After that, one or two other clubs came in for me but I made up my mind that I was going to sign for Forest. I had a gut feeling that it was the right club for me.'[19]

Asked about the League of Ireland and how the standard compared to cross-channel, Keane didn't hold back.

'It's years behind,' he said. 'The grounds are years behind. The Premier Division isn't bad but Cobh, who I used to play for, are in the First Division, and that's fairly poor.'

The production crew also trekked to Cork's northside to speak with Keane's parents, Mossie and Marie. As the pair gazed at Forest's team group photograph for the 1990/91 season and described how Keane was 'just in time' to be included in the top left corner, there was a palpable disbelief to their delivery, as if they were looking at something that wasn't real. At one stage, Marie pointed at Clough and said, 'There's the boss', like his presence was a mark of authenticity.

''Tis unbelievable,' Mossie said, straight down the camera lens while grinning wildly.

'It's magic,' chimed Marie, off-screen.

'And 'tis grand – we're getting a great kick out of it,' Mossie continued. 'We're not shouting about it ...'

'Ah, we are,' Marie interjected.

'But you'd have to be proud.'[20]

For much of the season, Keane had belied the innocence of his years. But walking into Wembley and surveying the playing surface with his teammates, he looked lost in a dark, baggy suit which seemed at least one size too big. An apt metaphor for the rest of his afternoon.

'Exceptional find this season, from nowhere, really. ... I just hope he's fit enough,' Bob Wilson commented on BBC's television coverage. 'I don't think Brian Clough would play him if he wasn't and he hadn't proved his fitness.'[21]

But the game on 19 May 1991 was forgettable for Keane as he desperately carried the damaged ankle. In his first autobiography, he describes the added pre-game stress of trying to handle the ticket demand from friends and family that was certainly an unhelpful distraction. But he wasn't the only one struggling.

As the teams walked out side by side, led by their respective managers, the tradition and pomp and ceremony all got a bit much for Clough, who grabbed [Tottenham manager] Terry Venables by the hand, clutching it tightly.

And when the game began, Paul Gascoigne – whose performances and profile had Lazio lining up to bring him to Serie A – lost himself in a haze of manic adrenaline.

'I'd played for the England Under–21s with Gazza and he was the same,' Steve Chettle says. 'Around the hotel, he'd be … excitable, shall we say? He was the centre of attention and just couldn't sit down and stay quiet for two minutes. But he was bouncing off the walls in the tunnel at Wembley. It was something I'd seen before but I still didn't expect what happened inside the first fifteen minutes where he could've been sent off twice.'

The first incident, where Gascoigne planted his studs into Garry Parker's chest, went unpunished by the referee Roger Milford, who merely awarded Forest a free kick. Shortly after, as Charles nicked the ball past him on the edge of the Tottenham area, Gascoigne lunged high and recklessly and immediately concertinaed in a heap. He'd snapped his cruciate ligament and though he was still on the pitch when Pearce sent the subsequent set piece ferociously to the top corner to give Forest the lead, he fell to the ground again moments later and was replaced by Nayim.

'If Gascoigne [had] stayed on the pitch, we'd have won the game,' Chettle maintains. 'They were playing with ten players because Gazza got overexcited for the day. The emotion of it all and the atmosphere, it was a huge game for him. There were a couple of surprises in our team and it was an early final for Roy to be playing in. But you trust the manager and after fifteen minutes, you think he's pulled another masterstroke and he's got everything right again.'

Milford later admitted he got the Gascoigne decision wrong, dwelling on the minutiae of the situation as the medical staff tended to the prone midfielder, rather than taking immediate action and issuing a red card. Clough, expectedly, held onto the grudge for a long time, later referring to Milford as 'a referee copping out of his responsibility'.[22]

Already in a state of high anxiety, Clough was unnerved too by Forest's early goal. It didn't help that Forest conceded a penalty, which Crossley saved from Gary Lineker, and the striker also had an equaliser incorrectly waved away for offside. 'We're going to get done here,' he told Alan Hill in the dugout, in keeping with his miserabilist mood.

But Forest had chances too. Gary Crosby missed a great opportunity to double their lead, while Keane had a sight of goal early in the second half when the ball ricocheted into his path. Bouncing up at an awkward height, he flicked it over the onrushing Erik Thorstvedt, but David Howells covered and cleared before Keane could finish to the net. Shortly after, Tottenham were level as Paul Allen was left in space to attack the Forest area and played in Paul Stewart, who shot crisply to the far corner.

Stewart, having received some specific pre-match instructions from Venables, had a superb game and was the dominant midfield presence at Wembley.

'For want of a better word, I was an enforcer,' he says. 'My job was to get the ball and give it to Paul [Gascoigne], really. But Venners [Venables] said that he wanted me to stop Roy Keane. He knew I was a fit lad and told me to go with him everywhere. We couldn't get an inch out of Forest. They always seemed to be our bogey team. Any important game, they seemed to have the edge on us. They always seemed to turn us over. And that's why we were going into the cup final as underdogs. We were conscious of it. So, I was like a rash all over Roy. Every run he made, I followed him. And he got sick to the back teeth with me. If I was able to stop Roy, and Gazza was able to get the space he needed, Venners thought it might give us a chance. But the plan went completely up in the air when Gazza went off injured. And if he didn't get injured, he probably would've got sent off anyway. But Nayim came on, we handled things very well and Roy did get fed up with me.

'It got to the point where I ended up with space which allowed me to score the equaliser because I think he'd just said, "I've had enough" and why wouldn't he have? He was nineteen. I was twenty-six and more experienced than him. As much as he was thought of as a great player, to play in the cup final at that age must have been a big occasion for him. When I was nine-teen, I was still playing in the Third Division with Blackpool and that's the magnitude of it. He's playing in the cup final when I would've been playing at Mansfield or Port Vale.'

With half an hour remaining, Clough replaced Woan with Hodge, but Forest were laborious and incoherent and incapable of working a way through Tottenham's cul-de-sac. Keane was irritable and largely anonymous, trudging through the game.

With fifteen minutes left, he found himself on the right side. Taking advantage of a slip from Steve Sedgley, he sent in a mishit cross that drifted over the bar. He was caught late by Justin Edinburgh, but much to Keane's frustration, there was no whistle from Milford, so he squared up to the full-back instead, pushing his head towards him and spitting insults. With violently protruding neck muscles and a vein bulging in the side of his forehead, Keane cut an intense and imposing figure, but Edinburgh, only eighteen months older, stood his ground. When Milford arrived to speak to both players, an animated Keane disputed the non-call as Edinburgh knowingly mocked his wild gesticulations.

'We always thought that even a ninety per cent fit Roy Keane would be formidable,' Stewart says. 'But he was just learning his trade and finding his own role, because he could play anywhere. He was so versatile. But you could see why inexperience might have cost him.'

At 1–1 at the end of normal time, it seemed a perfect moment for Clough – such a gifted man-manager – to provide some much-needed counsel to his wearied players. Instead, as Archie Gemmill and Liam O'Kane tended to the Forest group on the field, he remained on the bench, pensive and with arms folded. To some, it was 'typical Clough' – conjuring the unexpected, not overloading tired players with more instructions. To others, like *The Times*, which later referred to Clough's behaviour as a 'dereliction of duty', he'd bottled a crucial opportunity. Afterwards, he bounced between various explanations. In his autobiography, he said he didn't want to put additional pressure on his players by appearing on the pitch and reminding them of his own long-held quest for the trophy. But he revealed a different reason to Duncan Hamilton the following week. 'I thought we weren't going to win and that, somehow, whatever we did that day wasn't going to be enough,' he said.[23]

But he had used the same trick twice before – in a UEFA Cup game against Sturm Graz in 1984 and when he was in charge of Derby for an FA Cup tie against Tottenham eleven years earlier. It worked on both occasions. So there is the possibility that Clough, instead of admitting the risky strategy had simply failed at Wembley, cobbled together a range of excuses.

'We were told enough during the week to know what we were supposed to do,' Nigel said over two decades later. 'It was more of a statement that he trusted us.'[24]

Forest conceded just four minutes into extra time as Walker, trying to hold off Gary Mabbutt, inadvertently floated a header into his own net after Stewart had beaten Keane and Chettle to flick on Nayim's corner at the front post.

Forest were broken and failed to muster much of a response. During a late, frantic scramble, the ball broke to Keane in the area, but the whistle went for offside. He shot tamely at Thorstvedt anyway, much to the delight of nearby Edinburgh who laughed off the attempt. Keane offered up another volley of abuse to the full-back ('Fuck off, cockney prick') as Sedgley arrived and gleefully antagonised Keane further.

'Wanker,' he screamed at Keane, offering an accompanying hand gesture for good measure.

It was a sorry end.

'Justin was a lovely lad but Sedge was the ultimate fucking wind-up,' Stewart says. 'He's still the same now and he's in his fifties.'

'Keaney didn't have a great game but not many of us did,' Steve Chettle admits. 'It was kind of a dead final and nothing much happened but we came away bitterly disappointed that we hadn't won it.'

Keane later described how the occasion got the better of him, which certainly was a contributing factor. But there were other elements, notably his lack of match fitness. Ultimately, Clough's approach seemed poorly judged. Forest failed to create any decent chances and leaving Jemson out completely was short-sighted, restricting their options when they looked to change things.

'The day flew by me,' Keane said in *Have Boots, Will Travel* in 1997. 'People said I should take it in but I didn't. I was only a young fella. I didn't really play well. It just passed me by.'

Other reactions offered similar conclusions.

'Surprisingly anonymous, he had a bumpy afternoon in the company of Stewart,' said *The Independent* the following day, handing him a five out of ten rating. 'Young and unaccustomed to things not going his way and so lost his cool in the second half.'

With the exception of a handful of references to his temper tantrums, Keane's name barely featured in any post-game reportage. A damning indictment.

'Wembley's cruel hunger bled him dry,' according to the *Irish Independent*. 'Like a beaten fighter fumbling through the ropes, he had nothing left but tears.'[25]

But it was worth remembering that a crucial element of Venables' game-plan was having Stewart neutralise Keane's threat. At nineteen, it was a hell of a compliment.

'Without a doubt, he left an impression,' Stewart says. 'If somebody said to me, "Right, you're facing Roy Keane every week", I'd be like, "Jesus Christ, I need to find a better job than this", because he was something special. When it came to playing Forest and facing him, I knew I was in for a game. You had to be at the races. And he was a kid. I should have really been putting nineteen-year-olds to one side. I should've been able to control them. I was older and he was just learning the game. But he was well beyond his years.'

After the game, Clough confirmed he was staying on as Forest manager. Many had speculated that a cup final triumph would be the perfect ending to a storied career, but Clough was never the sentimental type. It's difficult to know whether he would have stepped aside if the circumstances had played out differently. He may just as easily have looked upon an FA Cup win as a two-fingered salute to his critics and the perfect reason to stay on.

With a handful of exciting young players and, at last, a decent chunk of money in the coffers, he remained optimistic about the future. 'You can only look forward in this game and there's no way I'm quitting yet,' Clough said. 'If football thinks it's seen the back of my big head it can think again. I'll do my best to be back next year, doing the same things.'[26]

There would be similarities, but ominous differences too.

8

BACK UP THE LADDER

A sort of homecoming.

St Colman's Park.

Late July.

Keane scored twice for Forest in the 5–1 pre-season friendly against Cobh on the twenty-seventh of the month, a fixture arranged a year earlier during transfer negotiations between the clubs. Clough wasn't there, preparing instead for a trip to Buckingham Palace where he was receiving an OBE for services to football.

Not that his absence mattered much to the 4,000-strong crowd. They'd come to see their adopted son.

Keane's family was there too, but only after a sitcom-like escapade. Having travelled from Cork by train, the group were unable to find a taxi at Cobh station and, with kick-off approaching, it was left to Mossie to improvise. He walked to a nearby undertakers, explained the situation and managed to secure a black funeral car to escort the entourage to the ground.[1]

It wasn't an omen for Keane, though, and it took him just four minutes to make an impact as he set up new signing Teddy Sheringham for the opener, sprinting to the by-line before cutting back for the £2 million arrival to dispatch. After Woan doubled Forest's lead, Keane swapped passes with Nigel Clough before cleverly flicking his finish over goalkeeper Giles Cheevers. Despite his old Rockmount teammate Eric Hogan pulling one back for Cobh, Sheringham headed home his second shortly before the break while Keane tapped home Forest's fifth after good work from Pearce.

Afterwards, Keane chatted politely about the intensity of the summer training regime and how Clough had warned him that he'd be a 'marked man' during the forthcoming campaign. But there was a bigger storyline Keane voluntarily brought up.

A controversy that needed addressing.

'Hopefully I can stay in the [Forest] team for the first few months of the new season and, then, get back into the international scene.'[2]

Days after the cup final defeat back in May, Keane had made his long-awaited senior debut for the Republic of Ireland. But in the build-up to the friendly against Chile at Lansdowne Road, Charlton retained an odd sense of anxiety about Keane's ability and mentality. 'If he can't handle it, we'll have to pull him off,' he told reporters, after revealing Keane would start the game. 'If we're going to give a player his first cap, he might as well be on from the start to see how he can handle it – there's no better place to learn than this.'[3]

Keane was now being trumpeted as 'the heir-apparent to Liam Brady's midfield throne'. The comparison seemed solid, especially as Charlton had been so suspicious of Brady too. Ball-playing, creatively minded midfielders filled him with a special kind of stress.

A few months prior to Keane's senior debut, and just days before the Euro qualifier with England at Wembley, Charlton gave a detailed inter-view to the BBC and explained his approach. 'We have a very simple way of playing, played by good players,' he told John Motson. 'They understand it. They know what's necessary. If any of them does anything [that goes] against the way we're supposed to play, they will immediately look across at us because they've done something they know I don't like. ... I believe in discipline on a football field. I believe in good players on a football field.

But they've got to fit into the discipline. You can't have the discipline surround them.'[4]

He even felt the innately talented Paul Gascoigne, whom he signed as a teenager while he was manager of Newcastle United, was a risk. 'In order to fit him into the England team, you've got to adjust everything round about him. ... Gazza likes to play with the ball anywhere. ... And sometimes that can be very unsettling in a team, when you've got a player like that who wants the ball in all sorts of different areas.' Previously, again while discussing Gascoigne, he proclaimed that 'sometimes a player can be too good for your team'.[5]

So it was strange for him to declare Keane as 'my type of player' ahead of kick-off and profess his admiration for how good he was on the ball, supporting attackers and scoring goals. All three attributes seemed completely at odds with Charlton's entire philosophy.

Still, he did seem somewhat intrigued by Keane's potential and, probably owing to a spate of withdrawals more than anything else, handed him a free role as part of a midfield five alongside Andy Townsend and John Sheridan, with David Kelly as the lone striker.

The day before the game, Keane trained at Lansdowne Road – remarkably revealing afterwards that it was his first time at the venue – and admitted that a pending senior debut was more nerve-wracking than the cup final. 'I feel more apprehensive and nervous about this game than I did about Wembley,' he said. 'To play for your country is a great honour and I'm thrilled to bits with the news. Last summer I was in my local pub in Cork cheering on my heroes in the World Cup. Today I trained with them and tomorrow I'll be playing alongside them. I still have to keep pinching myself to believe all that has happened.'[6]

Going by his demeanour, he was genuinely excitable. He did seem – somewhat uncharacteristically – to revel in the build-up surrounding his senior Ireland debut. Perhaps, given the frequency of his underage disappointments and setbacks, there was a special significance. Like the Belvedere game at Fairview Park or facing Arnold Town for Forest's reserves, it was another example of Keane proving a point. Ever since his mid-teens, he had felt under-appreciated by the key decision-makers within Irish domestic football. Now, in spite of those who had undermined him, here he was. A senior Irish international.

He enjoyed himself during the training session at Lansdowne and as the players' five-a-side began to wind down, he thumped a shot beyond Gerry Peyton and afforded himself a wry smile. It remained in place as a collection of fans rushed towards him for an autograph and it was still there as he lined up for the anthems the next day, standing between Kelly and Sheridan, the dark hair slicked into that impressive quiff. He was afforded a generous reception by the home fans and responded with a wave. Then it was down to business and he almost scored with his first touch, getting on the end of Kevin Sheedy's cross.

'It went closer to the corner flag than the goal,' Keane quipped after the relatively uneventful 1–1 draw. 'I'm not the nervous type and the occasion didn't get to me. You have to be able to adapt in every game and I felt I did reasonably well.'[7]

Charlton was furious at half-time, later describing the looseness of the performance as being akin to that of 'a Sunday morning team'. The second period was better, but his side went behind midway through and though Kelly equalised eight minutes from time, the near-post header from Sheridan's corner said much: the old way was still the best.

For Keane, there was no gushing praise. Instead, Charlton summed up his display as 'okay'.

'We tried a different way of playing, with David [Kelly] up front on his own, to give Roy a bit of room to operate in,' he told RTÉ's Ger Canning post-game. 'He was a bit strange in the first half. He didn't know when to go, where to go. It's his first trip with us, doesn't know the lads yet. But in

BACK UP THE LADDER

the second half he settled down better and made some good runs down the right side. So I was quite pleased with him today, actually.'[8]

From there, the plan for Keane was pretty straightforward.

He would be left out of the Irish senior squad's summer tour to the United States and instead captain the youth team at the World Cup in Portugal. He was given some time off to head home to Cork and was expected back in Dublin to join up with Maurice Setters' group in the first week of June, the tournament getting underway later that month.

Charlton was in Foxborough, Massachusetts when he learned that Nottingham Forest were preventing Keane from travelling because of a supposed knee injury. His Irish side had just drawn 1–1 with the United States and he was informed afterwards that the FAI were in receipt of a medical certificate from Forest maintaining Keane was unfit.

Inevitably, Charlton fumed and also claimed the club's behaviour could impact Keane's future with the senior panel. 'Nottingham Forest must understand that this jeopardises Keane's international career,' Charlton told reporters. 'I'll be contacting Brian Clough as soon as I get home to try and sort this out. He is our captain for the youth finals and our chances of doing well depend so much on Roy being in our team.'[9]

Charlton, speaking decades later, recounted the subsequent telephone conversation he shared with Clough when he was at the team hotel.

'I was in the bar and a girl came across and said, "There's a call for you, Mr Charlton." So I went over to the desk, picked the phone up and it was Brian Clough. And he said, "The boy Keane ... he's not going. He's had a hard season." So I said, "Come on, Brian. He's the captain of the youth side. They've qualified to play in this competition and he's very important to them." And he said, "He's not going." So I lost my temper a little bit and I swore at him and slammed the phone down. I walked back to the bar, the same girl goes, "Mr Charlton, there's another phone call for you." So I went back to the desk, picked the phone up and it was Cloughie again. He said, "I still love ya, but he's still not bloody going.'"[10]

Keane remained in Cork instead and spent a month embracing a lifestyle of drink and fast food.

'I indulged myself as never before,' he wrote in his autobiography.[11]

He even bumped into an old friend from the FÁS course: goalkeeper John Donegan, who'd signed for Millwall the previous October and was back home for the off season.

'Roy would always be talking about everything and anything,' Donegan says. 'He was just a really nice fella. And very, very funny. It was a grand aul' chat and nice to talk to him because it wasn't like the two of us had been somewhere and done something. We'd still done fuck all. All we'd done was gone across the water. But he was saying how much he was enjoying it at Forest, that he'd got a bit of a chance early on and he was delighted with it.'

Setters was understandably peeved at Keane's absence and lambasted Clough for what he felt was a hypocritical stance.

'Brian Clough has a lot to answer for,' he fumed. 'I just don't understand his attitude about releasing Roy. After all, he has released four other players for England's tour [to Australia]. Clough claims that he is worried about his players getting tired. If that's the case, why did he allow the foursome to travel yet deny Keane the chance to play in a big competition like the World Youth Cup? Of course Roy will be a big loss but we still have a squad of good, honest players and I feel we can do very well in Portugal. Maybe I will send Mr Clough a telegram to come out and see us when we reach the final?'[12]

Setters made a decent point, though the comparison between a handful of Forest players featuring in an end-of-season England tour and Keane captaining his country at an intense, elite but underage tournament was slightly unfair.

For Clough, he seemed intent on being mischievous just because he could, though it was another illustration of his fondness for Keane too. The decision to intervene here seemed a reflection of how much he appreciated Keane's impact, his ongoing awareness of him as a crucial player needing protection and being a young man who was understandably missing home comforts. For Forest's entire campaign, Keane had obeyed orders and done everything asked of him. Now Clough could step in and prolong the family time Keane treasured so deeply.

In the previous twelve months, he'd been on tour with the Forest Under–21 side in the Netherlands, played for Ireland youths at the European Championships in Hungary and then started forty-nine first-team games across the First Division, FA Cup and League Cup. In between, he had various other international assignments, and even though Clough allowed him some time off to return to Cork occasionally, it was still intense.

'He looked after him,' says Kingsley Black, who was signed from Luton Town that summer. 'After a game on Saturday, he'd say, "Right, you're all in on Monday – the usual time. Except you, Roy. See you Thursday." And he'd be back to Cork for a few days. These were his formative years. He needed time to relax and see his family. There was a mutual understanding of his talent. But everyone respected that Roy had come over from Ireland, was a young man, was away from his family and on his own. Cloughie was respectful of young players whose circumstances were a little different. And the thing about football is that when you're doing a good job on the pitch – which Roy obviously was – nobody really worries. If that player is getting you a win bonus on a Saturday, he can have all week off, really.'[13]

In the middle of June, Keane picked up the Jurys Hotel Cork Sports Star of the Month award, posed for some photographs and expressed his disappointment at having to miss the Youth World Cup while continuing to toe the party line regarding his supposed injury. 'I had little or nothing to do with the situation,' he said. 'I still don't think that my knee would be up to playing a full international game and obviously I'm bitterly disappointed that I can't play my part in Ireland's push for the youth title.'[14]

Keane found himself in a difficult spot. He certainly wanted to play for his country, but he also knew that arguing with Clough was pointless and almost certainly detrimental to his Forest career. He respected Clough, the man who spotted him in Sutton-in-Ashfield and changed his life. But the pair's relationship was only this strong because Keane kept his head down and did what he was told. He saw what had happened to Steve Hodge, a Nottingham lad with a long attachment to both Clough and the club, when he crossed the manager. No sentiment. No romance. Just an acrimonious breakdown. 'He was everywhere doing everything – the only thing he didn't confront or tackle at Nottingham Forest was me,' Clough later wrote about Keane.[15]

When long-serving disciple Stuart Pearce was asked what the secret to dealing with Clough was, his answer was a simple one: embrace the dictatorship. 'He's black and white,' Pearce said. 'As long as you do what you're told, he's quite easy.'[16]

When Dublin youngster Mark Reid was spotted by Noel McCabe in Fairview Park playing for Belvedere and then dispatched to Forest on trial, he spent time with Keane in Nottingham and gained some insight into his relationship with Clough. 'Roy brought up Cloughie and his style and how he carried a presence,' Reid says. 'He just told me to listen, do the right stuff and make sure everything was tip-top when the gaffer was around. I got the impression that all the players looked up to Clough and from what Roy was saying, he certainly carried immense respect for the manager. It was clear that he liked Forest and Clough because he was selling the club to me. I also had a trial lined up with Stoke so he had every chance to say, "Don't come here – go to Stoke instead." But he was trying to get me to come to Forest. He could easily have said, "Look, things are probably better there." Instead, it was nothing but good things about the club and Clough.'[17]

'There was always an element of "Is he being serious?" about Cloughie, but he knew Roy had talent and he knew he needed nurturing and looking after,' says Ian Kilford. 'If we were staying in Colwick Road, he'd often bring around all the Sunday newspapers and bars of chocolates and crisps and drinks to us in the digs. He'd go out of his way to do that. And it was especially for the young players who were staying in Nottingham for the weekend and were away from friends and family. Regardless of what Roy had in terms of his ability and what he contributed himself, maybe under a different manager things may not have gone so well? If you had the right attitude and worked hard, Clough would back you. He had that aura.'

Given the difficulty of Group A, the Irish youths would likely have found it tough at the World Cup even if Keane had made the trip. Drawn to face Portugal, Argentina and South Korea, they lost their opener against the gifted hosts – and eventual winners – in Porto. Memorably, a floodlight failure early on plunged the entire stadium into darkness for a ten-minute spell but, somehow, the game was allowed to continue. Managed by future Real Madrid manager and Manchester United assistant Carlos Queiroz, the likes of Luís Figo, Rui Costa, Jorge Costa, Abel Xavier, Capucho and João Pinto all featured, the latter pair supplying the goals in a 2–0 win as Setters was sent to the stands for abusing the referee.

Against the Koreans, Keane's childhood pal Paul McCarthy opened the scoring, but the Irish leaked a last-minute equaliser to severely dent their chances of progressing. They put up a spirited display in their final outing against an Argentinian side that boasted Mauricio Pochettino as captain and also had Mauricio Pellegrino and Juan Esnáider on the bench, but the 2–2 draw wasn't enough to see them through as runners-up.

When Keane returned to Cobh for Forest's pre-season friendly in July, he knew his absence from the tournament was still a talking point. Speaking to reporters afterwards, he reiterated that it was the club who deemed him unfit and he could do little about it, while he also seemed optimistic that Charlton would simply forgive and forget and bring him back into the senior squad.

'It was out of my hands entirely,' he told Noel Spillane. 'I had to accept the club's decision. That's my bread and butter. They sent a medical report to the FAI saying that I couldn't go because of the knee injury. I'd like to think that I'll be included in the [senior] squad for the friendly against Hungary in Budapest in September and I'd like to get in for the Sir Matt Busby testimonial match at Old Trafford on August 11. I really want to be involved in that particular match.'[18]

At the full-time whistle in Cobh, Keane was besieged by fans. They clambered around him on the pitch, desperate for an autograph. Then they waited patiently outside the dressing rooms and ambushed him again as he tried to make his way to the clubhouse. It took him twenty minutes to walk forty yards. That same evening, he posed for a photograph alongside Cobh's star athlete Sonia O'Sullivan, who was fresh from a gold medal performance in the 1,500 metres at the World Student Games in Sheffield.

The following night, Keane and Forest were at Tolka Park for a more muted friendly against Shelbourne that ended in a 2–0 win, with Sheringham again on the scoresheet.

The striker's arrival at the club had sparked a jolt of enthusiasm for the season ahead. Clough, who had finally pulled the trigger on a £1.5 million deal for Barnsley defender Carl Tiler, had openly discussed Forest's healthy financial situation and how it ensured they were still one of the First Division's elite clubs.

'It annoys me when I hear talk about the so-called big-five or top-six,' he said. 'I do not like those descriptions because I don't know who they are, or what the qualifications are for being a member. Our club has been to Wembley three times in the last three years. We reached the FA Cup final and finished eighth in the First Division. I doubt if there is another team in the country with a bank balance in such fine fettle. In my book, that makes us one of the top teams and we can compete with anyone, on the pitch or off it.'[19]

Clough's top attacking target was Derby's Dean Saunders and he bid just shy of £3 million for him. But he went to Liverpool instead and so Clough turned his attentions to Millwall's twenty-five-year-old Sheringham, the leading scorer in the English League the previous season with thirty-eight goals in all competitions and who was desperate to return to the top tier.

Sheringham enjoyed himself in pre-season, scoring nine times – including five in one game during a brief Swedish tour. But Keane looked sharp too, having worked hard to shift the extra stone he'd put on owing to his excessive summer relaxation in Cork.

The Forest positivity continued into the opening day of the season. With Steve Hodge sold to Leeds and Garry Parker unsettled, Keane was presented with a new central midfield partner in Scot Gemmill for a home clash with Everton, and as Sheringham partnered Nigel Clough up top, Nigel Jemson was pushed to the left wing. Unimpressed, he still managed to conjure the game-winner three minutes from time after Clough had made the most of an error by Neville Southall to equalise following Stuart Pearce's own goal.

Away to Leeds a few days later, Keane was subdued and found it tough against David Batty and Gary Speed. Forest's inconsistency was back with a bang as the home side picked up the victory thanks to an early goal from midfielder Gary McAllister, a player Clough had been keen to sign from Leicester City two years earlier but was then put off by the cowboy boots McAllister was wearing during their meeting. Clough had asked McAllister if he thought he was John Wayne and then launched into a series of inappropriate questions about his personal life.

But Keane was particularly excellent the following weekend as Nottingham enjoyed its first local derby for seven years. Neil Warnock had guided Notts County from Division 3 to the top flight in just two seasons and oversaw an aggressive, combative but limited operation. That was evident during the early exchanges at Meadow Lane when Nigel Clough was unceremoniously dumped to the floor by former plasterer Paul Harding with, as Tony Francis brilliantly put it in *The Sunday Times*, 'the subtlety of a stampeding wildebeest'.[20]

Scoreless at the break, Keane teed up Crosby for the opening goal ten minutes after the restart. His low cross from the right was glanced on by the winger, the ball kissing the upright before rolling to the opposite corner. Gary Charles added a second shortly after, before Keane expertly burst through with twenty minutes to go and latched onto Crosby's fine pass. He rounded County goalkeeper Steve Cherry, but the touch was heavy, which ensured a difficult angle for him to try to roll into the net. Despite this, he simply took a breath, took a glance, allowed players to commit to desperate diving lunges and squared for Sheringham to tap home his first league goal in Forest colours. Five minutes later, Keane had his own and it was almost a direct replica as he was too quick for County's ponderous offside trap once again. This time, it was Jemson sending a first-time ball through for Keane, who sprinted clear from halfway. With three magpie shirts trailing him, he approached Cherry, opened his body and calmly side-footed to the corner. He celebrated in front of the visiting fans, blowing a couple of kisses in their direction.

'When Forest finally broke free the chances were whole, made by their sweet timing of run and release,' went *The Guardian*'s match report of 25 August. 'Keane, impressive throughout, suddenly bestrode the stage.'

He had the spotlight in the days that followed too, but not for the right reasons.

First, he was publicly ridiculed by Clough after turning up late for training. 'The lad had an incredible first season but he still has everything to learn,' he said. 'Everyone else at the club knew what time they were reporting for training but he turned up late. He was the only one who didn't hear me so I'm thinking of buying him a hearing aid. If he continues not to hear me, he might just find himself back where he came from.'[21]

Then, the next day, Charlton named his Republic of Ireland squad for the friendly game against Hungary the following month.

Keane had been dropped.

'We have an embarrassment of riches at midfield and that's why I left out Roy,' Charlton said. 'He'll be back in the squad again on some other occasion, but I don't need him for this away friendly.'[22]

The slight was, ironically, as subtle as a stampeding wildebeest. As Charlton had effectively promised earlier in the summer, Keane was being punished for Nottingham Forest's decision to stand him down for the Youth World Cup.

Writing in his *Sunday Independent* column, Eamon Dunphy blamed Charlton and Clough – but mainly Charlton – for putting Keane in an impossible situation and failing to recognise his potential importance to his country at the European Championships, should Ireland qualify, and beyond. 'The youngster is in an unenviable position stuck between the rock of Clough's blustering arrogance and the hard place of Charlton's bullying insensitivity,' he commented. 'Charlton is most to blame. Ireland's demand that Keane play in an end-of-season international youth tournament was crassly insensitive. It was stupid of Charlton, and his assistant Maurice Setters, to create a fuss when Notts Forest claimed that Keane was injured. The player must have been emotionally drained beyond the point where he could have rendered useful service. Perhaps Charlton and Setters wished to make a point. Instead they have created a problem for the future.'[23]

Charlton's declaration that he had an 'embarrassment of riches' in midfield came back to haunt him when the squad was hit with a litany of withdrawals and he was forced to swallow his pride.

Ronnie Whelan – consistently struggling for full fitness – had a recurrence of a long-running knee injury and required surgery. Paul McGrath dropped out. Then Andy Townsend. So Keane was called up. Albeit very,

very late on. He had just returned to Cork to spend some time with his family when he was summoned and put on the next flight to London.

And, despite his less-than-ideal relationship with Charlton and the presence of long-time squad member Alan McLoughlin, Keane was handed a start alongside John Sheridan and played the entire game as Ireland came from behind to win 2–1 thanks to goals from Kelly and Sheedy.

'Roy Keane and [debutant] Terry Phelan were amazing out there,' Charlton said afterwards. 'The pair of them played very well and I'm very proud of them. I can't disguise my delight. They did us proud out there. It's very encouraging to see two young lads like them playing so well, especially when one considers the future. Keane had one hell of an influence on midfield. He did a lot of the sort of things that many people would not have noticed. It was one of the best individual performances I have seen from any of my side. There have been suggestions I don't think Keane is experienced enough to face Poland [in Euro qualifying]. I don't know where those rumours started but they are rubbish.'[24]

Keane's composure was especially impressive considering he'd been involved in a harrowing incident just a few days earlier.

Leaving training on the previous Friday morning, he totalled his new car, unidentified in reports but more than likely a black Volkswagen Corrado, in a two-vehicle road accident at an intersection close to the City Ground.

'He wasn't driving when he first got to Nottingham but when he passed the test he got a white Ford Orion Ghia,' Darren Barry remembers. 'Top of the range. A very nice car for a first one. And for a nineteen-year-old in 1991, it was lovely.'

'He couldn't drive it very well at the start and we used to have a nightmare with him,' Ian Kilford says. 'I'd be panicking when he'd be trying to park in a space where you could fit six cars.'

But the Orion was a club car and Keane moved on later that year, treating himself to the sporty coupé.

'It was like lightning,' Kilford says. 'I remember the first time he took me out in it. It had leather seats and he was saying, "Can you believe how fast this goes?" And I was sliding from one side to the other in the back because it was that quick.'

But now, just weeks after picking it up, it was smashed to bits, along with the other vehicle involved that had a mother and child inside. All parties fortunately walked away unscathed.

Speaking to *The Cork Examiner* a few days later, on Monday 9 September, Keane's parents said he was 'shaken but okay'.

'He's lucky to be alive,' Marie said.

'He got an awful fright – he said he just saw the car coming towards him at the last minute,' Mossie revealed.

'I was lucky enough to get out of it with a few cuts and bruises,' Keane told Noel Spillane the following day, playing the accident down. 'Thankfully I was wearing my seatbelt and that saved me. Mr Clough has said nothing to me about it – not so far anyway – so I'm hoping to keep in his good books.'[25]

Clough had other things on his mind, namely a mixed few weeks for Forest, and Keane was left especially irritated when Tottenham claimed a deserved win at the City Ground. As Clough had predicted, he was now a target for opposing teams who were intent on shutting him out of games. Just like at Wembley, Spurs were adept at it and in Paul Stewart they had a player who proved an unrelentingly effective shadow. With the game winding down and Forest trailing 3–1, Keane was on the receiving end of another reducer from Stewart that went unpunished.

Pearce stepped in to have Keane's back and furiously vented to the referee, Vic Callow. 'Young Keane, who had taken a battering, was lying on the ground and the referee delivered a mild rebuke,' Pearce wrote later. 'I was incensed and let him know in no uncertain terms. He sent me straight off.'[26]

Clough was miffed, particularly because before kick-off, Pearce had been presented with the PFA's Fair Play Trophy for the club's 'exemplary' disciplinary record the previous season. 'There's no excuse,' Clough said. 'He's an international and captain of this club. It was ironic after the award we received for being best-behaved team in the league. You might have thought that after eighty-nine minutes, and with a player down who'd been tackled from behind, the ref would have had other things on his mind.'[27]

Stewart again played the role of pantomime villain to a tee. 'When we'd first arrive and walk on the pitch, I'd just get the ultimate abuse from the Forest fans,' he says. 'And after I scored at Wembley, it got even worse. It wasn't just that I was hated by the crowd but I wasn't very popular with the Forest team either. There was always a niggle between me, Stuart Pearce and Nigel Clough, and to say that we weren't on friendly terms would be an understatement. I always found myself in an argument with at least one of them. I was there just to wind them up and they did take the bait because they got sent off. Because Roy was young and easier to wind up, we did have some proper, old-fashioned, ding-dong battles. My job was to get the ball at all costs. I'd be prepared to do anything to gain that advantage. Whether that was winding Roy up or some other players, my only concern was to gain possession, hopefully supply Gazza with it and he could do something magical with it.'

That week, Keane was entrusted with keeping an eye on Mark Reid, the young kid from Belvedere who was on a week's trial. And for five days, he offered a comprehensive, all-inclusive chaperone service. 'My first day at the club, I was in the dressing room and he just tipped me on the shoulder and said, "Are you the Dublin lad that Noel sent over?"' Reid remembers. 'I said, "Yeah, that's right." And he goes, "Right, I'm to look after you for the week." I was staying in a hotel, about halfway between the ground and Nottingham city centre, so he said, "I'll pick you up in the morning" and he drove me to training every day. If he was finished at the same time, he'd drop me back as well. And that's what he did for the five days. He was chatty.

It was light-hearted and certainly not intense. We talked about Ireland, about Forest and how he was doing. But it was a bit surreal because Forest played Spurs under the lights on the Wednesday evening and they would put all the youth team players along the side, right beside the dugouts. So, as a trialist, I was sitting there watching and thinking, "This just looks incredible."

'Roy played in that game and the following morning was picking me up from the hotel again and chatting to me about how everything had gone. He didn't have any airs or graces about him. It was one footballer looking after another that had come over. He knew I was away from home. He asked how I was finding it, what else I was doing and how different clubs compared. He took an interest in being Irish abroad. There was that "we stick together" mentality. It was a case of "if you need anything give me a shout". And on the Friday morning when he picked me up, he asked if I was around for the weekend because he wanted to bring me out and show me around town. But I had a flight that night to take me back home.'

During his short time at the club, Reid did have an encounter with Clough. Like Keane had instructed, he was courteous and polite, though a bizarre episode ensued regardless, with Clough's idiosyncrasies to the fore. 'We were all in the dressing room after training and I remember the entire atmosphere changed when someone said, "The gaffer is around." And then I got summoned,' he says. 'Somebody tapped me on the shoulder and said, "The gaffer wants to see you in his office" and I actually had to ask someone where it was. I walked down to this big room and he wasn't there. But there was his desk and his dog – Del Boy – in front of it. I'm standing there and he walks in, sits down and says, "You're over from Dublin?" And I said, "Yeah." He says, "Noel [McCabe] sent you over?" I said, "Yeah." He asks, "How are you finding it?" I said, "It's great, I'm being looked after really well, thanks very much." He goes, "That's good." And he got up, walked around the desk and went to dig me in the stomach. So, of course, I flinched – as you do.

And he said, "You'll need to toughen up that stomach if you want to make it here." And he walked out. And that was it. That was the interaction. So I was left standing there and I remember thinking, "Do I just leave? Do I stay?" There was no, "Out you get." He was gone. The dog was still sitting on the floor, didn't even move. I stood there for a few minutes and thought, "Right, he's obviously not coming back," so I pottered off.'

'You'd rarely see Brian Clough,' echoes Darren Barry, who was still trying to catch a break in the Forest youth side. 'Generally, he didn't come into training except on a Friday. He'd arrive in with the dog but wouldn't take the session. He'd walk around with Del Boy and you'd hear him shouting at various players. You knew when he was around because the place would be buzzing. Our youth team coach would say, "The boss is in" and it was like the Queen was coming. It was a big deal and everyone was excited probably because it wasn't a daily occurrence. I remember when I was injured and was in the physio room getting treatment after a cartilage operation. He came in and said to me, "Do you like ice cream?" And I said, "Yeah, I don't mind it." And he turns to the physio and says, "Graham, go get the Irishman some ice cream" and Graham Lyas had to head off and pick me up some. It was pretty weird. But I think it was his way of making a young lad feel good.'

It was a shame Mark Reid didn't get to stay in Nottingham that weekend, because Keane scored in a 3–1 victory over Oldham, again timing his run to perfection to reach a through-ball from Jemson and slide past Jon Hallworth for his second league goal in five games. But there were back-to-back defeats against Manchester City and Sheffield Wednesday.

As Forest hosted Wimbledon on 14 September, Clough was already fielding questions about pressure. 'We're not into excuses around here,' he said. 'We've just got to do better.'[28]

Keane, probably buoyed by the midweek praise he had received from Charlton after his exploits in Hungary, put on a memorable show.

His performance in Forest's 4–2 victory was greeted with breathless appreciation by the Wimbledon players, who lined up to offer a multitude of compliments.

'Keane is the new Bryan Robson,' declared their captain, John Fashanu, while goalkeeper Hans Segers seemed stunned at what he'd just witnessed. 'We were talking about him afterwards in the dressing room and couldn't believe the kind of things he was doing. When Forest scored their first goal, he was heading clear from their defence and sprinting sixty yards to take the ball in a goal-scoring position and whack it past me. What a player.'[29]

Wimbledon boss, Ray Harford, revealed with a weary sigh that they knew all about Keane's capabilities but the game plan to stymie his involvement had been completely eviscerated. 'We talked about how we could curb him, but we just didn't succeed,' he said post-game. 'We knew what he was capable of doing before the match, but we have to admit that he ran the show.'[30]

Forest were down a goal after just three minutes, but Keane equalised quickly, sprinting from one end of the pitch to the other after a Wimbledon attack broke down, and sending an expert finish across Segers after Sheringham spotted his support run and slipped him through. Just before the interval, Keane turned provider and pinged an inch-perfect cross to the far post for Kingsley Black – the £1.6 million summer signing from Luton – to volley home. Two minutes into the second half, Keane had a brace as he tucked away what was becoming a signature goal. He was too strong and quick for John Scales and when Gemmill sent the pass into his path, he took a touch to settle himself before side-footing past Segers. Then, that wide-armed celebration again and a thumbs-up to the fans. Rinse and repeat.

'I was seeing a player dominating a game,' says Warren Barton, who played against him that afternoon. 'His determination, his quality, his drive. At Wimbledon it was a physical battle, it wasn't a purist's game. But he never shied away from any tackles or responsibility. There are just certain moments in your career when you play against someone and think, "He's a player." And you sensed there was a special player there with Roy. We always fancied going to Forest and using our physicality and maybe getting a win. But he seemed to relish that type of attitude. He quite enjoyed the physical element. We always knew that somebody like Pearcey would come over if anything kicked off, but we weren't sure about the others. Then we quickly found out that Roy wouldn't back down either. He was never bullied or overawed.'[31]

'He was the attacking midfielder, really,' Black says. 'And what people didn't realise was how quick he was. He was like lightning. We used to do sprints in training and you'd be split into groups: the quick ones, the slightly slower ones. But Roy was always in the top group, along with Des Walker and Gary Crosby. He could break so quickly and outpace defenders. But also, there's the decision-making aspect. Roy made the right ones. The right runs, the right timing, the right pass. If it's simple, play it. If you need to beat a player, do it.'

So impressive was Forest's display that afternoon that some wondered whether they were league contenders. *The Guardian* talked of the team's 'silky skills that may yet land Brian Clough the championship', while praise was also lavished upon Keane, who, it was noted, was 'still not a first choice with the Republic of Ireland'. The article continued, 'At the heart of a marvellously uninhibited Forest performance was Roy Keane, again proving that he is one of the game's outstanding talents. He virtually ran the show from start to finish. He is usually thought of as a midfield player but that description hardly does him justice.'[32]

With no midweek fixture, Keane headed back to Cork – his previous trip home having been hastily interrupted. Speaking to the *Irish Independent*, he acknowledged the glittering reviews in the English papers but warned against the machinations of the tabloids, some of which had carried 'The

New Robson' as a headline to accompany their coverage of the Wimbledon game.

'You can go from up to down very quickly,' he said. 'You can't take any of it to heart. A few weeks ago they were against me when they blew something the manager said out of all proportion,' a reference to Clough's admonishing of Keane because of his tardiness.[33]

Keane's extended break meant he was planning to catch Cork City's UEFA Cup 1st Round clash with Bayern Munich at Musgrave Park, but only, he added wryly, if he could land himself a ticket.

When he returned to Nottingham in early October, he picked up his fifth goal of the season in a League Cup first-leg win at home to Third Division side Bolton Wanderers, which was the start of a four-game unbeaten stretch. In a 2–2 draw with West Ham, Keane's influence was curbed late in the opening period when Billy Bonds dropped Steve Potts from midfield into a sweeper role just to monitor Keane's runs. It was becoming a recurring theme.

'It's a little bit harder this time around,' he admitted the following week. 'I notice I'm closed down much more with man-to-man marking. But, remember, I've learned a bit too. Yes, last season I was niggled. But the intimidation thing doesn't worry me. I can look after myself.'[34]

When Forest headed to Burnden Park for the return leg of their League Cup clash with Bolton, Keane was scintillating. Scoring twice, he set up two more as Forest romped to a 5–2 win.

'His level of performance had to be seen to be believed,' Clough said afterwards.[35]

He turned one defender and sprinted clear of another before sending in a low cross for Sheringham to finish. Later, as a ball was played into the feet of Tommy Gaynor forty yards from goal, Keane had already begun his run in behind and when the pass was clipped over the top, he held off a challenge, rounded the goalkeeper and rolled to the empty net. Before the break, Gaynor capitalised from close range after Keane's shot was fumbled and, after the interval, the pair combined again as Keane ran through and stabbed decisively through the keeper's legs.

'I just wanted to wrap him up in cotton wool for ten days until our next game,' Clough said. 'But he wants to play international football and I realise it's an important part of his education.'[36]

This time, with John Sheridan and Ronnie Whelan both ruled out, Charlton had little hesitation including Keane in the squad for Ireland's crucial penultimate European Championship qualifier against Poland in Poznań.

'He's a much better player than I thought he was,' Charlton said, offering a startling admission. 'He gets better every game. I have no worries about throwing him in. He convinced me that he is a bloody good player against Hungary last month. Roy will play from the start. He has impressed me with his strength – mental and physical.'[37]

Keane was adamant that he wasn't nervous or apprehensive. 'I am ready for it,' he told Noel Spillane. 'I feel I have adjusted to international football now and even though I've only played twice with the seniors, the experience of playing with the Under-21 team over the last two years has stood to me. I can't wait for kick-off time to come around now and we can get down to business.'[38]

But after the squad met in Dublin, Keane did do something out of the ordinary and put in a call to a friend.

'He phoned me out of the blue,' says Tony Gorman. 'We'd exchanged a few letters at that time and he phoned me from the hotel before the team headed for the airport. We had a chat and he was saying how much he was looking forward to the game and other bits and pieces. We spoke a few times after that and there were some more letters and they were the usual stuff, nothing out of the ordinary. Pretty much a letter to home, telling me how he was getting on and asking me how I was doing.'

There may have been a degree of anxiety for Keane, owing to the importance of the fixture and the pressure of an unfamiliar system. Charlton's plan was to play five across midfield and use Tony Cascarino as a lone striker. He assigned Andy Townsend to the runner role instead of Keane, while Paul McGrath sat deep and Chris Morris and Kevin Sheedy slotted into the wide areas.

A packed Irish midfield hadn't exactly gelled on Keane's debut against Chile and it had been a while since he had to suppress his attacking inclinations. Under Clough, he was afforded a freedom to make incisive runs and get creative, but things would be more rigid in Poznań. Though Charlton maintained a draw was still a decent result, nobody was buying it. And it was clear from early on that Poland had flattered to deceive during the scoreless draw in Dublin and were very beatable.

To his credit, Charlton's strategy worked to perfection for the majority of the game as Townsend's dynamism led to him going close after just eight minutes following Cascarino's flick-on. After McGrath put Ireland in front with a close-range header, Townsend again burst through to get on the end of Keane's pass. He finished coolly but the goal was disallowed due to a contentious offside.

Conceding early in the second half, it was Townsend again who popped up to reclaim the lead for Ireland, rifling low to the corner from twenty yards after Cascarino had glanced on. And with twenty minutes left, they seemed assured of victory when Keane somehow won an aerial dual following Irwin's lofted corner and helped the ball into the six-yard area. Cascarino managed to stay onside and tucked the finish into the far corner.

But then the mistakes started. David O'Leary's sloppy clearance led to a deflected Roman Kosecki strike from distance that Bonner could only touch into the path of Jan Furtok who made it 3–2. Then, with just four minutes left, Bonner shouted at Kevin Moran to leave a cross from the right side, only for Jan Urban to get there before him and equalise.

Charlton tried to remain optimistic but the draw – Ireland's fourth in five qualifiers – meant that, to reach the Euros, they needed to beat Turkey in Istanbul and have England lose in Poland in the final round of Group 7 fixtures.

Keane wasn't available, having injured his ankle ligaments in Forest's 4–2 defeat away to Sheffield United in mid-October. He expected to be out of action for two weeks, but the recovery proved problematic. Earmarking a Thursday night reserve game against Manchester United in early November as his last chance to prove his fitness ahead of the Ireland trip the following week, Keane didn't even get stripped and went for a hospital scan instead.

After officially pulling out of the Irish squad, Clough refused him permission to travel to Dublin for the FAI Player of the Year awards and his parents accepted the Under–21 accolade on his behalf.

The following Tuesday, Keane managed seventy minutes for the reserves, but by the time he got back to competitive action, Forest were languishing in the bottom half of the First Division table and Ireland had failed in their quest to reach another major tournament.

But, regardless of the fortunes of both club and country, Keane's stock had never been higher and, as the end of the year approached, admirers began to linger.

PART 3

9

VIP LOUNGE

It was late November when Brian Clough got an early Christmas gift and dispatched his assistant, Ron Fenton, to unwrap it publicly. Forest excitedly revealed that they had been approached by Liverpool about a possible swap involving Dean Saunders and Keane. 'We dismissed the deal straightaway because Roy is a much better player than Saunders and he will get better,' Fenton told the press. 'He is worth more than Saunders, so the deal didn't make financial sense to us.'[1]

The striker had turned down the opportunity to join Forest in the summer but was struggling at Anfield, just four months after his record £2.9 million move from Derby.

Liverpool boss Graeme Souness didn't just have concerns in attack either and because of Ronnie Whelan's seemingly indefinite absence and Steve McMahon's general fitness issues, he considered a move for Forest's Garry Parker at the start of October and reportedly bid for him. Clough turned it down because he'd already allowed the forlorn Nigel Jemson to join Sheffield Wednesday, while his own son and Scot Gemmill were both nursing injuries at the time.

Floundering in mid-table, Liverpool badly needed an injection of energy and goals. And it wasn't the first time that a swap deal involving the clubs had been mentioned, though Keane had never seemed a top target before. The previous month, Souness had been linked with moves for either Nigel Clough or Des Walker.

Saunders had been under immense pressure for weeks, having netted just two league goals since arriving on Merseyside. Ahead of a midweek UEFA Cup third-round tie against Swarovski Tirol in Austria, Souness offered some tough love to his misfiring attacker. 'He's a boy who needs encouragement,' he said. 'He's had that in the past, but it doesn't work like that at Liverpool. You're told it's time to grow up.'[2]

Forest leaked the Keane story on the morning of the UEFA Cup game, Clough tickled pink by Liverpool wanting to trade a British record signing for a player he'd bought for a song. But it didn't have the desired effect and Saunders scored twice to give Liverpool a 2–0 first-leg victory. 'That will have knocked the smile off my critics,' he said afterwards. 'I am a Liverpool player and want to stay one.'[3]

Souness was seething at Forest's behaviour but, given the chance, fell short of denying he had made an offer for Keane. It was widely known he was in the market for a new midfielder and would eventually bring in Michael Thomas from Arsenal for £1.5 million in mid-December.

'I have not spoken to Brian Clough since the second-to-last game of last season,' Souness claimed. 'There has been a lot of speculation but there is absolutely no truth in it. We spent a lot of money on Dean Saunders and it is ridiculous to ask whether we want to keep him.'[4]

Keane had required five stitches to a head wound after a clash with Crystal Palace's Andy Thorn during a 5–1 Forest victory and had been afforded some time off back in Cork to recuperate when the story broke. Speaking to Noel Spillane, he suggested the whispers about a possible Liverpool move had started earlier in the month. 'I'm the same as everyone else and just getting the word from the newspapers,' he said. 'I'll have to wait and see what develops but I'd find it strange to move from Forest after just eighteen months there. At the moment I just want to carry on and continue to play well for Forest. I have heard talk about a possible move, okay, but there's been nothing definite yet. The rumours started two or three weeks ago but it's been getting stronger in the last week or so. I know Graeme Souness watched us play once or twice, but the talk at the club was that he was looking at Des Walker. I'm in the dark, really, and no one has spoken to me about a possible move. It's between the two clubs and out of my hands.'[5]

Later in the week, Clough confirmed Liverpool's offer and reiterated Keane wasn't for sale.

'We turned it down flat,' he said. 'As long as I'm team manager here, Keane will stay put. We are trying to build up our team here and you don't do that by selling off your best players and Roy Keane comes into that category. We still feel that the gap between us and the top clubs in the First Division can be bridged and Roy Keane has a part to play in that aim.'[6]

Especially in his dealings with the press, Clough was liable to say one thing and do another. For instance, in that same chat with reporters, he said there was no truth to the suggestion Garry Parker was set to leave the club. The next day, Parker had completed his move to Aston Villa.

Though he would have found it difficult to turn down a substantial Liverpool cash offer for Keane, Clough had allowed quite a few midfielders to leave the club and there was certainly a lack of depth to the squad. It made sense to keep hold of Keane for the moment, safe in the knowledge that his valuation was only going to go in one direction. Already, the Liverpool link had ensured Forest could probably command a fee in the region of £2.5 million for a player they'd signed eighteen months earlier for £20,000. Other clubs that were suddenly, and coincidentally, 'interested' in him included Manchester United, Arsenal and Aston Villa.

Meanwhile, Keane himself was still struggling with his fitness. He was forced off because of injury with twenty minutes to go in a 1–0 loss against Chelsea at the end of November and then missed the midweek League Cup stalemate against Southampton too. He returned in the impressive 3–2 win at home to champions Arsenal but sat deeper, allowing Gemmill and Woan make the powerful runs and assist Sheringham. The plan worked well as all three found the net.

Keane was back in the goals in a Zenith Data Systems (ZDS) Cup win away to Tranmere in December, netting twice and missing a pair of decent late chances to complete his hat-trick. But Forest's form was disjointed and after playing with plenty of energy against Arsenal, they were limp in their next league fixture at Liverpool and lost 2–0, with the entire squad having left Anfield within half an hour of the full-time whistle.

'I'm not allowed to say anything,' Woan hastily told reporters as he breezed past. 'We've been read the riot act.'[7]

Late on, as Forest attempted to rescue something from the game, Clough replaced Sheringham with centre-back Carl Tiler. He'd done something similar earlier in the season, when Walker was sprung from the bench against West Ham and Forest managed to find a dramatic equaliser. However, this was different. It seemed a pointed display of irritation from Clough and if it was intended to motivate Sheringham, it certainly back-fired. He wouldn't score again until late January.

The year ended in anti-climax for Keane also, as he felt the after-effects of another bad challenge from an all-too-familiar adversary. He'd set up Nigel Clough for the opening goal against Tottenham at White Hart Lane on 26 December, only for Paul Stewart to level affairs. With less than ten minutes to go and the game seemingly headed for a 1–1 draw, Stewart – as he'd done in the reverse fixture at the City Ground back in August – caught Keane with a 'shuddering foul'. After receiving treatment, he was eventually replaced by Darren Wassall and, just like in London, an incensed Forest teammate was punished for retaliation.

'I'd readily admit that I made a career at Spurs of getting the ball and giving it to Paul Gascoigne,' Stewart says. 'Now, if it was Roy Keane in the way or any other player, I didn't really care what happened to them. It was about my job and keeping myself in the team. I looked at it from my point of view rather than Roy's.'

On this occasion, it wasn't Pearce but Nigel Clough who delivered some wholly uncharacteristic violent retribution. He sought out Stewart, cemented him from behind and left him in a crumpled heap. Referee Ray Biggar showed him a straight red card, the first and only one of his entire career.

But, because of the time added on for both incidents, it allowed Pearce to step up in the ninety-third minute and rifle a superb free kick to the top corner to secure the three points.

Afterwards, a sheepish Clough Senior – so hell-bent on his players treating the game with respect – apologised for his son's actions, though Ron Fenton merely suggested that Nigel's motivation was sound and it was his timing that was off.

'It was too early to take retribution ... he should have waited for another ten, fifteen minutes and gone in a little bit more fairly.'[8]

Pearce scored again – his fifth of the season – away to Oldham in their final game of 1991, a close-range finish after Keane had smartly played him through. But two excellent crosses from Rick Holden either side of the interval set up headers from Graeme Sharp and Paul Bernard, and Forest lost for the ninth time in twenty top-flight games. Keane spent the bulk of the game shadowed by Nicky Henry and was unable to make much of an impact, suffering a recurrence of his persistent ankle problem too.

Though it had been a difficult start to his second season, Keane was settled. He enjoyed the city and had assembled a small but dedicated group of allies who were intent on embracing the thriving social scene. Darren Barry, plying his trade in the Forest third team, would tag along occasionally. 'The nightlife was really good for young people and very similar to Cork,' he says. 'Nottingham is a similar size, a bit bigger. You can walk around the city centre and there's so many pubs, bars and nightclubs. We'd go out on a Saturday night after a match and, if you had a midweek game, you could go out on Wednesday. And I don't mean for a couple of drinks.

'You had a few regular places. On a Saturday, quite often we'd start at the Trent Bridge Inn, which is five minutes from the City Ground, before heading into town. Then there was a wine bar called Browns, which was very lively and good fun. But I found it a bit odd myself, a working-class boy from Cork. You'd be thinking, "Why are we going to a wine bar?" But you'd manage to find something that you liked.'

Kingsley Black would also join Keane and his cohorts for an occasional night out. 'Tony Loughlan and Ray Byrne, another Irish player, were his big mates at Forest and continue to be to this day,' he says. 'He'll trust them implicitly and they're good, loyal friends. He chose them wisely, his close mates. And I had some nights with the three of them.'

'Roy's friendship group was Monday nights at The Black Orchid and Saturday nights at The Black Orchid,' according to Steve Chettle.

Located in an industrial estate in Lenton, about ten minutes outside Nottingham's downtown core, The Black Orchid was usually a twice-weekly haunt for Forest players. Prior to its opening in 1989, a memorable billboard teased the club as 'a night time adventure into dancing, eating and cavorting'. Rather unfortunately, the venue went through a rebrand in the late nineties and infamously reopened as Isis.

'Nottingham's got 238 pubs and clubs in one square mile, so it's very much a party town,' says Steve Campion, who worked as a doorman at the venue for over a decade. 'People came from everywhere. Sometimes we had ten to fifteen coaches parked outside from all over the country. It was always full by 10.30. I'd get there at nine o'clock and they'd be queuing around the block. It was mayhem. The Forest players usually came on a Saturday and a Monday. They'd get there at about eleven o'clock and we'd have them in a roped-off VIP lounge upstairs. Then, after we had a big refurbishment, that area got big glass doors and staff at the front. The players were all given a black VIP card and that allowed them to admit two guests. There was a group of Forest lads like Mark Crossley, Teddy Sheringham, Ian Woan, Steve Stone and Roy. I called them The Rat Pack.

'I remember meeting him for the first time because people had started to talk about this raw, skinny lad from Cork and he turned up one night. I think it was one of the first times he'd been out with the more senior pros. He was standing behind them and he was just like a schoolkid with his hands in his pockets. The lads took him into this big city that's supposed to have five or six women to every man. He's playing for Brian Clough. For a football club that's won back-to-back European Cups. And he's standing in this nightclub that holds almost 3,000 people. He looked like the proverbial deer caught in headlights.'[9]

Keane's profile was on the rise, as evidenced in late January 1992 when it was revealed that he'd signed his first major commercial deal and partnered with an Italian footwear company, Kronos. It was a three-year boot contract worth £100,000 and he had been approached along with Dean Saunders and Tony Adams as Kronos looked to make a splash in the UK market. He had previously been courted by a range of companies like Umbro and Diadora, as well as French manufacturers Line 7, whose biggest client was German World Cup winner and Juventus defender Stefan Reuter. They offered Keane a two-year contract, but he went with Kronos instead, admitting at the time that it was 'an extremely good deal'.[10]

He wore the new boots in a turgid FA Cup fourth round victory away to Hereford and again for a humiliating 5–2 home defeat to Sheffield United – Forest's heaviest City Ground loss in Clough's entire seventeen years in charge. Keane scored his tenth of the season that afternoon with a headed equaliser, though Sheringham was dropped (despite having ended his dismal run with a goal the previous weekend) and they were now winless in seven top-flight games, aimlessly adrift in mid-table and still just six points from the drop zone. But the idea of falling through the trapdoor was dismissed by the critics.

'Relegation? Forget it,' declared the *Daily Mail*. 'Forest have too much class and experience where it matters to go down.'[11]

The Kronos relationship did not last long for Keane, who was back wearing his trusted Pumas within a few weeks. And he wasn't the only one reverting to type.

From the seven games Forest played in February, only two of them were First Division fixtures, as they became the only club across all four divisions to remain in contention for each domestic cup competition. It provided some respite from a litany of sterile league performances. They breezed past Bristol City in the FA Cup to set up a quarter-final against Portsmouth. Meanwhile, a 3–1 aggregate victory over Leicester City ensured another Wembley appearance in the ZDS decider against Southampton. And in the League Cup, they faced very familiar opposition in the semi-finals.

Ahead of the first leg at home to Tottenham, match referee David Allison was asked about the simmering tension between the teams and how their previous two league games had seen two red cards. 'I regard this semi-final as just another match and will have no pre-conceived ideas,' he said. 'I always aim to finish a game with twenty-two players on the field but can make no promises that will happen because you can always be made to look foolish. However, I don't believe professional footballers tend to carry feuds from one game to the next.'[12]

At the City Ground, the sides were well-behaved. Despite being roundly booed every time he touched the ball, pantomime villain Paul Stewart applied another rigorous man-marking job to Keane and kept him quiet, though, with the score tied at 1–1, Keane did go close to a second-half winner when he forced a fine near-post stop from Erik Thorstvedt.

The second leg was a strange affair, played on Sunday 1 March against the backdrop of three separate IRA bomb attacks in London in a little over forty-eight hours.

During Friday morning rush-hour at London Bridge station, an explosion left twenty-nine people injured, four seriously. A subsequent series of hoax calls caused widespread pandemonium in the city and an unattended briefcase at Victoria Embankment was later destroyed by the bomb squad as a precaution.

The following evening, a smaller device was detonated at Furnival Street, in the High Holborn area, causing damage to various buildings and shop fronts, including the Crown Prosecution Service offices, believed to have been the target of the attack. Again, it had been a day of unease and tension with police evacuating thousands of shoppers from Oxford Street and its surrounding areas due to another suspected bomb threat.

In north London, kick-off was set for 3.30 on Sunday afternoon. But, hours beforehand – as more than 30,000 fans travelled for the game – a member of the public spotted a suspicious package on the tracks at White Hart Lane station. By the time a telephoned warning was registered with a hospital switchboard, bomb disposal experts had already diffused it. As police closed off and searched various streets in the vicinity, a second device was also located. The stadium was searched too.

'I don't think we were too aware of the bomb scare but I remember being on the coach, stuck in traffic and late,' recalls Kingsley Black. 'And then we got to the ground but weren't able to get through. But you're focused on the game and what's at stake more than anything else.'

Momentarily, it seemed the game could be postponed. But fans – after a two-hour wait outside – were eventually allowed to filter into the venue and kick-off was put back until 4.30.

By that stage, a hard rain had been falling for much of the day. It meant the pitch was already a muddied mess by the time the players emerged from the tunnel. ITV's live coverage was affected in a couple of different ways: the delay ensured that the latest *Hannah Hauxwell* episode, about the Yorkshire hill farmer's first trip outside the UK, and Sir Harry Secombe's religious chat show *Highway*, were both postponed until a later date and, probably more importantly, one of their two studio guests – Middlesbrough manager Lennie Lawrence – didn't arrive in time. So Manchester United boss Alex Ferguson, whose side were drawn to face 'Boro in the other semi-final, flew solo and wondered whether the surface would actually ensure a memorable battle.

'It's looking a bit heavy now and there's a bit of wear and tear in the middle of the park ...' he told Elton Welsby. '[But] sometimes in these conditions, it makes even a better game, you know?'[13]

He was right.

After ten minutes, Lee Glover gave Forest the lead with a low left-foot strike that zipped past Thorstvedt, kissing the near post on its way. But five minutes later, Tottenham were level when Gary Lineker slipped the wrong side of Darren Wassall and beat Stuart Pearce in the air to send a downward header past Mark Crossley. And they should have been in front shortly after when Paul Stewart swivelled in the area and sent a half-volley towards the corner, only for Crossley to brilliantly tip it onto the upright and then block the follow-up from Nayim too.

'We always enjoyed playing Tottenham, especially away from home,' Steve Chettle says. 'The cup final was proper dour, but they were usually very good football matches between us. Spurs were a great team with a good brand of football and the games were normally pretty open. It was a horrible night, horrendous weather. But it was another occasion where Roy showed his capabilities.'

For long periods, Forest struggled to cope. The conditions made it difficult to pass crisply and break quickly, and they were badly exposed by Tottenham's aerial prowess but also their midfield set-up, as David Howells sat deep to track Nigel Clough, Stewart pushed higher and Gordon Durie roamed to support Lineker. Inevitably, Keane found little space to exploit and was repeatedly on the back foot. And it wasn't just him. Sheringham was anonymous, usually battling both Gary Mabbutt and Steve Sedgley, while Gary Crosby rarely gave Pat van den Hauwe much to worry about on the flank.

By the start of the second half, the entire central strip of the pitch – from one goalmouth to the other – was a soggy, brown swamp. Some Tottenham players changed their sodden shirts during the break, but Clough, with that regimented football code, didn't allow it for his side. As the period wore on, things became farcical. At one stage, referee Joe Worrall attempted a drop ball with predictable difficulty. Both Stewart and Durie's drenched and dirtied shirts hung down around their knees while Durie's number was completely indecipherable. There was no breakthrough from either team and with the aggregate tied at 2–2, the game trudged to an additional thirty minutes.

As Nigel Clough and Sheringham gathered in the centre circle to re-start, the camera zoomed in for a close-up of the Mitre match ball. Encased in a lumpy mass of unrelenting sludge, it seemed the perfect metaphor for what had been an energy-sapping battle.

Unlike in the cup final the previous year, Clough did speak to his players on the pitch this time and whatever encouragement he offered certainly had the desired effect.

With ten minutes gone, Forest had rallied and were camped deep in Tottenham territory. When they forced a second corner in quick succession, Keane lingered close to the penalty spot. The routine was fairly straight-forward. Sheringham would hang back towards the eighteen-yard line before making a late dart to reach Gary Crosby's delivery to the near post. As before, Stewart stayed along the six-yard line and kept his eye on Keane.

Tottenham's Howells manned the upright but glimpsed Sheringham's position, and once Crosby sent in the corner, he raced to try to cut off the striker's arrival. But it was too high for Sheringham, and the gaggle of off-white shirts around him. Behind them all, Stewart – who'd delivered another excellent performance – seemed to anticipate a clearance or a second ball and was caught flat-footed.

'It was my job to pick him up at the corner but he lost me and did what he ended up doing very well for the rest of his career: scoring a massively important goal,' Stewart says.

Keane sprinted in front of him and, although the trajectory was low, stooped to power a thunderous header beyond Thorstvedt. The connection was so fierce that the microphones behind the goal picked up the thunk of skin against leather. There were shades of Rockmount Under–15s, of that near-post header he had no right to score. It was a magnificent finish and as he celebrated in the direction of the away supporters, he lifted a strong left arm in the air.

'You didn't expect anything but you realised he was capable of anything,' Chettle says. 'He was your go-to man. Nigel [Clough] was our catalyst at the top of the pitch but Roy could produce anything from anything and score a goal at any point. Various different goals too: from the edge of the box, him making a run after the striker drops deep, headers. And you realised at that point that the kid was something special.

'He was the best header of the ball that we had. He was so athletic and this was before we had a sports science programme. This kid was just naturally athletic. We didn't have a conditioning programme or a weights programme. He was just a natural athlete with the most unbelievable talent.'

In the ITV studios, Ferguson agreed. 'He's had a free run but what a header,' he said, watching a replay of the goal that booked Forest another Wembley appearance. 'The boy is exceptionally good in the air and brave to go there too.'

'It's a bit like the semi-final header against Juventus [when Keane pulled Manchester United back during the UEFA Champions League semi-final second-leg by expertly glancing home at the near post] in 1999,' says Black. 'In a big game, he wouldn't let you down. When something was needed, he stood up. That was an early sign of him being the match-winner. Taking it on his shoulders.'

'When you look at midfield players and talk about box-to-box, he was the ultimate,' Stewart says. 'And that's very rare. He could defend and score goals. When you think of the players that had that in their lockers, maybe only Bryan Robson springs to mind. When you look at that era, he was possibly the perfect midfield player. You either get somebody creative and who doesn't track back, or somebody who defends but who doesn't get forward. Roy did both better than most.'

Keane enjoyed the moment and what it meant. A victory over Tottenham, and in those circumstances, was particularly sweet. And it ensured a return to a stadium where he'd underperformed the previous year, something that still rankled with him. Forest were already assured of a Wembley appearance in the ZDS Cup final at the end of March, though the prospect of a League Cup decider carried a much greater impact.

'It's fantastic to get to Wembley again – and to beat Tottenham to do it makes it even more special,' he told *The Cork Examiner*. 'It can't make up for what happened but I feel a little bit better about it now.'[14]

Meanwhile, he brushed off both his winning goal and the tense atmosphere surrounding the game, preferring to concentrate on what the result meant for his manager. 'I feel so good for the boss,' he began. 'I know how much he wanted us to reach Wembley again.'[15]

'In terms of the goal, I just stuck my head out and it flew into the top corner,' he told Spillane. 'I couldn't believe it because I rarely score goals with my head. I suppose it was one of my best so far in England ... I didn't really think about the bomb scare or the fact that I was an Irishman in London on the day. At 1.50, we were told the match had been delayed for an hour or so because of the scare and we just went back to the hotel. The seriousness of the situation only dawned on us when the referee came onto the coach to tell us that the match was touch and go.'[16]

Keane enjoyed himself that afternoon, perhaps a little too much.

'We're back on the bus … and I'm on the card table … and Keaney's in the seat a couple back,' Craig Bromfield, the teenager from Sunderland who Clough had taken in, said in May 2019. 'He's just poked his head through and he's gone, "Lads, lads, lads, I've got a bit of a stupid question. Do any of you ever get a semi on when you're playing?" And the lads are looking at him, like. You can just see Pearcey's face is like "What the … what are you talking about?" And anyway, everyone is, "Roy, just no. Bloody hell, like. What do you mean?" And he's gone, "Well I do and I did today. … All that happened was that I won a corner," he said, "and I looked down … and I had pretty much a full erection. And," he said, "I'm trying to, like, find ways to hide it in my shorts." And anyway, the lads are absolutely giving him dog's abuse. … And I mean, that just sums it up. The lad used to get an erection when he was playing football. He enjoyed it that much and he wanted to win that much.'[17]

Keane grabbing the headlines wasn't a new phenomenon, but as journalists were desperate for fresh detail in his story, they simply invented some.

'There were muddied heroes all over the place and no one deserved to score the decisive goal more than Forest's Roy Keane,' went the *Daily Mail*'s match report. 'The brilliant young Irishman once had a trial at Tottenham – the kind of irony which comes back to haunt so many managers, coaches and scouts. He did not come up to expectations in North London, went back to Cobh Ramblers and, eighteen months ago, joined Forest for £25,000 [sic].'[18]

Keane never trialled with Tottenham, but it made for a good angle to the story. And in the context of myths being curated around him in England, it was an early turning point.

Still, some elements remained indisputable. Like his stamina.

Just forty-eight hours after the exhausting semi-final victory, Keane was a standout in a scoreless league clash against Crystal Palace. He set up Gary Charles for two excellent chances, the first of which was cleared off the line and the second brilliantly kept out by Nigel Martyn.

Palace boss Steve Coppell, probably expecting to face a relatively strained and off-form Forest, was thoroughly impressed and took time to single out Keane once again. 'After what Forest had gone through physically on Sunday it was a terrific achievement,' he said. 'I was amazed to see Roy Keane bombing around in the ninetieth minute. He runs back quicker than he runs forward.'[19]

Although the praise was nice, it didn't change much. It was early March and Forest were still without a First Division victory since 26 December. It got worse the following weekend when the novelty of still being involved in all three cup competitions was quickly extinguished. With a place in the semi-finals of the FA Cup at stake, Forest were understandably weary given it was their third game in seven days and succumbed to a 1–0 defeat to second-tier Portsmouth at an electric Fratton Park. Only ninety-six seconds were gone when Crossley dropped a harmless, floated free kick from the right side and Keane's international teammate Alan McLoughlin – on loan from Southampton after a turbulent time at The Dell – tapped home from two yards.

'My heart went out to the keeper,' a sympathetic Clough said afterwards. 'No one had to tell him he had dropped a clanger. We have all got to remember that less than a week ago he was making the saves at Tottenham that got us to Wembley. He'll get over it.'[20]

In terms of results, the rest of March was a lot better as Forest put together four consecutive wins prior to their ZDS Cup final against Southampton and the mood improved considerably. Before a home clash against Norwich, Clough was curiously presented with the Manager of the Month award for February, despite Forest's mixed form, while Keane picked up another Young Eagle of the Month accolade from Barclays, receiving more silverware and another £250 donation to the charity of his choice. Keane scored against Norwich that afternoon – another perfectly timed run from deep, another Nigel Clough through-ball for him to chase, another calm finish – and impressed again when both Manchester teams came to the City Ground in the space of seventy-two hours.

Against City, he set up the opener for Gary Crosby, before grabbing a close-range header late on to secure a 2–0 win. Just eighteen months earlier, during his debut at Anfield, Keane was caught in the moment as he watched Steve McMahon run alongside him. Now part of the City midfield, it was McMahon left in the dust as Keane's pace and purpose stole the show. Word was spreading and new admirers began to hover.

When he joined up with the Republic of Ireland squad the following week for a friendly against Switzerland at Lansdowne Road, rumours swirled about his Forest future amid reported interest from Serie A side Genoa. The Italians had just eliminated Liverpool from the UEFA Cup the previous week but needed reinforcements. High-profile assets like Stefano Eranio and Carlos Aguilera were linked with moves elsewhere, and with David Platt proving such a success following his switch from Aston Villa to Bari (hitting double figures from midfield), Genoa looked to England in the hopes of finding something similar, particularly a player who could support their Czech striker Tomáš Skuhravý. A club spokesperson later confirmed Keane had been watched and was of interest to them.

'We consider Roy Keane to be a very exciting and skilful player and we believe he could do an even better job for us than David Platt is doing for Bari,' they said.[21]

Unlike when Liverpool batted their eyes at him earlier in the season, Keane admitted to having no knowledge of Genoa's pursuit, though he was certainly fascinated by the prospect of a move to Italy and didn't exactly play down the possibility of an exit.

'Of course I'd like it but I don't know a thing about it – I'll have to wait until I get back to the club,' he told *The Cork Examiner*, before adding he 'would be mad' to ignore Genoa's advances.[22]

The interest soon fizzled out, and during Genoa's UEFA Cup semi-final exit at the hands of eventual winners Ajax, they were impressed enough by John van 't Schip to sign him in the off-season instead. But Keane wasn't the only Forest player courted by a Serie A side. Des Walker had been a long-time target for Sampdoria. The previous summer, Clough had turned down a £5 million offer for him, but a clause in his contract meant he could leave within the last twelve months of his deal for just £1.5 million.

Walker's probable departure lingered as Forest returned to Wembley for the ZDS Cup final against Southampton on 29 March. The team made quite the sartorial impression upon arrival with a memorable three-piece suit which included a canary-yellow, patterned waistcoat.

'Paul Smith the clothes designer is from Nottingham,' Steve Chettle says. 'We used to go down and get a couple of suits every year because of how successful the team was. But we went to that final all dressed as Rupert the Bear, basically.'

'It was a beautifully cut suit and I've actually still got that waistcoat,' says Kingsley Black. 'We went up to a warehouse just outside of Nottingham, not too far from the ground, to get measured. At the time, we had no idea who Paul Smith was. He was a bit like Roy – an emerging talent. They weren't quite the white Armani suits that Liverpool wore to the FA Cup final in 1996, but we looked the part, I think.'

Keane was central to Forest's opening goal in the final as a set-piece routine worked delightfully after just fifteen minutes. As Crosby prepared to take a throw close to the corner flag, Keane took up a position along the by-line, about halfway inside the area. When Crosby picked him out, he beat Barry Horne in the air and glanced a header towards the corner of the box. The target was probably Ian Woan, who would have supposedly whipped in a cross or, given the sweetness of his left foot, fired in a shot. Instead, Scot Gemmill moved towards the dropping ball and hooked a superb volley across Southampton goalkeeper Tim Flowers to the far corner. Just before the break Kingsley Black added a second and Forest seemed to be coasting. But they conceded twice in the second half, displaying their frailties under a high ball once more as Matt Le Tissier and Kevin Moore scored from close range. But with ten minutes left in extra time, Gemmill arrived at the far post to meet Gary Charles' cross and crack a powerful first-time strike past Flowers.

The silverware – Keane's first in England – was nice but, in truth, the Wembley visit served as a costly distraction. Pearce damaged knee ligaments early on and wouldn't play again that season, while Forest's fixture list remained unsustainably intense. Later on Sunday, Clough attended the PFA dinner at the Grosvenor House Hotel to pick up a Merit award and couldn't resist a dig during his speech: 'I shall now go home because I've got those shits Arsenal on Tuesday, and those even bigger shits on Thursday: Wimbledon.'[23]

Forest were forced to play four games in seven days and the win at Wembley was the best it got. Fatigue was already creeping in away to Arsenal, where they surrendered a commanding lead. Woan cancelled out Lee Dixon's early penalty with an outrageous strike from distance before Nigel Clough's deflected effort looped over David Seaman. Keane sprinted from midfield twenty minutes from time to support Sheringham and when the striker pounced on Seaman's spill, he set Keane up for a simple tap-in and Forest seemed out of sight. But they leaked two goals in the final four minutes and were forced to make do with a 3–3 draw.

Forty-eight hours later, against 'the bigger shits', they were torn to shreds as John Fashanu wreaked havoc. Before the game, he presented Clough with a colourful caricature – autographed by the entire Wimbledon squad – of Clough sitting on the toilet, a reference to his PFA speech. Fashanu was wearing flip-flops, so Clough thanked him before stepping on his toes and playfully punching him in the stomach.[24]

Fashanu, the younger brother of Justin, a player who had an immensely difficult relationship with Clough when he signed for £1 million in 1981 and lasted just thirty-six games, was a battering ram all afternoon and scored twice in the 3–0 win. Limp and lifeless, Forest also lost two more defenders – Chettle and Charles – to injury. As the players trudged off, Clough pointed a finger in their general direction.

'Roy Keane,' he bellowed.

Keane prepared himself for a dressing down, a dig to the midriff or a clip around the ear.

'Tuck your shirt in.'[25]

Relieved, he did what he was told.

Two days later, the exhaustive run of games came to an end with another defeat: this time at home to Sheffield Wednesday.

A 1–0 win over Southampton prefaced their second trip to Wembley in a fortnight on 12 April for the League Cup final against Man United. Forest's defensive crisis meant Brett Williams returned to the starting line-up for the first time since September, while Clough also pondered using his son as an emergency centre back should the casualty list get any worse. He took a gamble on Charles' fitness for the clash with United, but the full-back only lasted twenty-three minutes after a recurrence of his hamstring problem.

By that stage, United were already in front thanks to Brian McClair's low left-foot strike. But Forest had started brightly and should have scored early on. Even though Alex Ferguson had been so concerned by Keane's influence that he selected Mike Phelan alongside Paul Ince in central midfield rather than the more offensively minded Neil Webb, Keane managed to evade them long enough to go close to an opener.

On a quick breakaway, he found enough time and space to swap passes with Clough and raced into the area, hounded by three United defenders. Panicked by the presence of the blue shirts [United's away jersey at the time], he hurried his low shot and even though Peter Schmeichel failed to gather at the first attempt, it was straight at him and he pounced quickly to smother. It was Keane's most meaningful contribution as Forest – with one goal to show from their previous three games and still recovering from the overwhelming volume of recent fixtures – struggled to create much. Phelan and Ince gamely stuck to their defensive task and Ryan Giggs' consistent weaving in-field was another headache to contend with. Keane was stronger and better than his Wembley experience twelve months earlier, but still came up short.

Two days later, Forest were back to the grind and travelled to Kenilworth Road for a meeting with relegation-threatened Luton Town. This was their seventh game in seventeen days. Before kick-off, Forest were without six defenders and were forced to start Nigel Clough at centre-half and Gary Crosby at right-back. Added to their anxiety was a playing surface that seemed better equipped for water polo than football. However, they took the lead after just two minutes when Keane dodged some challenges and puddles before releasing Toddy Örlygsson, whose cross eventually fell for Black – the former Luton player – to volley to the corner. But by half-time Forest had conceded twice and lost Des Walker to a knee injury. So Clough instructed Keane to drop back and partner his son in a makeshift central defensive pairing. Forest didn't concede again, though they failed to muster an equaliser.

Clough was so impressed that he kept Keane there for the visit of Aston Villa four days later. Forest racked up a clean sheet while Gemmill and Sheringham found the net.

'Some local variant of Dutch elm disease had felled Forest's centre-backs, but the unlikely combination of Nigel Clough and Roy Keane gave the impression that they had always yearned to play at the back,' wrote

Dave Hadfield in *The Independent*. 'With Keane strong in the air and surprisingly combative and Clough's vision and intelligence as valuable in his own penalty area as in the other, the odd couple were a testimony to the adaptability of Brian Clough's latest team.'[26]

The players weren't surprised by Keane's flexibility.

'Timing, basically,' says Black. 'It was impeccable. The run, the leap. He was fantastic at centre-back. Superb. He may have had a relatively slight upper body but his legs were extremely strong. But we missed him in midfield.'

Alex Ferguson labelled it an 'incredible result' as he prepared to host Forest two days later in a must-win game. In command of the title race for so long, United had suddenly started to splutter. With nearest challengers Leeds hitting their stride and the team facing into three crucial fixtures in the space of six days, it was a momentous game. United's nervousness was evident as a Schmeichel blunder resulted in Woan grabbing the opener after thirty-three minutes. Almost immediately, McClair headed home from close range to equalise after Steve Bruce had evaded a subsequently furious Keane at the far post to tee him up. But Keane – back in midfield – played a part in Gemmill's match-winner ten minutes from time that silenced Old Trafford. United slipped to second in the table and never recovered.

Keane finished the domestic season with two home draws. The first, against Liverpool, again saw his high energy and timed runs consistently cause problems. When Ray Houghton undersold a back-pass to goalkeeper Mike Hooper, it was Keane who got there first and he ended up winning a penalty that Sheringham converted. Ian Rush conjured an equaliser but Keane had chances in the second half. Only a last-ditch challenge from Nicky Tanner prevented him from finding the net after he expertly broke the offside trap, while Hooper denied him with a smart save later on.

It had been a different, difficult and long campaign. Like Clough had predicted at the start of the season, teams had persistently attempted to shackle him. But as much as it had been a substantial challenge, it led to that initial youthful exuberance being replaced by something more resolute and complete. His first year was built on a wide-eyed earnestness and a willingness to buzz around every inch of the pitch. But there was more control to his sophomore stage. An awareness of a more specified and impactful contribution. Effectively, he was developing and flourishing as a player. Clough was there to offer an embrace, instruction or insult and it helped that with Sheringham as an attacking focal point and Gemmill an under-rated midfield partner, Keane could concentrate on a more minimal to-do list. But, for the most part, the growth appeared innate.

'Generally, Cloughie didn't have to coach him much,' says Duncan Hamilton. 'He didn't do much anyway but the most important thing for Clough was that if you were having a bad day, even if you weren't on the top of your form, providing you shed sweat, you could get away with a lot. With Keane, he never pulled out of a challenge. He didn't argue when Clough asked him to play centre-half. He kept going. Maybe other technically gifted players were a bit soft and tended to sulk. And he saw in Keane somebody who didn't do that. That is the difference.'

And Keane was in demand. Liverpool had wanted him. Badly. There had been confirmed interest from Serie A. And at the end of the season – one that on the outside may have looked a lot less than his debut campaign – he was recognised with a high-profile award.

'Some youngsters, and sometimes even the more experienced players, excel for one season, but what a lot of them find it very difficult to do is to show it for another year,' Graham Taylor eloquently explained, as he announced the Barclays Young Eagle of the Year winner. 'But that is what Roy has done. Not only is he good from box to box and a good passer of the ball, he knows how to intercept and tackle, and he scores his quota of goals. Jack Charlton is a lucky man. Barring injuries, this lad could play the next eight to ten years at the highest level.'[27]

As the season wrapped, things were changing. The cocooned existence was waning. For a while, it seemed that Keane was Forest's little secret. A quiet, unassuming guy who blended into the background. But he was a fully fledged public figure now and a target for big clubs. The dynamic was shifting. Some friends remained, others moved on. There was a feeling that what was next would be different.

'There's mythology there and the stories grow, but if you looked at Roy at the time, you'd have seen a nice fella and a normal, decent, sociable guy,' Darren Barry says.

It had been tough on Barry. Another prospect from Cork. Another youngster who'd played for Rockmount. Signed in the same summer.

'A few people did comment to me. When a young Irish player went to a big club, it would be a big deal in your local community, even if you weren't in the first team. But because I had Roy above me, it certainly overshadowed me. But I'm not sure if that was a bad thing. And it kept me grounded, that's for sure.

'We were never close friends, but when I was released by Forest and went back home, he drove me to Birmingham Airport, which was a nice gesture. That's quite a drive and he didn't have to do it. I remember when I was back in Cork and I used go around on a mountain bike at the time. I was on the northside of the city and going up a really steep hill – and there are many of them. Roy went whizzing past in his white Mercedes. And there was some sense of irony to that.'

The day before the League Cup final, Keane had turned up at the team hotel sporting a dramatic new haircut, much to the delight of his team-mates. The Tintin-style mound had been replaced by a tight crop, which would become a signature look for the remainder of his career. It also seemed a timely statement of sorts. No longer was he one of Clough's neat and tidy brigade with their short back and sides.

He was standing out and, more importantly, beginning to acknowledge the worth of his individuality.

10

TRADING PLACES

Boston in early June.

Having failed to qualify for the European Championships, Keane had been named in the Republic of Ireland squad for the US Cup, a four-team tournament taking place in Massachusetts. But he only lasted seventy-eight minutes of the first game – a 3–1 loss to the host nation – after picking up an ankle injury. Speaking to Noel Spillane afterwards, he was concerned by the possibility of two things: that Forest might demand his immediate return to Nottingham for treatment and that they'd disrupt his upcoming holiday plans too.

'I had to fax a message to the City Ground to keep them posted on what's happened me but I am terrified they will call and tell me to get back over to Nottingham for treatment,' he said. 'If Cloughie hears of this, he might insist on me going back to the club. It's all down to the physio, Graham Lyas, really. I've told him it's not that serious but I am worried about it. When I get back to Dublin, I'm heading off immediately for two weeks' holiday in Cyprus but I just hope the club don't force me to cancel that now.'[1]

Keane wasn't summoned and remained on the tour, despite not being able to feature in the remaining games against Italy and Portugal. He was thrilled. Without the pressure of playing, he could enjoy himself in the US. Though the tour was immensely innocuous, Keane himself ensured it took on mythical status. In his autobiography, he detailed how he and

Steve Staunton went out the night before the team was due to depart and were inevitably late for the bus the following morning. It led to a furious Charlton confronting them about their behaviour.

'I didn't ask you to wait,' Keane replied.

When the team captain, Mick McCarthy, told him he was out of order, Keane offered a four-word riposte.

'Go and fuck yourself.'[2]

But there's another memorable story from that trip that Keane didn't include.

'We'd go for a walk in the afternoon and there was a second-hand jewellers shop,' Alan McLoughlin recounted in an interview with Portsmouth's in-house media team in November 2013. 'And he [Roy] kept stopping at the shop and looking at the watch [in the window]. ... So I said "What are you looking at?" and he said, "There's a nice little Rolex there and it's $1,200." I said, "Are you buying it?" And he said, "I can't afford to buy it."' At that point Roy was still 'on [a] pittance at Nottingham Forest'. So two days later, 'he stopped again [at the jewellers] ... I felt a bit sorry for him. ... I was earning a bit more money and could afford it, so I stumped up the agreement with him that I would buy the watch and he would pay me when he came [on] the next five Irish trips. ... He wore it back to the [hotel] room. ... We were going out that evening ... and he decided he would leave the watch in his room. I told him no, put the watch on ... [but] he decided to leave it in his room. And, lo and behold, what happened? All the rooms got robbed and his lovely Rolex went. Unfortunately, he still had to pay me. ... I think his next watch was ... about twelve grands worth! ... I could see he was a nice lad and I decided it was the right thing to do.'[3]

In total, over $25,000 worth of cash and other valuables were stolen from the Irish players at Boston's Park Plaza hotel that night. Five of the rooms were raided and Keane was one of eight team members affected along with Packie Bonner, Gerry Peyton, Chris Morris, Kevin Moran,

Dave O'Leary, Tommy Coyne and Niall Quinn. Morris, who had planned to head to Florida on a holiday the next day, lost $6,000 in hard cash.

The players were partially refunded after an agreement was hammered out by the FAI, the tournament's organising committee and the hotel. But the FAI did acknowledge that some players had been irresponsible and it was revealed that sixteen key cards had been issued to one room.

It was a shambolic end to a dismal and wasteful tour.

After his Cyprus sojourn, Keane was back in Cork to help out on a week-long FAI coaching course at St Mary's Park in White's Cross, about a ten-minute drive from his family home in Lotamore Park. By this stage, his Forest future was again the subject of much debate.

Having squandered the First Division title with a late-season collapse, Alex Ferguson was intent on making changes at Manchester United in time for the launch of the new Premier League and identified midfield as a problem area. Desperate to replace Bryan Robson, he had also lost faith in Neil Webb, while the likes of Mike Phelan and Danny Wallace seemed nothing more than fringe players. Keane's name was mentioned as a possible target, as was his nemesis at Tottenham, Paul Stewart, but Ferguson's top choice was a player Keane knew very well.

Ferguson spoke publicly about a possible move for Andy Townsend, revealing he had talked to Chelsea 'several times' about securing his services. But they slapped a price tag of £2.5 million on him and Ferguson felt it was excessive for a twenty-nine-year-old.

Still, the whispers set the tone. Keane would spend the majority of the 1992/93 campaign at the centre of feverish transfer speculation.

Before that, however, there were some lower-key affairs to tend to.

On a July evening at Oriel Park, Forest took on a Dundalk side that boasted two of Keane's ex-FÁS cohorts, Tommy Dunne and Richie Purdy, in their back four. But it was a difficult night for them. After Nigel Clough opened the scoring five minutes in, Keane deftly lobbed Eddie van Boxtel midway through the half to double their lead, while Teddy Sheringham and Brian Laws completed the rout.

'I'll never forget the game because the difference in the size of him was incredible,' Dunne says. 'He'd bulked up and bulked out. Whatever he'd been doing, everything was bigger. We'd talked beforehand about watching his runs from midfield. But there was nothing you could do because they were timed perfectly. He was outstanding. Every time the ball went into a striker's feet, he just took off. You knew it was happening but there wasn't a huge amount you could do about it. He was just so powerful in his movements and his runs. After a while we said, "Hang on a minute, if we leave space in behind, he's just going to be in all night" so we dropped off completely as a team. Otherwise he would've torn us asunder. But that was an extremely good Forest side.'

For Purdy, there was something else that caught his eye about Keane: the influence he was wielding on the pitch, despite the fact he was still only twenty.

'Brian Laws had a throw-in,' he says. 'Roy was in the middle and showed for it but Laws never threw it to him. Well, you should've heard what he said to him. This was Brian Laws – an experienced player. Roy was only a kid. But he fucking lambasted him. He called him a langer and every other fucking name under the sun. He didn't care who it was. They had Teddy Sheringham, Stuart Pearce, Nigel Clough. Roy was going around the middle of the park and if he got a bad pass, he'd lash anyone out of it. He didn't care about anyone but himself and you need that selfishness to do what he did.'

Dundalk were so excited by Keane's involvement that the cover of the match programme was a photograph of him, wide-mouthed, celebrating after scoring the winner against Tottenham in the previous season's League Cup semi-final second leg.

But the reception was slightly different when he turned up at the RDS, situated close to Lansdowne Road in leafy Dublin 4, two nights later for a game against Shamrock Rovers. Forest were left frustrated by a strong performance from Ray Treacy's side and the affair ended scoreless.

There was a needle to proceedings from the off. Inside the opening minute, Keane was on the receiving end of a forceful challenge from Rovers' midfielder John Toal and was sufficiently wound up thereafter.

'It was a normal game against an English team,' says Toal. 'You let them know early on that it wasn't going to be easy and that they weren't coming over here to fanny around and take the piss out of us. We weren't "only" a League of Ireland team. You raised your game and got stuck in to them. That was the bottom line, whether it was Roy Keane or Cinderella you were facing. And for us, playing against a twenty-year-old who'd been cross-channel for a few years wasn't a big deal. Roy had a name for himself at the time but we had some fellas that had won the league, like John Coady and Peter Eccles, as well as a few other seasoned pros.

'I do remember that before the game, Ray Treacy said to me, "This fella Keane in the middle of the park, he won't get on the ball much but he'll get it, send it out wide and then bomb into the box. And if you lose him, just pass him onto Gino [Brazil]." And, Jaysus, he was very fit. The engine on him. Up and down. There were a lot of little niggles in the game and a lot of tackles going in from either side but not because it was Roy Keane. He was in the middle of midfield against me and when you got a chance to make a tackle, you took it. There were a few verbals. I remember something being said about Cork and Dublin – just a bit of slagging and banter. And he gave as good as he got. Just the usual joking on the pitch. It was all in good spirits. But he did lose the rag later on.'[4]

Given his style, Keane should have appreciated and applauded Rovers' attitude. Instead, he cut an irritated figure and when he clashed with Martin Bayly ten minutes before half-time, referee Oliver Cooney brandished a yellow card. Immediately, Ron Fenton – in charge of the Forest side in Clough's absence – replaced Keane with Scot Gemmill. As Keane walked to the bench, he was roundly booed by a section of the crowd. It wouldn't be the last time it happened in Dublin.

'Martin would have been an easy kick at the time because he was a cultured, lovely footballer,' says Toal. 'He'd stay on the ball and throw some shapes. It was a tough challenge on him and I remember myself and John Coady running over to Roy. We were in like Flynn and got very close, standing over him. It was all "Fucking referee" and that kind of outrage because Martin was a fella you'd be looking to protect. He was excellent on the ball but timid and if there was a tackle there, he wouldn't go into it. But it could've been anyone tackling him. It just turned out that it was "the famous Roy Keane". He was making a bit of a name for himself but still only twenty. And he had a bit of a nark about him. A bit of a spice.

'In terms of the booing, maybe it was the Irish way of begrudging? Sometimes we don't like to see a fella doing too well? But I was definitely disappointed when he was taken off because I wanted to see more of him. You liked to see these guys play. He was only a young fella but he had a bit of a chip on the shoulder, that hunger. Maybe Forest were protecting him, felt he was worth a fortune and didn't want him getting injured.'

Teddy Sheringham didn't play in Dublin as he seemed set to join Tottenham. They'd offered £2 million and Clough was happy to sell, but he wanted a replacement before allowing him leave. With Spurs looking to add a striker quickly owing to Gary Lineker's move to Japan, the deal went cold and Sheringham returned for the four-team Makita Tournament in early August that also featured Leeds, Sampdoria and Bundesliga-champions Stuttgart.

Forest faced the Italians – who lost the European Cup final to Barcelona just two months earlier – in their opener at Elland Road. Included in the tourists' starting line-up was debutant Des Walker, who'd completed his transfer from Forest earlier in the summer. Sampdoria were already in front when Keane was forced off at half-time due to injury, and they added a second late on. The following day, Sheringham missed a host of chances as Forest went down 1–0 to Stuttgart.

There were concerns, not just about the underwhelming pre-season results, but the club's wider recruitment drive. Darren Wassall, who had been groomed as a successor to Walker and featured heavily throughout the previous campaign, moved to nearby Derby amid rumours of a clash with Clough, though he maintained Forest had merely dallied in offering him a new contract. And despite losing two first-choice centre-backs, when Clough did enter the transfer market, he brought in young Scottish midfielder Ray McKinnon.

There was another new signing by the time Forest headed to Northern Ireland for two more friendlies in early August, but the acquisition of thirty-two-year-old striker Gary Bannister on trial from West Brom hardly whipped supporters into a frenzy, despite him netting on his debut against Ards at Castlereagh Park.

Despite suggestions Forest would struggle, Keane claimed that a solid start to the league campaign could ensure a title push. But he also seemed to hint that while he was a long way from the finished article, he was ready for a greater challenge.

'I'm not stupid enough to think that I know it all,' he told the *Evening Herald* on the eve of the very first Premier League weekend. 'It's within me to be better, to play at a higher level. There's a lot more to come from Roy Keane.'[5]

As it turned out, the same was true of Forest and they impressed in their opening fixture at home to Liverpool. The Premier League revolution was televised and the game was the first of its kind shown by Sky Sports. Billed as a 'TV spectacular', the coverage was five hours long. Initially, the broadcaster wanted to show the champions, Leeds United, hosting Wimbledon, but they couldn't get local police to agree to switch the game to Sunday because of a Michael Jackson concert taking place at Roundhay Park that evening.

Though it wasn't their first choice, Sky did still land a decent clash to which Keane contributed a fine performance. He should have scored after just three minutes, when a typically excellent angled run took him right through the heart of Liverpool's back three, but his low left-foot strike was blocked by David James, making his debut after a £1 million switch from Watford, who then saved two follow-up efforts from Nigel Clough. Just before the break, Gemmill curled in a cross to the far post where Keane climbed above Nicky Tanner and sent a strong downward header towards the bottom corner, but James again was equal to it. And inside the last ten minutes, Keane popped up in the area once more, rounded James and was upended by the keeper, though referee Mike Reed felt there was simulation and ignored the penalty appeals, much to Keane's fury.

At times, he did seem pent up and when he went in recklessly on Ronnie Whelan, an irate Graeme Souness jumped from the dugout and vented his anger. Keane was booked, but it could have been worse.

'A ball came over, I knocked it down and next thing he just splattered me,' Whelan said decades afterward. 'I wasn't hurt but I sort of let on that I was because I knew he had tried to do me and I knew he was going to get booked. So, I knew then I had half a chance to do him back because he'd be on a booking and wouldn't be able to go in full whack for the next ball between us. This is the way the mind works, you see. He was booked but he finished the game and afterwards Dean Saunders said to me, "What's going on there with you and him?" And I said, "I don't know. Why?" And Deano said, "Because when you were down, he was shouting as he was walking away, 'That's for fucking kicking me at Anfield!'" See, Roy didn't forget.'[6]

Whelan had clattered him on his debut. Keane waited two years to clatter him back.

Writing in his newspaper column the next day, John Giles revealed Keane was his man of the match but offered the 'Cork youngster' a warning. 'The last thing he wants is a reputation of being a hard man.'[7]

Forest did enough to claim a 1–0 opening day win, as Sheringham fired a superb strike beyond James just shy of the half hour. Arguably, it was the high point of the team's entire season.

'We don't work on scoring goals like that,' opined Clough later. 'They come out of the blue from pure ability. Edward Sheringham stuck it in … bang! That's what strikers are paid for.'[8]

But he was paying lip service. Clough wasn't interested in Sheringham's 'pure ability' or his prowess because the proposed move to Tottenham was resuscitated at the end of the month after the Londoners were depressingly thumped 5–0 by Leeds. A price of £2.1 million was agreed and the player who struck twenty-two goals in his debut season was pushed out the door. It was an alarming departure and a defining moment for both the manager and the club. Also, it was another example of Clough going back on his word. He'd maintained Sheringham would only be sold once he had lined up a replacement, but one wouldn't arrive until March.

'Selling him [Sheringham] was the right decision,' Clough later argued in his autobiography. 'It was right then and it would still be right, in the same circumstances, today. He wanted to leave. His heart was obviously not with Forest and in a situation like that there is only one decision for a manager to make – you get rid! He'd been with us barely a year but, separated from his girlfriend and able to see his little boy just at the weekends, he was unsettled. Once he knew he could get a move to Tottenham his enthusiasm and commitment to Nottingham Forest were bound to be affected.'[9]

Clough was immediately linked to a range of attackers. One rumoured target was Duncan Ferguson, then at Dundee United. Dean Saunders was again suggested and available as Liverpool looked to offload him while it was even mooted that Forest could re-sign Nigel Jemson, a player they'd sold to Sheffield Wednesday a year earlier.

But it seemed Clough had a soft spot for Alan Smith at Arsenal, who had a year remaining on his contract. George Graham was reluctant to sell but did enquire about a possible swap deal. Forest would get Smith, centre-back Andy Linighan and £1 million in exchange for Keane, a player he'd admired ever since Arsenal won 2–0 at the City Ground in September 1990.

Given the chance to play down the story, Keane elected to pour petrol on the flames instead and, once again, confirmed he would be prepared to speak with any team about a switch.

'I'd be the last to know what's going on in terms of a transfer,' he told *The Cork Examiner*. 'I'm in the dark, really, about this latest paper talk. But if an offer did come in from another club, I would have to consider it. In the past, Manchester United and Liverpool have been linked with me but this is the first time Arsenal have shown an interest.'[10]

It was an intriguing package and, as part of the deal, Forest would gain much-needed reinforcements at both ends of the pitch. However, Clough had already identified a centre-back that would ease their problems.

Laurent Blanc, the French sweeper, had lost his place at Napoli and was allowed to look for a new club. During their dismal time at the European Championships in the summer, England had drawn 0–0 with France and Nigel Clough, who was an unused substitute, was impressed by Blanc's calmness, composure and intelligence. Forest were keen on an initial year-long loan, like Eric Cantona's arrangement with Leeds, to gauge whether Blanc could adapt to the Premier League. But Nîmes represented less of a gamble for the twenty-six-year-old and he went there instead.

Having failed to replace Walker and Wassall, fringe figures like midfielder Terry Wilson were back in the fray and tasked – ridiculously – with central defensive duties. The squad seemed seriously lacking in depth or progress.

And when another injury crisis brewed, Clough again turned to Keane.

By that stage, the team weren't being beaten but humiliated, especially away from home. In their third league fixture against Oldham on 22 August, they were 5–0 down midway through the second half, only a late three-goal spurt putting some relative respectability on the scoreboard. At Ewood Park against Blackburn, it was a similar story. They conceded an opener after four minutes and trailed 4–1 shortly after the hour mark.

Behind after one minute and forty-one seconds in Norwich, it was Keane who brilliantly constructed an equaliser for Nigel Clough on the half hour. Sprinting to fetch a Pearce pass into the left channel, his first touch took him back towards his own goal. But after a quick glance, he spotted Clough's run into the area. A second touch gave Keane a kinder angle to work with before he curled a deft pass over the top. Clough allowed the ball to bounce and, for a second, it seemed like the chance was gone. But he stretched and hooked a powerful strike across Bryan Gunn that nestled in the net via the inside of the far post.

It was a brief interlude in another awful display, evidenced by the Canaries' second goal, when Toddy Örlygsson inexplicably kicked his standing foot on the edge of his own area, fell to the ground and inadvertently pushed the ball into the path of Lee Power, Keane's underage international teammate, to slide past Crossley. David Phillips, who would sign for Forest the following year, added a third.

There had been a tame 2–0 loss to Manchester United – where Keane exchanged verbals with Peter Schmeichel after a penalty area dust-up – as well as home and away defeats to Sheffield Wednesday. Even when a fragile Forest arranged an innocuous Monday night friendly against second-tier neighbours Derby County to build some much-needed confidence, they lost 2–0 at the City Ground.

It was Forest's worst start to a season in almost forty years and they were rooted to the bottom of the table with one win from seven games.

Against Coventry, Keane was deployed at centre-back alongside Carl

Tiler as Clough desperately tried to stop the rot. 'He was still a bairn,' Clough later wrote. 'We were struggling for central defenders and I remember putting a question to the staff: "Who's the best header of the ball in this club?" They all came up with the same answer: Roy Keane. "So that's who we'll play at centre-half," I told them. No hesitation, no qualms, no reservations. He had ability and, even at such a tender age, he could solve an immediate problem.'[11]

Other reactions weren't as positive.

'The experiment was not a conspicuous success,' opined *The Independent*. 'Keane's surges from midfield were badly missed, and his aggressive instincts did not always serve him well at the back.'[12]

But it was a harsh review. Adjudged to have obstructed Peter Ndlovu in the penalty area just before half-time, Keane conceded the indirect free kick that the guests scored from. But other than that, it was a relatively painless evening for him. His comfort in possession, positioning and speed ensured Forest were able to push higher. Later in the game, Keane stepped up and essentially played at the base of midfield, though the loss of his offensive verve was a severe drawback. The central midfield pairing of Gemmill and McKinnon failed to provide much in the way of high energy or creativity and Forest offered little from open play as Nigel Clough's acrobatic equaliser, inevitably, came from a corner kick.

The draw papered the cracks, but whispers were growing ever louder regarding a managerial change. The run of poor results, coupled with how the squad had been allowed to shrink so quickly and severely, led to an inquest. And when it was announced Clough would be receiving the freedom of the city the following spring, it appeared he was being shepherded towards the exit.

'I'll out-see the lot of you,' Clough said after the Coventry game. 'All this speculation about my future is ridiculous. We've got a good bunch of lads and they've got a good manager.'[13]

Beforehand, he'd revealed he was contemplating boycotting the Coventry fixture because of the damage inflicted on the City Ground surface by the Sky Strikers, the team of dancers employed by the broadcaster to provide on-pitch entertainment during televised Monday evening games.

He had a point, but it was easily dismissed as him merely raging against football commercialism. But Clough was also feeling a wider loss of control. As much as he was struggling to remedy Forest's newfound malaise, the game was starting to slip from his hands too. It was unrecognisable now and while his idiosyncrasies had always made him stand out, they didn't carry much currency any more. He'd always been prepared with a quip or a witty rebuke, but now he was ponderous and unsure.

There were more sinister reasons for Clough's sluggishness, as Teddy Sheringham revealed later on when describing his memories of the opening day victory over Liverpool. 'What I do remember about that day was coming in first at half-time, with the gaffer standing there, me picking up the nearest orange juice, knocking it back and spewing it straight out shouting "Fucking hell! I think that's your one, gaffer,"' he said. 'It was nearly all vodka. I was sweating my bollocks off, just wanting a quenching drink and that screwdriver was a hell of a shock to the system.'[14]

'He was just trying to hold his life together,' says Duncan Hamilton. 'I remember going to watch them against Man City at Maine Road and they played so abysmally. They were already in the bottom three at that stage and you thought, "Crikey, this team is going down." I wrote that and got an absolute bollocking for it. But it was just so obvious. They didn't have anyone to score goals and they were struggling at the back.'

And when it came to signings, Clough just didn't know any more. The difficulty in trying to replace Sheringham wasn't a one-off and there was the same indecisiveness in his search for a centre-back. He tried for Craig Short, but he went to Derby instead for £2.7 million. Then he thought about bringing back Colin Foster from West Ham, but the player failed to agree personal terms. Finally, in early October, it seemed like Clough was about to push a deal through when Mark Wright became available. Clough had tried to sign him from Southampton in 1987, but the defender went to the Baseball Ground instead. Now struggling at Liverpool and dropped by England, he was looking to press the reset button. A £1.8 million fee was agreed but Clough, again, changed his mind at the eleventh hour.

Languishing at the bottom of the table, new club chairman Fred Reacher acknowledged the less-than-ideal circumstances but offered Clough his full backing. 'People keep saying that the manager has shot it but nothing could be further from the truth,' he said. 'Now is the time for him to keep a cool head and not panic. And he's the perfect man for the job. There's money available for strengthening the team and we're working overtime at all levels to find them. Hopefully, before very long, there will be one, possibly two, new faces at the club. But there's no point rushing out and signing players in a panic. He's too good a manager for that. Others might in such a situation, but not Brian Clough. No one in his right mind would be happy with the results and I am as disappointed as anyone. But let the manager get on with the job. I'm sure he will sort it out.'[15]

With Keane retained in the centre of defence for a stretch of games, things improved slightly. There were draws against Chelsea and Manchester City, but a sense of foreboding still hung in the air. When he returned to midfield against Division 2 side Stockport County for the second leg of their League Cup second round tie, Forest were on edge and the 5–3 aggregate win was wholly unconvincing. The performance was languid and disjointed and Clough berated the players at half-time because of the carelessness of their passing. Giving an insight into just how bad things were, after the game Pearce described the result as a breath of fresh air.

Still, there were a litany of issues, Pearce included.

The captain was earning £4,000 per week but wanted to renegotiate better terms. With three years left on his deal, the club offered him £300,000 spread over the remainder. But he turned it down and Clough was irritated.

'I took exception to Stuart Pearce's attitude,' he wrote later. 'We just had the feeling that "Psycho" wasn't quite as enthusiastic or committed to the cause as he always had been. Maybe Stuart just felt things at Forest weren't as they should be, and the standards of old weren't being retained. Maybe he was affected as much as anyone by the depression that descended on the place.'[16]

Pearce himself believed the club's nosedive had been signposted for a while, beginning with the sale of Des Walker, while he referred to Sheringham's departure as 'a monumental mistake'.

'We had a real high from 1988 up until the 1991 Cup final when things began to wane,' he wrote. 'Clough was Clough. He ticked along while the fans were demanding he sign new players and we realised we had lost too many quality players to maintain our previous high standards. In typical style, he ignored the demands and the obvious failings.'[17]

It had only been two months since the opening day positivity following the win over Liverpool. But the atmosphere was now frigid.

'We didn't really replace Sheringham and we didn't have a figurehead,' says Kingsley Black. 'When you're not scoring, the confidence goes. The first game of the season, Sheringham scored and we won and everyone was buoyant. You think, "Cor, we're in for a good season here." I remember Mark Crossley in the big bath after the game and he said, "I think we could really do something this year." And we all agreed with him.'

Turning his nose up at alternatives, Clough persisted with Keane as a makeshift defender and enjoyed basking in the afterglow. It seemed another inspired decision as Forest picked up some momentum and lost just once in eight games. The defeat came at home to Arsenal where Alan Smith – ironically – netted his first of the season. Afterwards, George Graham offered a critique of Forest under Clough that dripped heavily with condescension, but also carried a forthright difference in opinion that Clough certainly wasn't hearing at the City Ground. 'I feel sorry for Forest,' he said. 'They play some lovely stuff and I admire the way they push the ball around. But my philosophy is probably a little different from Brian Clough's. I don't want to be playing good football and be at the bottom of the table. They're a good side and I'm sure it won't be long before they move up. They just need a bit of luck and a few wins to restore confidence, though it seems a shame Roy Keane has to play at the back.'[18]

Graham hinted at an oxymoronic element to Clough's approach. How could he extol the virtues of an aesthetically pleasing style of play but confine his best creative outlet to the centre of defence? How could he bemoan the combative, long-ball strategy of other sides but wilfully oversee the huff-and-puff, half-baked efforts of his own players? Of course, Graham may also have been being purposely mischievous by dropping Keane's name. He'd already made a tentative move for him and things would only intensify as the season progressed, as Keane's contract situation became a story in its own right.

But Clough was undeterred by Graham's comments and declared Keane 'the best centre-half in the country'. It was another way of reminding dissenters that he could still make insightful decisions when required. However, while Keane's ability was never in doubt, he and his teammates agreed with Graham and felt the strategy was misguided.

'It proves how high his football intelligence was that he stepped straight in there like he'd been there forever,' says Steve Chettle. 'Roy was aggressive in the air, could make tackles, had a great range of passing. He had all the attributes to be whatever he wanted to be in whatever position he played. But, we were putting square pegs in round holes just to get results. We could've done with three Roy Keanes. We had to take him out of his favourite position – where he could potentially grab a goal and win a midfield battle – to try and counter how productive the opposition's centre-forward was. You were taking him from where his strengths were to try and neutralise somebody else. Roy was crucial in terms of our attacking prowess and goal-scoring and he was playing in the centre of defence. It's not great in terms of a winning formula, but it was great for the other team. We were in a no-win situation. It wasn't perfect. We picked teams to get results.'

Keane was growing agitated, especially as Chettle was fit again but still being left on the bench. He publicly reiterated his desire to return to his best position, though he remembered his place too and acknowledged that he'd gladly fall in line with Clough's wishes. 'I don't see central defence as my position for the future,' he began. 'I consider myself a midfield player and I look forward to getting back there as soon as possible. It's at midfield that I made my mark so far in football and it's the position where I feel most comfortable when I'm out on the park. I will carry on playing in the centre of defence as long as Brian Clough wants me to stay there but the only reason I feel comfortable playing there is the support I am getting from all the other players in the defence.'[19]

But Clough did seem quite taken with the idea of Keane as a long-term stopper and made moves to sign another central midfielder that month. He'd watched Alf-Inge Haaland impress as Norway's Under–21 captain in a 2–0 win over England in Peterborough and a deal was quickly ironed out with his club side, Bryne. Haaland even posed for photographs outside the City Ground alongside Clough and Ron Fenton later that month, but a protracted registration meant he didn't arrive until December 1993.

Meanwhile, Clough had second thoughts anyway and Keane was eventually reinstated to his preferred role after an illuminating loss to Ipswich, their eighth defeat in fourteen league games. The result was hardly surprising, but the reaction at the full-time whistle certainly was.

Forest had been in the dirt for months, but Clough still had the fans in the palm of his hand. In September, prior to a game at Hillsborough, the side were on a run of five straight losses. But he was greeted with a rousing reception from the away supporters as he made his way to the dugout. 'Other managers would get hate mail in Forest's position,' Duncan Hamilton said at the time. 'Cloughie walks out and gets a standing ovation. There is a great residue of goodwill for him.'[20]

However, it had all but worn away by Halloween.

'We're at the bottom of the league because we're crap,' Clough said. 'We're not good enough to be anywhere else. The nation I can put right overnight but I can't get a win. I am in the shit. If it meant getting three points on a Saturday I would shoot my grandmother. Not nastily, I would just hurt her.'[21]

The wry humour was still there, but not many were laughing any more. As he marched towards the tunnel after Jason Dozzell's solitary goal at Portman Road spoiled another Saturday afternoon for Forest, the crowd booed intensely while some cheered sarcastically. It was a telling shift. Even the loyalists were losing faith.

Before the next game against fellow strugglers Everton, Clough faced the gravity of the situation in his usual way. 'Come twenty-to-five, Howard Kendall or Brian Clough might get the sack,' he told reporters.[22]

But after the subsequent defeat, his chairman seemed less convincing about the future than he was only a month beforehand. 'I will honour Brian's contract. We have a written agreement to the end of the season and a verbal agreement for a further twelve months,' Reacher said. 'I believe in letting managers manage – and that is what Brian will continue to do. In the early days he could have left us. But he stood by Forest. Now it's our turn to stand by him.'[23]

But the message was clear: Clough was okay until the end of the campaign but nothing was guaranteed beyond that.

Increasingly, it seemed to be something similar with Keane.

11

FANCY DRESS

In demand.

The Sunday newspapers carried word that Blackburn wanted him, while long-time flirts Arsenal lay in the long grass. Any deal would be a transfer record.

Keane claimed he knew nothing about the reported interest. And he wasn't behaving like he was eyeing an exit either. In late October he bought his first house – The Stables – on Chapel Lane in the tiny village of Scarrington, about a thirty-minute drive outside the city, motivated by its distance from the trappings of Nottingham's core.

For a twenty-one-year-old, it was a curious choice.

With its collection of sprawling farms and imposing manors, it's a picture-postcard quaint English parish but, with the exception of the local church, devoid of any social setting. No pub, no restaurant, no cafe. Scarrington is a place for garden fetes, sports cars and secrets, a likely setting for one of Chief Inspector Barnaby's *Midsomer Murders* investigations. If Keane was searching for self-imposed isolation, he certainly got it.

'It was a barn conversion,' says Ian Kilford. 'At the time it was quite trendy for a footballer to get one and there were a lot of them being built. It was probably a case of him wanting to get involved in the housing market too, a little bit of property. Also, in football, it never does you any favours to live right in the city that you play in, but I don't think he wanted to move anywhere that was too far out either. We were still young and he liked to go and have a night out and Nottingham was a good place for that. We'd actually head to Bingham, which was nearby, and the local pub there – The Wheatsheaf – was run by Ian Storey-Moore, the ex-Forest player. It was quiet and we'd pop in for Sunday lunch and a few drinks. He was very humble and he always looked after people, so we'd often have a lot of his cousins, uncles and brothers come over and a lot of the time you'd sit in this country pub and have some of the best afternoons just drinking Guinness. I thought I could drink Guinness, but obviously I couldn't. By that stage, I'd left my digs and moved to a housing estate close to Trent Bridge, but we'd usually end up in Roy's for the weekend. You'd just end up staying over and I have a lot of good memories, some I can't remember.'

Keane had to put a proper housewarming on hold because of international commitments. The Republic of Ireland were unbeaten after three World Cup qualifiers, a straightforward 4–0 thrashing of minnows Latvia followed a tense 2–0 opening win over Albania, while there was also an impressive scoreless draw in Copenhagen against the reigning European champions.

The clash against Denmark was memorable for the pre-game skittishness surrounding Keane's 'biggest career test'. *The Irish Press* deemed it 'a gamble' for Charlton to select him as a midfield anchor, in the absence of both Paul McGrath and Ronnie Whelan. Keane himself referred to the game as the biggest of his brief career, even placing it – rather ludicrously – ahead of the 1991 FA Cup final in terms of importance.

Keane was excellent, as were his teammates, in the stalemate, but a greater test lay ahead in mid-November. By the time he reached Seville to prepare for a clash with Javier Clemente's group favourites, Keane was the subject of feverish transfer talk after Clough had lavished praise upon him during an appearance on the 11 November edition of BBC's *Sportsnight* television programme.

'He's the best centre-half in the country,' Clough reiterated to John

Motson, after being quizzed on Keane's newfound defensive role. 'Keane fits the bill so much I believe he should think about making his career at the back. We have been conceding goals like a sieve so he had to go in the back four, although we missed him in midfield. He can't play like Beckenbauer yet, but that will come. He gets a bit frustrated when he loses the ball but he's quick and talented.'

Then Motson pressed him on the rumours surrounding a potential move away from Forest.

'Keane is going nowhere,' Clough began. 'If Kenny [Dalglish, Blackburn manager] wants to buy him, he'll have to pay a lot of money and still throw in the Trent, the Thames and whatever river flows through Blackburn.'

Increasingly, it appeared Keane was available for the right price. A 'source close to Forest' offered a withering response when asked about Arsenal's reported £3 million package of cash plus players. 'For that kind of money, Brian Clough wouldn't even take a phone call. Arsenal would want to be talking £5m by today's transfer market values before Forest would even consider opening discussions for Roy, who still has well over a year to go on his contract.'[1]

The chatter overshadowed Keane's preparations in Spain and facing a barrage of reporters' questions about a possible transfer, he offered the usual platitudes about being flattered but unaffected. However, the positional switch at Forest remained a sore point for him. 'The truth is, I can only play in one position, really,' he said. 'When I was first put at the back, the manager said it was only for the short term. Obviously, I have to do what he asks. I have to help out the team in whatever way he decides. But I can't get forward at all from centre back.'

Playing under Charlton, Keane cut a much more sober figure. There were no gut-busting runs from deep, no centre-forward dropping to create space for him in behind, no neat passing combinations on the edge of the area. And having screened the defence so competently in Copenhagen, he was tasked with the same role in Spain. It meant the natural inclinations were curbed even further and the mere suggestion of offensive contribution shelved. He operated in a tight area, with only Andy Townsend allowed to push higher occasionally. He showed and laid off. He shadowed. He tackled. He ran. He was a lesser version of himself. And Keane admitted that it grated occasionally. 'In Denmark, I was the man who stayed in the deeper role and Andy had the free rein to get forward now and then,' he said. 'It's frustrating sometimes but I know I'll have a specific job to do against Spain.'[2]

Despite feeling restricted by the defensive obligations, Keane was excited at the high-profile nature of the qualifier. 'The bigger the match, the more I like it. And that's the truth,' he told Noel Spillane ahead of the game. 'For me, this is what international football is all about. Players like [Emilio] Butragueño and Michel are world class and it's great for me to step out on the same pitch as them. I'll recognise most of their players because I watch all the Spanish stuff on the telly every week.'[3]

As it turned out, Michel was quiet, while Butragueño proved a bystander and his eventual substitution led to some famous commentary from an excitable George Hamilton during RTÉ's coverage: 'He's pulling him off. The Spanish manager is pulling his captain off.'

In the intensity of the Ramón Sánchez Pizjuán Stadium, a fortress where the hosts had never lost, Keane was the revelation, the heartbeat of a wonderfully spirited Irish display that deserved more than another 0–0 draw. Niall Quinn missed a gilt-edged chance in the first half, side-footing wide of Andoni Zubizarreta's upright when clean through, while John Aldridge had a goal harshly called back for offside after Keane and Quinn combined to set him up. The hosts failed to create anything of note and played the last half hour with ten men after Juan Manuel López cynically brought down Aldridge. It was a herculean effort from Charlton's side, but the plaudits were reserved for one man only.

In an Irish context, it was Keane's coming-of-age party.

'The superb Corkman, seemingly armed with bottomless lungs, covered every blade of grass with a performance that will long be remembered and cherished,' declared an effusive *Irish Independent*.

'The lad's a marvel,' Charlton said afterwards. 'The boy never stops running. He is always putting his feet in and has the close control needed to make himself a bit of room. I lost count of the number of tackles and the number of runs that he made. You have to remember he is only twenty-one and still learning his trade. He is only a boy and has a lot still to learn but he gets better by the day. I like the boy. I like him a lot.'[4]

Perched by the dressing room door in the immediate aftermath of a draining night's work, Keane sipped on a water bottle and seemed non-plussed by the experience. If anything, regardless of the calibre of his dis-play, Keane felt restrained and confined. 'I was happy enough with my own game but I have to change my style for Ireland against foreign opposition and it is never easy,' he said. 'I still feel like I've got something to prove. This was my tenth cap but I know some people still say there is a question mark over me. It's two months since I played in midfield and it was just great. Tonight I was back where I wanted to be. I was knackered in the first half but got my second wind and felt very strong after half-time.'[5] He added, 'There are many questions about me as an international. Like, am I old enough? Can I adapt to Ireland's game when Forest's game is so different? Out there tonight the ball fell nicely for me. It was like I was always getting it in space.'[6]

In the days that followed, things got weird.

After serving a fifteen-month ban for cocaine use, Diego Maradona had signed for Sevilla in the summer. He watched the qualifier with interest and took particular notice of the industrious number six in the green shirt. 'There was nobody to touch Keane on the pitch,' he said. 'He impressed me with everything he did … He was a long way ahead of the rest – especially for a player who's so young.'[7]

The rumour mill went into overdrive and forty-eight hours after the game, the UK tabloids reported that Sevilla wanted Keane to sit alongside Maradona and provide support for Croatian striker Davor Šuker up front. They were prepared to pay him £3 million, spread over a three-year deal. Included in the reports were quotes from the club president Luis Cuervas. 'Keane was the number one player in the game and was very strong,' he said. 'Obviously, we would be very interested in bringing him here.'[8]

Everything was beginning to spiral and while Keane had been primarily linked with Blackburn and Arsenal up to that point, it wasn't long before Europe's elite were rumoured to be chasing him. Real Madrid and Inter Milan were added to the shortlist, while Manchester United were apparently back in the mix too.

That weekend, the wall-to-wall coverage continued and Keane was the subject of an in-depth profile in the *Mail on Sunday* newspaper on 22 November. While similar background pieces had previously delved into his time in Cobh primarily, this one was more revealing and thoughtful, with Keane opening up and showing equal parts vulnerability and gratitude.

'I was very depressed and frustrated,' he told Bob Cass about his teenage years. 'I had left school without the prospect of ever getting a job. I went on a government-backed scheme where I was given coaching in football. It was just for kids who were unemployed. It was better than having us hanging about the streets but I only had a couple of months left doing that when Forest offered to take me on trial. I've never felt so happy or excited.

'A few other clubs started taking a bit of notice and they got in touch with me when I went back home. But I felt they were only showing interest because Forest had offered me a deal and I never went back to them. I signed the contract; got my first team chance within a few weeks and thankfully I haven't looked back since … I don't know what the future holds. I don't let all this talk about price tags bother me. You don't let things like that go to your head when you know how different things might have been. I was a nobody until Forest took a chance with me and I'll be grateful to them and Brian Clough for that for the rest of my life.'

This genuine warmth was mutual. During an interview with *The Observer*, Clough was asked about Forest's poor start to the season, criticism from supporters and rumours he was facing the sack. He responded with a story about a recent visit to a children's special needs home. 'I took my son and Roy Keane,' he began. 'They can't talk, walk, move. We lit the place up. But they lit us up also. When I came out I felt a million dollars. Then I went home to babysit [his grandchildren] and thought how lucky I was.'[9]

For the visit, one which Clough would make regularly, it was inevitable that Nigel – polite, pleasant and polished – would be there alongside him. But Keane's presence was striking. Stuart Pearce, the club captain and an England international, wasn't brought along. Neither was an older, more experienced figure like Steve Chettle, born and bred in Nottingham. Instead, it was the raw twenty-one-year-old with a reputation for late nights and fistfights. Perhaps that was one of the reasons Clough had him there, though it wasn't a PR event. Perhaps Keane simply added a degree of glamour to proceedings as Forest's in-demand superstar. Or, perhaps Clough felt Keane's humility was well-suited to such an occasion. Maybe it was a mix of all three. Still, it required a certain sensitivity and maturity that went against Keane's off-field caricature.

After a run of relentless compliments and high praise, Clough ensured Keane's ego was kept in check by banishing him to the right wing and rendering him largely ineffectual when he returned to club action for a trip to Crystal Palace. At least he was back in midfield, though it said much about Clough's priorities that when he eventually parted with some money in November, it wasn't to invest in defensive cover but to buy back midfielder Neil Webb from Manchester United instead, despite his well-documented injury problems.

Keane quickly found his rhythm again and when Forest turned in a vibrant midweek performance against Tottenham in the League Cup – a competition that was a seemingly persistent shelter from the storm – he was central to it.

The City Ground surface was heavy, but the hosts were nimble on their feet. They created two goals of real quality, with Ian Woan played through by Nigel Clough for the opener. Midway through the second half, Clough deftly did likewise for Keane, who sent a thunderous strike past Erik Thorstvedt for his first competitive goal since March. He enjoyed the moment – particularly given the opposition – and after a celebratory knee slide, he turned to face down the thousands of baying Spurs fans behind the goal and, almost apologetically, held his arms out wide. Smiling mischievously, he flicked a V-sign at them before turning to salute Clough and the Forest bench.

Afterwards, a supporter from Hertfordshire wrote to Nottingham police to complain about Keane's 'obscene gestures'. Not that he cared too much. He was in high spirits, Forest's form was improving and he had two friends in town: Noel Spillane and Eddie O'Hare.

'There wouldn't be much sport on over Christmas so we'd go over to the UK around the end of November or the start of December and spend time with eight or ten different players,' Spillane says. 'We'd get the interviews and the photographs and then they'd run in both the *Evening Echo* and *The Cork Examiner*. We'd drip-feed the pieces between Christmas and the New Year – filler items, if you like. You'd have Brian Carey, Denis Irwin and Roy too.'

Though the pair made quite a few trips together, their 1992 adventure in Nottingham is an especially fond memory.

'We were doing this before any other newspaper and it was brilliant stuff,' O'Hare says. 'We'd regularly meet up with Kieran O'Regan in Holmfirth, where they used to film *Last of the Summer Wine*, because he was with Huddersfield at the time. But I remember we were fascinated to see Keane on the front cover of *Shoot* or *Match*. And we were saying, "Jeez, look at him." We were chuffed, like. One of our own on the front of a big soccer magazine.'[10]

Arriving into Nottingham's train station, a five-minute drive from the City Ground, Keane was waiting and whisked Spillane and O'Hare to his country house in Scarrington for coffee and a chat.

'I decided to move out of the city centre because of the temptations and so on,' he told Spillane. 'I had an apartment with all my furniture in there but I changed my mind at the last minute. Living in town there are just too many temptations for me. Every night you can find something to do. It doesn't have to be the nightclub scene or the pub but you're always out and about. I wanted something more homely, I suppose, and that's what prompted the move to Scarrington. I was in digs, in a rented house and a flat, but I would never stop in at night in those days. I was always on the go, flying around in the car, doing silly things like calling around to the lads to watch a video, going for a drink, to the pictures. It was all to kill and pass time.'[11]

Ray Byrne, who was a close friend since joining Forest as a trainee in February of the previous year, became Keane's housemate, while Tony Loughlan and Ian Kilford were regular weekend lodgers at the four-bedroom, open-concept property.

'I'm much happier and content in myself now that I've made the move into my own house,' Keane said. 'It's much more relaxed and I'm very much my own man. There's just a scattering of houses in the village – there's no pub, no shops, no nightclubs and nothing in the way of temptation to distract me.'[12]

Keane was at ease in his new surroundings and happily posed for an array of photographs. Whatever O'Hare suggested, he agreed to and the result was a stunning collection of intimate images. Outside, with the various sheds and sprawling greenery ensuring a striking background, he propped his crossed arms on an iron gate and smiled for the camera. In another shot, with the scale of the site adding perspective behind him, Keane – dressed in a Hugo Boss sweatshirt, light-blue jeans and a leather jacket – nonchalantly draped his left arm across the side of his white, soft-top Ford Escort convertible.

Inside the house, O'Hare snapped Keane in the kitchen, carrying a tray filled with coffee cups and biscuits. Upstairs, obeying various directions, he lay on his bed, surrounded by a selection of his game-worn Ireland jerseys. He sat on the bedroom floor, perching beneath the slanted window, and flicked through his CD collection. Clutching U2's *Achtung Baby* in his hand, other albums were strewn around him – Bob Marley and the Wailers' *Legend*; The Eagles' *Best Of*; *The Commitments* soundtrack; some dance compilation; Michael Jackson's *Thriller*; and *Back to Front* by Lionel Ritchie.

Then, spotting one of his Irish caps on display, O'Hare had another idea. Moments later, Keane was grinning proudly for him with the cap on his head.

That night, after watching Keane score against Tottenham, Spillane and O'Hare waited for him outside the dressing rooms as he dealt with a relentless range of obligations, much to their amazement. ITV wanted an interview on the pitch. Local radio needed their sound bites. Ian Edwards from the *Nottingham Evening Post* waited with his Dictaphone. A local supporters' group wished to make a presentation to him. And he also needed to pose with the sponsors – Lamcote Motors – who handed over the Man of the Match award to him. Then there was a multitude of jerseys, footballs and programmes to be autographed, fans and corporate guests to mingle with. When Keane finally approached Spillane to chat briefly, reporters followed and hovered.

'We experienced first-hand the enormous demands that are made on the young Keane after matches,' Spillane later wrote. 'And to be fair to him, he handled everything with a charm and authority that belied his tender years.'[13]

As they wrapped up at the stadium, Spillane asked if a meeting with Clough could be arranged.

'Two fucking chances,' Keane replied, before having second thoughts. Forest had won and the performance had been impressive. Clough, more than likely, would be in a good mood. So Keane escorted his visitors through the bowels of the City Ground.

'I remember going through a warren of little passageways before the space opened up and I spotted a door with a marble entrance,' Spillane says. 'Clough was inside but Ron Fenton came out to us and said, "Lads, I don't know if Mr Clough is up to it, he's a very busy man." So, we just accepted that and said, "No problem, we just wanted to take a chance as we're here with Roy." And the next thing, yer man appears at the door. He comes over and we get introduced. Eddie is trying to stop him from moving around so that he can get a picture and finally, we're all standing together – myself, Roy and Clough. Eddie has everything framed up and ready to go and, the next thing, Clough comes up behind me and grabs me by the balls. So I'm struggling with him and trying to get him off and meanwhile Keane is rolling around laughing. Eventually, we all calm down and Eddie is lining up another one and Clough comes again. But this time he picks Keane up in a bear hug and he's saying, "My boy, my boy" as he wheels him around.'

'There's something about Cloughie, an aura,' Keane had told Spillane. 'He's larger than life and a living legend when it comes to football. That's no understatement – I mean it. People talk about him in the same breath as Sir Matt Busby and Bill Shankly. It's hard to explain but he's got a special presence whenever he steps into a room. We get on really well together. You have to know him to understand him. He's eccentric, okay, but most of the time he's just an ordinary bloke. All the talk of a crisis at the club is rubbish.

We are too good a side to go down and we'll get out of this mess alright.'[14] Keane seemed to be talking sense.

Forest faced the champions at Elland Road in early December and made it back-to-back wins for the first time since mid-April as Webb and Keane gelled magnificently in midfield. The former pulled the strings from a deep position and constantly spotted his partner's probing runs. After Nigel Clough gave them a first-half lead, Webb deftly flicked in to Keane's path in the second half, but as Leeds' goalkeeper John Lukic raced towards him, Keane uncharacteristically sliced the shot wide. Furious with himself, he kicked the turf in frustration. But moments later, Webb looked to release Kingsley Black over the top only for Keane to veer into his lane, take a touch and tuck inside Lukic's near post. After Black added a third less than a minute later, Keane strode beyond a hapless Leeds defence after being put through by another astute Webb pass and rolled to the far corner.

'Perhaps the nearest in the Premier League to Bryan Robson: dynamic; all-action; producing goals,' said *The Independent*. 'Keane spent much of Forest's miserable early season at the back, a role Clough believes he fills with considerable authority. The same applied to the young Robson but surely you do not stifle such rare talent and inspiration?'[15]

The Robson comparisons were coming thick and fast.

'In Keane, Forest have the most exciting talent in the country,' said Aston Villa boss Ron Atkinson, ahead of a league clash between the two sides. 'He is the nearest I have seen to Bryan Robson at his best.'[16]

At Villa Park, he backed up the pre-match pleasantries with another sparkling display. After nine minutes, Nigel Clough spotted Keane's run and sprayed a diagonal ball from the halfway line. Galloping clear of Steve Staunton, he spotted goalkeeper Nigel Spink's wayward positioning and sent a delicately cushioned lob to the net.

'He's just too hot to handle at the moment,' roared commentator Clive Tyldesley on BBC's *Match of the Day* later that evening.[17]

But his fourth goal in three games still wasn't enough. Some more calamitous Forest defending cost them an equaliser before Paul McGrath got on the end of a set piece and thundered a header past Crossley. But Keane seemed set to grab a late leveller when he sprinted clear inside the last ten minutes, only for McGrath to catch him from behind on the edge of the area. It was a clumsy challenge, a possible red card offence and an ideal position for Pearce to thump home a free kick, but referee Joe Worrall waved play on. Once the ball went dead, an incensed Keane chased him to remonstrate and was quickly joined by a group of Forest players. The respite had been brief, the momentum was gone and the side remained bottom of the table.

Still, the players felt a decent run could get them out of the mire. The previous season there had also been talk of relegation, but they managed to turn things around with a late surge. So, when they headed to Nottingham city centre for their Christmas party in midweek, the group remained in good spirits.

'We went to the Old Vic pub in the Lace Market,' remembers Steve Chettle. 'And it was fancy dress. Most of our Christmas parties were because you could disguise yourself when you were in town. But that year we went dressed as dwarves and ended up getting barred. I'm not sure if it was Pearcey who had an argument with a bouncer, but they ended up throwing about thirty dwarves out of the same pub.'

'A lot of the lads went out as Snow White's seven dwarves, with the masks on,' says Ian Kilford. 'But I can remember there was me, Gary Charles and another young lad called Chris Hope, and we went as George, Zippy and Bungle from [children's TV show] *Rainbow*. And I was George, the pink hippopotamus. So we went out drinking and we're in and out of the Nottingham pubs all day. You can imagine. But our escapades made the paper and my dad rang me all concerned. They'd said Steve Stone took my head off and threw it on the top of a double-decker bus and it had gone all around Nottingham city centre. But I had to reassure him that it was the hippo head and just part of my George costume.

'There was a lot made of the entire episode, but the coaching staff had realised we were out and the Notts County boys were too. So, the next day, we got a phone call to come to the City Ground immediately. We were all hungover, but the coaches had arranged a friendly against Notts County. I think we played for about an hour and it was awful. I don't think the ball moved out of the centre circle and it was 0–0. The coaches were just there having a laugh and taking the mick.'

The following weekend, on Sunday 20 December, Norman Fox penned a glowing feature for *The Independent* on Keane and his rise to stardom. Under the headline 'The last jewel in Clough's treasure chest', he quoted Graham Taylor, who described Keane as 'the outstanding find of recent years'.

'For him [Taylor] and those of a certain age, comparisons with Duncan Edwards are irresistible, but a young Bryan Robson also comes to mind,' Fox wrote. 'As Taylor points out, the assets of all three are similar: power, control, fitness, a fine sense of timing and positioning and the ability to score goals.' He continued, 'With the [Forest] defence conceding soft goals and the attack not scoring enough to compensate, Keane's responsibilities are wide and his strength is crucial. There is an element of misfortune in Keane's ascent being associated with Forest's decline, but he says: "I still find it difficult to believe where I am. It seems only yesterday that I could only watch teams like Manchester United and Liverpool on the television."'

But the timing of the piece couldn't have been worse. The previous day, it was revealed that Keane had been hauled to the local police station in the early hours of Thursday morning, as Forest's festive knees-up was winding down. The press – particularly the UK tabloids – had a field day, with the added detail of a beery, bleary and belligerent Forest squad dressed as dwarves sprinkling some potent surrealism on an already impressive story.

Nottinghamshire police later confirmed they'd been called to the scene of a public disturbance outside Ritzy nightclub and had picked Keane up 'to prevent the incident getting out of hand'. He was taken away, warned as to his future conduct and released without charge.[18]

'When you'd be in town with your mates, were full of beer, had a curry but still wanted a drink, you'd head to Ritzy,' says Steve Campion. 'Because The Black Orchid was situated about two-and-a-half miles outside the town, when you came there, it was a planned night out, while the city centre had various pubs and clubs, with Ritzy one of them.'

Clough was furious, but Keane protested his innocence and said he'd reacted to abuse from Notts County fans. His version of events was backed up by the police and he avoided a substantial fine, though Clough did issue him a nightclub ban.

'It was the first time I've ever been in trouble over here,' he told *The Cork Examiner*. 'And even though it wasn't my fault, it looked bad for me in the papers here and back home. I was worried about my Mam and Dad and the impression it might give. My name is clear today and I have nothing to worry about. No punches were thrown, or anything like that, and the club have left the whole thing lie. There's no question of disciplinary action and I won't be losing any sleep over it. I think I was singled out when I was with a few of the lads. Whether it had anything to do with being Irish or not I don't know. I should just walk away from situations like that, but it's not easy.'[19]

Keane was certainly affected, however, and was noticeably out of sorts in a 1–1 Sunday afternoon draw against Wimbledon. But he had plenty on his mind, not least discussions over a new contract. He'd paid £100,000 for the Scarrington property, a price that left him overdrawn at the bank. He was still earning a paltry weekly wage of £700 and Clough had suggested he discuss new terms with Ron Fenton.

With his transfer value skyrocketing and a multitude of teams lining up to sign him, Keane felt overwhelmed and sought the assistance of the Professional Footballers Association (PFA). They assigned Brendon Batson, the former Arsenal and West Brom player, to offer counsel during Keane's contract talks with Forest.

'I remember seeing him "live" for the first time against West Ham in the FA Cup semi-final in 1991 and he made a huge impact on me,' Batson says. 'Not just in terms of his ability on the ball and his influence on the team as a young lad, but also the way he covered the pitch. He reminded me – in the way he went box-to-box – of Bryan Robson, who I'd played with at West Brom. He had such determination and he was dragging people along with him. For a young guy, you could see the other players around him being affected by the way he conducted himself on the pitch. You felt you were seeing something special in the making. His whole persona was bristling with intensity. Robbo was probably less animated in terms of how he conveyed his feelings on the pitch, but in terms of personal performance and looking to get the best from himself and others, they were very similar. They were generals, on and off the pitch.

'Forest won comfortably that day and he was instrumental. And then, probably about eighteen months later, Roy somehow got in touch with me and asked me to help him with his contract negotiations. At the time, the PFA were acting as agents in a very low-profile type of way. Our only concern was getting the very best deal for our members. It wasn't commonplace, but our role was to advise players and give contract advice to those who didn't have an agent, or to those who did because, at the time, not all agents were acting in the best interests of their client. We would try and act as a balance, just saying, "Look, here are the things you should be aware of and this is what you need in terms of specific wording."'[20]

By this stage, Keane had already met Blackburn's management team of Kenny Dalglish and Ray Harford to discuss their interest. According to him, the pair said that if he was going to sign a new deal, he needed to insert a clause that allowed him to leave if Forest went down. They also hinted at what they'd pay him, should he decide to move to Ewood Park. It gave Keane an edge in negotiations with Forest and while Fenton tried to lock him down quickly, he was in no rush to sign.

'Our time together was very limited as there weren't a series of ongoing meetings and a lot of it was done over the phone,' Batson says. 'But he was very strong-minded for a young lad and definitely knew his value and his worth to a club. I found him very focused on what he wanted the outcome to be. Keaney was good and there was certainly not many like him, at that time. But that doesn't happen overnight. There was this chatter around Roy and that would've filtered down to him.'

As Christmas approached, Keane began to speak publicly about the stand-off. 'I do need to think things over very carefully,' he said. 'I love the club and the offer made to me is an incredible one financially. Any transfer talk is just speculation at the moment, but, even so, I need more time to weigh things up. I rushed into signing a contract last time and I don't want to do that again. The reason I have taken so long to sort out my situation is that I want everything to be right. When I first came over from Ireland, everything was rushed and that was a mistake I was determined not to repeat. It was Brian Clough who brought me to England in the first place and gave me the chance of building a new career for myself. Additionally, I like the city of Nottingham and the people who have been so good to me.'[21]

Forest wanted Keane to sign a three-and-a-half-year extension, keeping him at the club until the summer of 1996. With some reports suggesting he was asking for as much as £7,000 per week, Keane was happy with £5,000 plus incentives. But he also demanded a substantial signing-on fee, as well as the relegation clause to be inserted. In public, at least, Clough was chagrined.

'He is being a greedy child,' he later said. 'Keane is like a kid who wakes up on Christmas morning and finds an apple, an orange, a box of Smarties and fifty pence in his stocking. He wants more. Keane is the hottest property in the game right now but he is not going to bankrupt the club.'[22] In private Clough took a softer stance and, the day after the comments were carried by every major newspaper in the UK, he pulled Keane aside at training and denied having anything to do with the story. Given his own history with financial compensation – he spoke openly and proudly of how his substantial pay-out from Leeds United in 1974 (£100,000 after tax, plus the club Mercedes) had set him up for life – it was pretty rich for him to criticise Keane's attempts to hold out for the best deal.

'I quickly discovered that he [Clough] was obsessed with money, as if he feared he might wake up one morning and find himself a pauper again,' Duncan Hamilton wrote in *Provided You Don't Kiss Me*. 'It wasn't purely greed but a form of self-protection against the dreadful insecurity he felt. Money was his armour-plating against life's hardships.'[23]

Keane was increasingly annoyed by the battering his reputation was getting and tried his best to change the narrative. 'I am not a greedy individual by nature and that's the truth,' he told Noel Spillane. 'Forest know what I want but money is not the major stumbling block at this stage.'[24]

Keane's future added another layer of uncertainty to Forest's battle against the drop. Along with Clough's rapid deterioration owing to his personal demons, the tension between Clough and Stuart Pearce, and the club's lack of new signings, there was no let-up from the gloom. The players couldn't even enjoy a night out together without it becoming tabloid fodder.

Acknowledging the sorry state of the club, Clough himself was devoid of the usual sparkle and was unable to muster a pithy line or colourful quip. The greyness had even got to him. 'Our heads won't drop and we'll never give up,' he said, reduced to well-worn clichés. 'We'll just keep battling until we get it right.'[25]

But when they rounded out 1992 with another defeat – this time at

White Hart Lane – it left them five points adrift at the foot of the Premier League table. Forest's continued belief in a passing game was still greeted with admiration, but without someone to apply the finishing touch, it remained a stunted strategy. They finished the Spurs game with a five-man midfield and Nigel Clough – so much more effective in a deeper role – left to scavenge by himself up front.

'Like the condemned man who salutes from the scaffold there is an almost tragic nobility about the way Nottingham Forest continue to play pure football as their position at the bottom of the Premier League worsens by the week,' determined *The Guardian*. 'The Marquess of Queensberry rules never did count for much in a street fight and that is what Forest face now.'[26]

12

WE COULD HAVE BEEN
SO GOOD TOGETHER

Keane's contract situation was unhelpful to Forest's plight.

Though it was primarily played out on the back pages, the various rumours regarding wages and bonuses seeped into the dressing room. It fuelled a general sense of frustration and irritation that had already been lingering for some time: basically, the players felt that Keane was destined to move on anyway, even if Forest stayed up.

'There were some unhappy people and, at times, if you're not playing well yourself, you'll look to deflect your own performances onto others, which could have happened,' says Steve Chettle. 'I don't think Roy's personal situation would have helped. But results were the major factor. And performances. The atmosphere wasn't great. We weren't used to being where we were in the league. Everyone was scratching their heads and we couldn't put our finger on it. But I don't think we'd have put it down to Roy not signing a contract. We were aware he wasn't signing the deal but we were bottom of the league and he was going to go somewhere else. It was one of those simple scenarios. We knew what was being said in the newspapers and knew he was going to go to one of the big four if we went down. It's just natural. A player in Roy's situation is not going to sign a deal to stay at a club that's slipped down another division. They want to play at the highest level and that's fine.'

Forest's best hope of salvation came – as usual – in the cup competitions. And drawn to face Southampton in the Third Round of the FA Cup on 3 January 1993, Keane – with his impeccable timing – commandeered the headlines once more.

Trailing to a close-range finish from Matt Le Tissier, it was Keane who equalised, rising superbly to plant a downward header inside Tim Flowers' near post following Gary Crosby's corner. As he celebrated, he pointed furiously towards the Forest supporters, grabbed the badge on his shirt and kissed it twice. A few moments later, he brushed off the attentions of his teammates, turned to face the fans again and pulled the badge to his lips one more time.

Webb grabbed the winner two minutes later, expertly curling home from inside the area for his first goal since rejoining the club. But with his contract situation unresolved and so many stories linking him with a move elsewhere, Keane's celebration ensured reporters clamoured for some clarity.

'A couple of weeks back, it was in the press that I'd agreed a contract and was just thinking things over,' he told the BBC's Ray Stubbs afterwards. 'And it looked bad from my point of view because I hadn't agreed the right terms in the first place. It looked like I was waiting to see if we were going to go down. But the truth is I hadn't agreed and I still haven't agreed. So I'm just waiting to see what happens. It's up to the club now. I've told them what I want and it's up to them.'

'Have you got an open mind on it?' Stubbs asked him. 'Would you like to stay at Forest?'

'They were the first club to give me a chance and I love the place,' Keane replied. 'Good manager and good coaches. I'm still only twenty-one and still learning. I don't think I can learn anywhere better than at Forest. If I get the right deal, I'm prepared to stay.'[1]

Later that week, despite his team being rooted to the bottom of the table, he was voted the Barclays Young Eagle of the Month for the fifth time in two years.

'He's playing in a team that's in this strange position for them ... and everybody's talking about Roy Keane,' Graham Taylor said, as he handed over the award. 'There have been so many superlatives spoken about him, it's difficult to follow them. What I would say is he can do a bit of everything: it looks to me like Roy is Jack of all trades – and Master of them all. Something I really liked about him was last Sunday after scoring the equaliser in their FA Cup victory against Southampton he went out of his way to show the Forest fans where his heart lay – kissing the club badge on his shirt before the Trent End spectators.'[2]

Keane buckled under the weight of the contractual impasse. When he'd remained silent, others shaped the story arc and he was portrayed as ungrateful. But when he stepped in and attempted to redefine it, nobody seemed to listen or care anyway. So, towards the end of January, Keane issued an update and revealed he'd make a decision at the end of the season.

'At this stage I don't feel there is any rush or panic to commit myself. Just because I haven't signed doesn't mean I won't stay with the club.'[3]

But it wasn't that easy to push the situation to one side. In a League Cup clash at Arsenal – a team chasing his signature – Keane was anonymous as Ian Wright's double ensured a comfortable 2–0 win, eliminating one of Forest's lifelines in the process. Then, at Old Trafford, he was a ball of frustration as Manchester United battered their guests for long periods. Paul Ince's deflected long-range effort broke the deadlock just after the interval, while Mark Hughes added a second with twenty minutes left. Shortly after, Keane was involved in a clash with Ince and Steve Bruce and exchanged heated verbals with both players. Almost immediately, Clough, so often emotionless throughout the campaign, instructed Gary Crosby to warm up and, moments later, Keane was replaced. As he traipsed towards the dugout, Clough walked onto the pitch and escorted him to the bench.

'By his own standards he was not having a particularly good game,' Clough said afterwards. 'But I also felt he might get himself into trouble. He's only twenty-one and is still learning his trade. To an extent, I could understand his feelings because he was becoming frustrated. We all go through that, even me at fifty-seven. But in this game you have got to be able to curb yourself. He'll learn. It's the same in life, and the best thing Roy can do is get himself a steady girlfriend, have a courtship, and even think of settling down to married life. Believe it or not, that will help him more than any help he can get from me.'[4]

Thankfully, Clough's comments were treated with the silliness they deserved. The *Evening Herald* even ran a competition and asked readers to send in their suggestions for whom Keane should marry and why. The winner, Tom McLoughlin from Glasnevin, put forward Mary Elizabeth Mastrantonio, who played Maid Marian in *Robin Hood: Prince of Thieves*. The reason? 'She's had experience dealing with outlaws from Nottingham Forest.' For his trouble, Tom won a romantic night out in Dublin city centre restaurant Dobbins Bistro.[5]

Keane could have done with it.

The irony was that earlier in the month, he'd broken his nightclub ban. Clough fined him a week's wages, which – temporarily at least – substantially inhibited his chances of finding a life partner.[6]

'In The Black Orchid, the players would stay in the VIP area for most of the night but Roy did like to mingle,' says Steve Campion. 'One night, he came to me and said, "I've got this girl walking around and she won't leave me alone. She said she only wants a kiss but if I say the wrong thing it's going to be in the papers tomorrow." So we went and found the girl and she kept saying, "I just want a kiss. I just want one kiss, just to say that I've kissed Roy Keane." And that's what he had to put up with. He was just a young lad wanting to go out and have a good time. That's all.'

While Keane was on his self-inflicted hiatus from Nottingham's nightspots, he didn't observe an entirely monastic social life.

'He was really into his music and did listen to a lot,' says Ian Kilford. 'He'd go into HMV and if anyone had released something he liked, he'd buy all their albums and singles and listen to them. Sometimes he'd come out with about fifteen or twenty CDs and in his bedroom they'd be lying around everywhere. We'd laugh about it because I'd be saving up to buy the one I wanted that month and he'd walk in and grab about twenty in one go.

'He always had Big Country on in his car. And it was Roy Keane, so I wasn't going to argue with his selections. There were a few Irish bands and artists that he enjoyed, like Van Morrison, but he did seem to have Big Country on all the time. And we had a few trips to Rock City in Nottingham, which was terrific for live music. There was one night we went to watch The Shamen [Scottish dance act] and we came out sweating after dancing the entire time. But I think it was Gary Bowyer's car that had been clamped, so we couldn't get back home for a bit. There was another time when we went to see Madness and I remember Stuart Pearce and Mark Crossley coming back in to The Black Orchid doing all the Madness moves.

'Nottingham was a great, vibrant night out, but we had to be careful because we knew that if we said something or stepped out of line, the papers would want to know. And for us, the one place you didn't want to be on a Monday morning was Brian Clough's office. You just didn't want to be in trouble because it was the ethos of the club. They would look after you and back you.'

As the press suggested that Keane would become a millionaire within a few short years, owing to the size of his improved contract, RTÉ cameras were dispatched to Lotamore Park in Mayfield on 3 February to get the thoughts of his parents.

'There are times I'm thinking I'm in a dream, like,' Mossie said. 'This money is ridiculous, because we're ordinary people, like. He was just playing AUL football here. Now he's over in Nottingham, in three cup finals in twelve months. They're talking about Italy, about this money ...' He paused, holding carefully for the punchline. 'We'd be delighted to get a hold of it, like.'

But Marie seemed concerned by her son's mindset, that it might all be a bit much for him.

'I feel sorry for him,' she said. 'He's over there and none of the family are with him. He's only looking for people to advise him. But he doesn't talk about transfers. I'll say something to him about such a thing and he'll just go, "Mam, paper talk."'[7]

Back at Forest, Clough did continue to show his affection for Keane and was particularly sensitive. The out-of-character, off-colour performances against United and Arsenal proved to him just how much Keane was affected by the pressure and media scrutiny. So he gave him a long leash.

Against Oldham, Clough retained Gary Bannister in a wide role and tasked Keane with playing up front, alongside Nigel. The 2–0 win – a fourth in seven games – moved them off the bottom of the table for the first time in four months and, unsurprisingly, the twinkle returned to Clough's eyes as he chatted to reporters afterwards. Briefly, it was just like old times.

'I've got snowdrops and crocuses coming out in my garden and I was anxious to be able to look at them knowing that my side had made a move up the table,' he said. 'Roy Keane came to see me on Friday morning and said he was unfit because he had a bad ankle. I told him I've got two bad ankles and a couple of bad knees. I asked him to play up front and he said he couldn't turn, but would give it a go anyway. What happened? He was crap, but we won. It was a tactical triumph, all my vast knowledge came into play. But don't tell the board, you might get me the sack. Afterwards Keane asked me if it would be all right for him to go back to the Nottingham nightclub from which I have banned him so that he could find a nice girl with whom to settle down. I told him it would be a fine of not one, but two weeks' wages if he went in there again.'[8]

'I don't know how I'm supposed to meet anyone when the boss has banned me from The Black Orchid,' Keane responded.[9]

For a little while, it looked like Forest might just survive. A rousing 3–0 replay win over Middlesbrough on 3 February ensured a meeting with Arsenal in the Fifth Round of the FA Cup and the momentum continued with a decent league point at Anfield, though it really should've been three but for Bannister missing a great chance late on. Even when Ian Wright conjured a brilliant brace – just like he did a month earlier in the League Cup – to eliminate Forest from another domestic competition, they responded by picking up successive league wins against 'Boro and the high-flying QPR, and pushing out of the drop zone completely, with Keane stepping into the centre of defence again in both games due to a spate of injuries. The previous week, it was the same story when he returned to Dublin to play in a friendly for the Republic of Ireland against Wales at Tolka Park. After David O'Leary was clattered early on by Mark Hughes and forced off, Keane dropped back and partnered the no-nonsense Brian Carey, who was making a rare appearance and looking to impress as a possible World Cup loomed on the horizon.

'Roy showed me how to do it,' Carey commented later.[10]

'I let Brian attack the ball and he didn't miss much,' Keane said. 'I felt we did okay at the back together. It was a good night for Cork.'[11]

Back in Nottingham, results may have improved, but the toxicity that had been kept within the Forest walls finally began to seep through. A group of 'rebel' shareholders had grown increasingly concerned at the club's ill health and called an Emergency General Meeting, the first in twenty-three years. They wanted a committee to investigate Forest's day-to-day operations and the reasons why no one at board level 'dared challenge' Clough's authority, despite 'his decisions and manner during Forest's alarming slump'. The board handsomely won a subsequent vote, but there was still a sizable number of shareholders desperate for Clough to go. And the situation pushed him over the edge.

Before the next game against Crystal Palace, Clough signed a striker. But it wasn't Southend's exciting Stan Collymore, a player they'd monitored and mulled over for weeks. Instead, Robert Rosario arrived from Coventry City for £400,000. If Clough was trying to placate fans, it was an underwhelming attempt.

Rosario provides some insight into the move. 'Forest were looking to sign me and Collymore at the same time – they thought the two of us would work well together. But his deal fell through and they ended up getting him in the summer instead,' he says. 'I loved it at Coventry and I didn't want to go to Forest. So when I got there, I wasn't happy. The atmosphere was so laid-back. It wasn't doom and gloom. There was still a buoyancy there. Mr Clough was left-of-centre and very unorthodox, but I don't think he knew he signed me. I don't think he was running the team then. His assistants – Liam O'Kane and Archie Gemmill – were doing all the work, which was sad. I was shocked. He wasn't there when I signed and I don't actually think he even knew my name. He never called me Robert, he just referred to me as "big fella".

'I was fully aware of how much of a hero and an icon he was, but the players were in control of the situation. Mr Clough wasn't really at training, though he might turn up on a Friday. My first experience of him was when we played Palace and we were all in the dressing room. Mr Clough had a cricket ball and he'd just throw it around and you had to catch it and throw it back to him. So you got changed facing him or otherwise you'd get a cricket ball in the back of the head. It was an eye-opener for me.'[12]

Keane popped up with a trademarked equaliser in the 1–1 mid-week draw at the City Ground on 3 March, striding onto Ian Woan's lobbed pass over the top, waiting for the bounce and then hammering the strike to

Nigel Martyn's bottom corner. But, given how they'd dominated the game, it was a crucial opportunity missed by Forest.

Clough cut a jaded and disorientated figure and at half-time remained in the dugout watching a penalty shoot-out contest instead of motivating his players. It wasn't a gimmick any more. He just didn't seem to care enough.

And compounding the weirdness of the situation and the overall lack of leadership, it transpired that Forest would be without Rosario for the next two league fixtures after he picked up a booking in his final outing for Coventry. Keane was in the same boat, while Clough was also without the injured Webb and Stuart Pearce, whose appearance in the cup loss to Arsenal would prove his final one of the entire campaign due to a persistent groin problem.

However, Keane did provide some good news and revealed he'd decided to sign the Forest contract, keeping him at the club until the summer of 1996. The deal was agreed after Clough stepped in to negotiations one afternoon and, in a moment reminiscent of when Keane sat in the same room with the Cobh Ramblers contingent in the spring of 1990, told Ron Fenton to give him what he wanted.

'I am delighted to be staying with Brian Clough because I will never forget that it was he who gave me my first chance in England. I just hope that this will end all the speculation about my future,' he said.[13]

It didn't. Though when his name next appeared in the back pages, it wasn't transfer-related. It was worse.

With a ten-day break before Forest were next in competitive action, Clough felt a trip to Jersey would be good for team morale. A game was lined up against one of the local amateur sides, Jersey Portuguese, but the main purpose was to play some golf, socialise and relax. The squad were staying at the Grand Hotel, situated along the picturesque esplanade in St Helier.

Keane was immersed in a drinking session in the bar on the second day. Also present were some hockey players from teams in Jersey and Guernsey, as well as their respective partners.

Keane later claimed one of the women approached him and, after some chit-chat, threw her drink over his head. Worse for wear, he retaliated with his own pint before her husband intervened. The two men started to grapple.

'He enjoyed a drink but was hot-headed, and he could become argumentative when he wanted and that was one of the occasions where he proved to be,' says Steve Chettle. 'He became more loud and more excitable. I wasn't out with him all the time but I heard of occasions in The Orchid. When you see somebody like Roy Keane, he's there to have a pop at and people want to have a piece of him. And he wasn't backwards in coming forwards. He ended up being taken out of the hotel bar.'

Alan Hill, Forest's chief scout, was the man entrusted with diffusing the situation. 'He was sitting about ten yards away from me and I thought, "What the hell is going off here?"' he recounted years later for the *Inside the Mind of Roy Keane* documentary. 'Roy's saying something about a slag and, "Do you know who I am?" and all this business. I said, "Roy, it's time for bed." And he said, "I'm not going to bed." And I said, "Son, you're going to bed." So I stood up and physically got a hold of him and he tried to headbutt me. And that was the first time I saw Roy Keane in a different light.'

Rosario also witnessed the incident. He'd only been at the club for a number of days but had already been taken aback by the influence Keane had on the team and the responsibility he shouldered.

'Stuart Pearce was the captain but my take was that there was one person in control and that was Roy,' he says. 'I was blown away that a twenty-one-year-old ran the club. You had Pearcey, Neil Webb, Nigel Clough and it was this young kid who was running the show. But he had all the qualities to do so. They say that if you're good enough you're old enough, but there aren't that many twenty-one-year-olds with that amount of confidence. After a week of training with him, I remember thinking, "This guy is a rock star." But every successful, high-profile star player needs qualities that may not be liked by a lot of people. You had to be single-minded, ruthless and no one could get in your way.

'This is all subjective, but I think you need to have a craziness to you, but a controlled craziness. At the time, football clubs were like workingmen's clubs. That was the culture, particularly when it came to drink. And in Jersey I saw the other side of him. The crazy side. I remember being over by the elevators in the hotel and he'd lost his mind. Alan Hill had to pick him up, grab him and get a hold of him. It was a bit of Jekyll and Hyde and there would be that edge to him.'

When Clough arrived in Jersey the following day, he was briefed on the incident and immediately sent Keane home as the club attempted to keep the story under wraps. The incident did still make the papers, however.

'There was a fracas, but it was no big deal,' said the hotel manager Samantha Chatham. 'In fairness to Forest, it was the hockey people who were out of line. Some of them were very drunk.'[14]

Regardless, Keane was banished but, fortunately, was able to find some solace in Cork because of his two-game Forest suspension. Plenty of time to reflect on an expanding list of misdemeanours.

One of Clough's ex-Forest players, the no-nonsense centre-half Larry Lloyd, was running a Nottingham pub, The Stage Door, in the early 1990s and allegedly had his own memorable encounter with Keane. 'It was Forest's Christmas party, and let's just say I thought Roy was being a bit naughty,' Lloyd said. 'I asked him to leave. He gave me some lip. I had a word with his captain, Stuart Pearce, and asked him to get Roy to leave. Stuart said: "He's no harm." So I chucked all of them out.'[15]

'To be fair, Larry shouldn't have been barring anyone from his pub,' says Steve Chettle.

'That story has gone from Roy being asked to leave to him being barred. But there were these descriptions of him as a hellraiser and it couldn't have been further from the truth, but he was gaining a reputation as a bit of a drinker,' Steve Campion says. 'He got put out of a wine bar on one occasion and he fell against the window and it smashed. The next day, the story was in the paper and the doorman got paid £1,200. So, people were trying to cash in. But he was never put out of The Black Orchid for fighting. On a few occasions, I did have to put my arm around him and say, "Keaney, it's home time, pal." And he'd say, "Ah Steve, not yet." He'd be heartbroken. He didn't want to leave. And I'd just have to reiterate it. "Keaney, you've got to go. You're just starting to get on people's nerves and I'm a bit concerned that someone might give you a clout." Not everyone likes footballers and it was at the stage when he was attracting attention from other clubs and in the papers a lot.

'But we've all got that friend, don't we? The one you chat to afterwards and say, "You were a bit loud last night, weren't you?" And what I liked about Roy was that on a Sunday morning, the phone would ring and it would be him. He'd say, "Steve, last night … I'm really sorry. I had too much to drink." And I'd say, "Roy, you don't need to call." And he'd be adamant. "I know but will I still be allowed come to the club?" He'd always phone to apologise. And he hadn't done anything wrong. He'd just had a drink, like they'd all had.'

Keane had always enjoyed a night out. But during the 1992/93 season, his status changed. He became a consistent feature on the back pages and both the transfer and contract speculation offered up dizzying numbers. No longer was he described as an 'exciting midfielder' or 'talented youngster'. Instead, it was '£5m-rated star'. And that brought a different kind of attention.

'I'd been out on the town with him many times and I never saw Roy cause trouble, even with plenty of drink taken, and there were a lot of late nights,' says Darren Barry, who left Forest in the summer of 1992. 'He was never an instigator because he kept to himself. If somebody had a go at him, it was in his nature to have a go back. But that's about where you come from too. I grew up in the same place Roy did and if somebody has a go, you don't just walk away.'

For his latest indiscretion, Clough fined Keane a basic week's wage of £5,000 and the tabloids eventually got their hands on the story just as Forest prepared to face Everton at Goodison Park on 13 March. Things started badly when Clough named his son as sweeper and the 3–0 loss seemed almost expected.

Afterwards, Tony Cottee, who scored twice for the home side, turned the knife in Forest's gut with a withering and justified assessment. 'They were poor,' he said. 'You expect relegation-haunted teams to battle and while I know it's not Forest's style, I expected them to create a bit more than they did. They have to start putting results together because they're running out of games. They had a lot of players missing but they have got to start scrapping for points and winning their home games.'[16]

But in their next home game against Norwich, they also lost 3–0. It was energy-sapping. And the players were drained. Clough, effectively, had shrunk down to an invisible presence.

'He needed people around him to give him a boost and advise him,' says Toddy Örlygsson. 'When you look at history, when you have power for a long time, you need somebody to challenge you. In Cloughie's case, he just got too settled.'

'We knew he wasn't well,' Chettle says. 'Clearly decisions weren't being made by himself. And everyone kept saying the team was too good to go down – journalists, opponents, ourselves. But the history books speak for themselves. If you don't win enough games and get enough points, you're not a good enough team. The last three or four months were really, really hard work. Nothing really happened at all. We weren't catching up with the teams above us and it just got naturally worse. When you look at our line-ups at the end of the season, they were kind of makeshift. We didn't really have anything else to fall back on. And not having that man there to guide us through it, as he used to do, was awful. We were trying to sort things out for ourselves and just weren't good enough. It was a horrible way for things to end.'

When Keane returned for a home game against Leeds on 21 March, a fixture that coincided with Clough's fifty-eighth birthday, the manager – perhaps having read *The Observer*'s assessment that Sunday morning – had started to panic.

'Forest can no longer be said to be too good to go down,' Paddy Barclay wrote. 'They are, on the evidence of last Wednesday's home defeat by Norwich, too bad to stay up.'[17]

The crowd serenaded Clough with a rendition of 'Happy Birthday' as he walked to the dugout, but the cheery mood quickly evaporated. Forest conceded early once more and, despite Nigel Clough equalising from the penalty spot later in the half (Keane created it with an injection of pace down the right side and a cross-field pass to Woan, who was upended by John Lukic), the Trent End was appalled at their side's radical change of approach and the deployment of 6ft 4in Rosario as a mere battering ram. When Nigel – so uncharacteristically – lofted another long ball in desperation, the home fans booed him. On the bench, his father flicked a V-sign at them in retaliation. Earlier in the season, when George Graham had advised a change in strategy owing to their predicament, Clough gave him short shrift. 'We play football on the grass, we shove it around,' he said. 'If it were meant to be played in the air, God would have put grass and cows up there.'[18]

But Forest were now in free fall and the frenzy continued when they tried to resuscitate the Collymore deal, only for Southend to dig in their heels and demand £2 million for the twenty-two-year-old. Clough received the Freedom of the City of Nottingham and basked in the applause. But the same week, East Midlands Electricity – who had a six-year commercial relationship with him – announced an end to the partnership, days after breakfast cereal Shredded Wheat did likewise.

In need of an adrenaline shot, it was Keane who supplied it.

Against Southampton at The Dell, he raced onto Kingsley Black's cross, veered past Ken Monkou with his first touch and clipped the angled finish over Tim Flowers. It put Forest 2–0 up, and they needed the cushion as Matt Le Tissier pulled a goal back late on. Clough had doubts about Collymore and seeing his side pull out a crucial win that moved them to within one point of safety helped make his mind up. With the transfer window about to shut, he pulled the plug on a last-minute £1.75 million deal that Southend had agreed to and told the *Nottingham Evening Post*, 'We're sticking to what we've got.'[19]

In public, he seemed adamant about the transfer. But it was a different story in private, as he revealed to Duncan Hamilton. 'I could pick up that phone now and buy that bloke Stan Collymore,' he said. 'We've got the money. I just don't have the inclination. I don't know if he's right for us, I'm not sure he can play. And yet the thing is I used to know. I'm just knackered, mentally and physically. We've been absolute, total shit for most of this season. I've never been so depressed, so down. I have to accept I'm not as good as I was.'[20]

While Clough's descent continued at an accelerated pace, Keane was at the PFA Awards dinner in London where he finished third in the Young Player of the Year race, behind Nicky Barmby and winner Ryan Giggs. For the first time in his career, he was named in the Team of the Season, alongside compatriot Paul McGrath, who also claimed the senior individual accolade.

From there, Keane travelled back home to keep two appointments: a World Cup qualifier in Dublin against Northern Ireland and the Blarney

Sportstar of the Year awards at Christie's Hotel, where he was guest of honour and presented trophies to a range of local athletes. In the midst of all the mayhem, Keane was glad of the change in scenery. At Lansdowne Road on 31 March, he and his teammates made light work of their neighbours, scoring three times in the space of nine first-half minutes to leave them second in Group Three, having played two games fewer than leaders Spain. Afterwards, Keane grabbed a pint with his father Mossie and Forest teammate Kingsley Black, who'd played the last twenty minutes for Billy Bingham's side. And he ended the night in Rumours nightclub on O'Connell Street, along with Terry Phelan, Kevin Sheedy, David Kelly and Packie Bonner, as Mary Carr gleefully detailed in her AfterDark column in the following day's *Evening Herald*: 'Describing himself as "the most immature man in soccer", Roy couldn't contain his twinkle toes any longer when the strains of George Michael's "Careless Whisper" was blared,' she wrote. 'And grabbing his partner, the blonde Martina, made some strategic moves for the dance-floor. There he happily took his place among the gyrating bodies and flashing lights, remaining until Eric Clapton's sappy "Wonderful Tonight" was well and truly over.'

Now a darling of the Irish social scene, he was a long way from raves at Rock City.

13

AFTER THE LORD MAYOR'S SHOW

It was a Wednesday morning, the third week of April, when a number of Irish newspapers carried a story on their front pages.

The reports were short on details but maintained proceedings had been lodged at Cork Circuit Court against Keane pertaining to an incident that took place in May 1991, where he was alleged to have used a slanderous remark when speaking to a young woman during a night out on the Grand Parade.

The allegation, revealed later to have been made by a neighbour of Keane's, would linger until reaching a conclusion more than two years later, when it was thrown out in the Cork High Court. But it was a development that triggered a greater awakening in Keane: such was his status, his hometown wasn't providing the solitude or sanctuary that it used to. In fact, it was becoming more obtrusive than Nottingham.

'Roy used to call in to see me when he was home,' says Noel Spillane. 'He'd come to the *Examiner* offices on Academy Street and you'd get a phone-call, hush-hush, like. "Roy is below." And he'd come up and we'd chat away and we might even head for a couple of pints. But this one day, he was with me and we were in the far corner of the office. He'd been in a bit of trouble and we're chatting away. But I hear the clicks of a camera and it was another staff photographer – not a Cork-based one like Eddie [O'Hare] – who was there and snapping him. Roy looks at me, so I tell this fella to fuck off and that the conversation is private. And he's saying, "Just one more, Noely. Just one more." And I can see Roy's face and he's ready to go for him. So I tell him that we should head off and he agreed with that. So we're walking down Academy Street to grab a pint and the same fella is in front of us with the camera as we're going down the road. And he's saying, "Where are ye going now, Roy? Probably for a pint. Cashman's, is it?" And with that, Roy nearly went for him. He was very close to giving him a proper smack.'

There was another, more impactful incident around that time too. Unbeknownst to Spillane and O'Hare, Dublin-based tabloid newspaper *The Star* had contacted the *Examiner*'s editorial team looking for fresh photographs of Keane to accompany articles they were preparing for publication. An agreement was reached and their picture editor, Jim Dunne, travelled to Cork, where O'Hare's extensive catalogue of Keane images – the vast majority of which weren't even published yet – was put on display. He returned to Dublin with the best ones tucked under his arm and some featured in the paper not long after.

'I got a phone call and it was Roy,' Spillane remembers. 'He was so quick off the mark. Somebody tipped him off. He said, "You're some fucking bollix, you." I hadn't even seen *The Star* so I said, "What's wrong with you, boy?" And he goes, "What about Eddie's photographs? I suppose he got about ten grand for that, did he? Fucking muppets, the two of ye." I said, "Roy, hold on a while. I had fuck-all to do with it." But that was the end of it. Bang. The phone was slammed down. We were told it was some sort of reciprocal arrangement. It was unethical, unprofessional and our "in" with Roy was in danger of being completely blown out of the water. They sold us down the swannie.'

Keane was now a commodity in his own backyard and a mild paranoia began to sprout within him. His ascent dovetailed with the dawning of Ireland's tabloid age and he was already a prized target. Unwilling to be caught off guard again, he'd keep a distance from here on. Even those he went back a long way with would be kept at arm's length. The circle grew smaller.

Arriving to Cork ahead of a 1–1 World Cup qualifier draw against Denmark at Lansdowne Road, his family were hassled by national press at the Mayfield house, owing to the slander allegations. 'I suppose I haven't helped myself but it's quite difficult,' Keane told *The Cork Examiner*. 'Even when I come back home it's hard. But my family and friends know that I'm the same person I was when I left three years ago. People can write what they want but they don't know me. I don't go around looking for trouble and provoking people in pubs and dance halls. Unfortunately, I have gotten into trouble here and there, but people just want to knock me. That's all. But I have to live with that.'[1]

The trip home was especially irritating because he'd longed for some respite as Forest careered towards the First Division.

Keane confirmed – not that it was any great surprise – that he would 'definitely' leave the club if relegation was confirmed. That would happen if they failed to win against fellow strugglers Sheffield United in their penultimate game of the season. But, long before that, the death knell was sounding.

Earlier in April, there was a ninth home defeat of the season to Aston Villa, as Paul McGrath rose above Keane to head the only goal of the game. And a few days later, Forest lost 3–1 to Blackburn Rovers at the City Ground, where the fans booed mercilessly. They finished with ten men as Gary Charles was sent off and Clough tried to rescue things in the second-half by pushing Keane up front. Then, against QPR at Loftus Road, Keane single-handedly rallied the troops. Forest led twice but Les Ferdinand's unerring accuracy in and around the penalty area ensured his first hat-trick for the club and a dramatic 4–3 win.

That afternoon, Keane had battled an exasperated thirty-six-year-old Ray Wilkins for the first time. 'The ball was in midfield and Ray turned around to somebody – maybe Alan MacDonald – and he basically said, "Who is this that I'm playing against?" I cannot keep up with him. *Who* is this kid?"' remembers Kingsley Black. 'I had a little chuckle to myself because Roy was doing it regularly and nobody could keep up with him, really.'

Wilkins, who had spent three years with AC Milan in the mid-1980s, was asked about Keane after the game, particularly if he felt he could succeed in an environment like Serie A. 'Roy is a talented player and the way they play in Italy should suit him,' he said. 'Over there, the forwards are marked tightly, so players who can break from midfield and score are highly valued – people like David Platt. Roy made some tremendous runs against us and he is very similar to Bryan Robson.'[2]

The QPR game put Keane's future front and centre again. Blackburn were rumoured to have officially lodged a £3.5 million bid that Forest turned down, while Arsenal still hovered too. Manchester United were also included on the shortlist of suitors, as Robson himself declared his club 'would be mad' not to have an interest. 'Roy Keane is a winner, shows a good attitude and he wants to work hard at his game,' he said. 'He's quick, he's got good stamina, gets forward well, he can score goals and has a great engine between the penalty areas. He would suit United's style of play too and if we win the championship at the end of the season, I think that might strengthen our hand in any transfer talk.'[3]

But the whispers surrounding a switch to Italy weren't going away either. They'd started the previous season when Genoa briefly claimed an interest and, in the early part of 1993, both Milan sides were rumoured to be in the mix. The story was taken so seriously that Keane's parents were asked whether they'd like to see him move there.

'When he went to England first I didn't want him going there but Italy would break my heart,' Marie told RTÉ television on 3 February.

But Mossie was enthused at the prospect, smiling enthusiastically as he contemplated his son rubbing shoulders with Roberto Baggio, Marco van

Basten and Roberto Mancini. 'It would be marvellous,' he said. 'Everyone in Cork now is saying "Italy, Italy, Italy". And I'd be up in the clouds. Oh, God. Italy is … [the pinnacle]. The only thing I'd be afraid of is the media over there. The media are stone mad, I think. They'd nearly want to sleep with you. I saw a bit of pressure on Roy with this contract, just from talking to him. But reading some of the players in Italy, they say it's impossible to live there. Everything you do they [the media] are taking notice of it. You haven't a minute's peace, really. That's the only thing: the media pressure. But I'd still take a chance and let him go over. Just to see can he do it over there.'[4]

The transfer talk relaxed temporarily as Forest pushed back against the tide and mustered a rare home win against Tottenham on 12 April, only to suffer an embarrassing and hugely damaging defeat to a depleted Wimbledon the following weekend.

When Keane broke the offside trap at Highbury four days later, rounded David Seaman and rolled an equaliser to the net deep into injury time, his excessive celebration suggested there was still some hope. He had played like there was, a bundle of dangerous energy and described by *The Independent* as Forest's 'heart and soul'. Early in the second half, he snapped at Nigel Winterburn and inflicted a challenge on him so severe that it damaged the left-back's ankle ligaments and forced him off on a stretcher. And when he calmly tucked home the leveller, he kissed his Forest badge in front of the home fans – who'd abused him relentlessly since Winterburn went off – and cheerily expressed exactly what he thought of them. Later, just like what happened when Keane celebrated a goal against Spurs earlier in the season, a fan complained to police and he was interviewed by an inspector in the dressing room after the game. Unsurprisingly, Scotland Yard confirmed no action would be taken.

Arsenal had claimed the League Cup the previous weekend and George Graham admitted his side had shown 'after the Lord Mayor's Show' symptoms.

The same could be said for Keane. Embroiled in a relegation mess, he had a month or two to figure out his next career move, there was a court case pending back home and he was struggling to come to terms with his newfound celebrity status.

Having signed a two-year contract with energy drink Lucozade, Keane had agreed to film a TV advert for the company in Dublin on 22 April. It was an ill-advised decision and Clough stepped in, telling Keane that promotional work was out of the question given Forest's perilous situation. That story appeared on the front page of *The Cork Examiner*, along with the revelation he had been interviewed by police at Highbury and that he had also failed to attend a gala event in West Bromwich where he was being presented with the Midlands Young Player of the Year award.

Days later, there was another damning story in the press. But not about Keane this time.

When it eventually came, Clough's demise was sordid and sleazy and took the form of a horribly clichéd 'tabloid exclusive'.[5] *The People* reported that a Forest director, Chris Wootton – who was eager to force Clough out – claimed Clough's alcohol addiction had led to him narrowly escaping death on two separate occasions. Wootton, the paper alleged, also had a tape recording of Clough slurring his words as he tried to record a TV spot for Shredded Wheat. Frantically, Forest attempted to save face but only made matters worse. To the widespread shock of the assembled media, chairman Fred Reacher announced that Clough – apparently after lengthy discussions that had been ongoing for weeks – would retire at the end of the season, after eighteen years at the club. Following the weekend exposé, Clough had told Reacher of the plan, though without a public statement he was always likely to change his mind. So Reacher – later admitting the announcement had been mishandled – saw a window of opportunity and hastily arranged a press conference.

The players had no idea and captain Stuart Pearce found out while listening to the radio. Keane was with the Irish side in Dublin when he heard the news. He said he was 'shell-shocked and bitterly disappointed', immediately taking a moment to acknowledge that without Clough, his career would have been markedly different. 'Brian Clough was the man who launched my career in the English League and I will always be grateful to him for that,' he said. 'He's been brilliant to me over the last three years.'[6]

But Steve Chettle maintains the squad did feel something had irrevocably changed. 'I don't think we were shocked,' he says. 'We were fully aware that it was a possibility. For the benefit of his health, it was the right decision.'

Given his career, it was always unlikely that Clough's eventual departure from Forest would be a clean break, though the sour aftertaste hung in the air for a long time. His wife and children issued a statement distancing themselves from the club's behaviour and they expressed their hurt at the way his 'retirement' was handled. And the red-top rumours about his drinking weren't helped when Clough spoke to *The Sun* to address stories of him being found asleep in a ditch close to his home.

'I am not a boozer,' he said, as the accompanying close-up suggested otherwise. 'I often walk between my home and that of my son Nigel. It's about six or seven miles and bloody hard work when you get to my age. On the day in question, I had a kip in a field because I was tired.'[7]

Clough stayed away from the club for the rest of the week and didn't even see the players until twenty minutes before kick-off against Sheffield United on 1 May, the do-or-die fixture and supposedly the rousing home performance that might just keep Forest up. Pearce later described the atmosphere as 'creepy' and, once again, it's hard to know if it was some more faux-psychology from Clough or simply a snapshot of a drained man who was too exhausted to care any more.

'The performance was flat,' says Steve Chettle. 'I don't think emotion came into it. The damage was done previous to that.'

The reception from supporters was extraordinary: an outpouring of genuine love, affection and sadness. But, as noted by the *Daily Mail*'s Neil Harman, 'the only bit of the afternoon that wasn't right was the match itself'.[8]

Trailing to a neat Glyn Hodges' finish, Keane personified an anxious Forest display by missing a glorious chance early in the second half, after Woan curled in a perfect cross. With an open goal at his mercy, he headed over the crossbar and collapsed to the ground. Later, Brian Gayle added a second for United and Forest's fate was sealed.

'I hate to say it, but when I got there I think there was an acceptance that we were going down,' Rosario says. 'It wasn't as dour as I thought it would be. I can't remember there being any anger or disgust. I didn't see anyone sobbing or that whole woe-is-me thing. We were all professionals and disappointed. But I think they knew they could bounce back immediately and they had a strong nucleus. I wouldn't say it was a relief but it was inevitable and plans just turned to getting them back in the top flight.'

Those plans began quickly and within days of Clough's anticlimactic final game in charge – another loss away to Ipswich – Forest had announced one of his former players, Frank Clark, as the club's new manager. His first order of business was declaring he'd fight 'tooth and nail' to keep hold of Keane, as well as Pearce and Nigel Clough.

'I will be doing everything I possibly can to keep them here but they will have to show they want to stay,' Clark said. 'If they show they don't want to play for Nottingham Forest then I will sell them. There has already been contact from other clubs and it would take twenty minutes to read out the list of clubs interested in Roy Keane alone and I'm not surprised.'[9]

Perversely, Forest's dismal season only heightened Keane's qualities. He'd made the PFA Team of the Season, finished third in the voting for the league's best young player and still managed eight goals in all competitions, despite spending so much time at centre-back. He'd begun to blossom at international level too, becoming a crucial player for Jack Charlton in a radically different role.

'Roy Keane shone like a beacon through all the gloom of that desolate season,' Clough later wrote. 'I knew other clubs had taken note of his outstanding talent – they'd have been blind not to see it.'[10]

With no interest in remaining at Forest, Keane revealed, prior to a World Cup qualifier in Albania at the end of May, that his next move was already in the pipeline. 'I've yet to talk to Frank Clark and I plan to do that when I get back,' he told *The Cork Examiner*. 'I have a fair idea of where I want to go and I want to get things sorted out fast. There's been no change in the situation since our season ended and what with a few days back home in Cork and our World Cup matches coming up, I haven't spoken to anyone about any transfer.'

But others had.

Keane was 'the most coveted midfield player in the country', but, despite all of the various rumours, Blackburn seemed to have little in the way of direct competition for his signature. They had outlined their desire to sign him way back in December and the hard work had already been done. However, towards the end of May, Keane's head was turned by interest from abroad.

Clark had indicated that Forest's former centre-back, Des Walker, was a prime target. He'd struggled at Sampdoria and the Italian side were happy to let him go after just one season with them, though it seemed optimistic to think he'd swap an Italian giant for a First Division side. 'I'm prepared to move heaven and earth to bring Des back to Forest,' Clark told reporters. 'The best years of his career were with this club. I want to bring him home.'[11]

Under the terms of his renegotiated contract, Keane could only go to a foreign club for a minimum of £5 million, so it made financial sense for Forest to try to arrange a deal with Sampdoria.

Keane was ready to shun Blackburn amid the reported Italian interest, despite warnings from certain quarters that he should ignore the advances and stay in England instead. 'I've been told by Brendon Batson that Sampdoria are one of two Italian clubs interested in me,' he said. 'I might never get another chance of going to Italy. If this materialises, I'd go in the morning. People have urged me to stay on in England with one of the bigger clubs for another two or three years to gain more experience but I don't see it that way. I have made the right decisions in the past and I would hope to continue to do that now. I didn't think there would be interest from abroad. I just thought there would be English clubs involved. Obviously it's great there's another option for me.'[12]

However, Batson was only working on Keane's behalf so, regarding the Italian interest, he was being informed of it by Forest. 'There was a lot of interest in him but because he was still Forest's player, it was all done in a pretty orderly way,' he says. 'I wasn't aware of any particular frenzy and he was pretty calm himself. I was dealing directly with Roy, so anything else was through the club. I wasn't actioned as a mouthpiece for other teams. Any interest in him from other sides would've had to go directly through Forest.'

Forest's main objective was to instigate a bidding war for Keane, and Sampdoria eventually issued a statement to refute rumours they'd submitted a bid.

'These reports are completely unfounded,' they told Paddy Agnew of *The Irish Times*. 'Sampdoria is not interested in Keane and made no offer whatsoever for him.'[13]

But the rumours may not have been so far-fetched. The club were eyeing a goalscoring midfielder and later in the summer spent £5.2 million to take David Platt from Juventus, while they also offloaded Walker to Sheffield Wednesday.

Keane returned from Albania after a sluggish 2–1 Irish win, in which he was noticeably uptight and not 100 per cent fit. Though he was named in the squad for David O'Leary's testimonial against Hungary at Lansdowne Road just a few days later, Charlton allowed him travel to Nottingham to inform Clark of his decision to leave the club. And it seemed to release some pressure.

On the Saturday, 29 May, back with the Irish squad, it took him just fourteen seconds to make an impact against Ferenc Puskás' side. Some speculated that the transfer gossip would potentially inhibit his performance, though he quickly rubbished that.

'He was never overawed by anyone or anything, ever,' says Tommy Dunne, his old FÁS teammate. 'I remember Ronnie Whelan told a great story about that day against Hungary. The two of them were in central midfield so he said to him beforehand, "Just ease into it, we'll sit here and get settled" – exactly what an experienced player would say to a young fella. But straight from the kick-off, Roy was gone. He took off down the pitch and rifled in an unbelievable goal. Roy was basically telling him – by bursting down the pitch – "You play your game and I'll play mine." This was Ronnie Whelan – senior Ireland player, European Cup winner, Liverpool captain. Regarding mindset and character, Roy was already so mature.'

It was Keane's first senior goal and described by the *Sunday Independent* the following day as 'five seconds of genius'. He dashed from the halfway line, rounded one Hungarian defender and blasted beyond the goalkeeper from twenty-five yards, with the strike glancing the near post on its way.

Though the game would end in a 4–2 defeat, Keane didn't care. Having come to the conclusion that the Serie A rumours carried little substance, he'd agreed terms with Blackburn Rovers the previous day and confirmed the news over the weekend: 'Blackburn have offered me a four-year contract and the manager assures me that he wants the club to be up there challenging for major honours with the likes of Manchester United, Liverpool and Aston Villa,' he said.

'Mr Dalglish says he wants Blackburn to have a squad capable of winning the league and cup double. Blackburn are the first club to talk to me and there was no problem agreeing personal terms. I did not put pen to paper out of courtesy to the other clubs who have shown an interest.'[14]

Later, Keane backtracked on this version of events and said the only reason he didn't sign for Blackburn was because club staff had finished for the day and there was nobody left in the offices at Ewood Park by the time agreement was reached with Kenny Dalglish late on Friday afternoon. The transfer would have been a record fee and another substantial coup for Rovers after the capture of Alan Shearer the previous summer. Owing to its magnitude, surely key club personnel would have made themselves available to complete the deal, regardless of office hours? It seems more likely that Keane was simply unsure of the move.

The club had only just returned to the top flight and although bank-rolled by Jack Walker's bottomless resources, didn't exactly appeal to Keane's traditionalist ways. He knew there was wider interest, with United and Arsenal still reportedly in the picture, but no other club was putting an offer on the table. So his decision to go public with confirmation of his Blackburn agreement was either a silly error or particularly cunning. They'd approached him behind Forest's back and he was supposed to keep quiet until further notice. Inevitably, his reveal dramatically changed things. Forest chairman Fred Reacher, who wanted to keep pushing a bidding war, maintained the club had not given Blackburn permission to speak with him, that no fee had been discussed between the clubs, that Rovers' behaviour had left him 'incensed' and that Keane was still on the market.

'My take on it was that Roy was very interested in joining Manchester United,' says Brendon Batson, who was still advising Keane at that stage.

Others felt that way too.

Years later, Dalglish detailed a conversation he shared with Frank Clark after Blackburn's illegal approach had been revealed. 'I got a phone call to say Forest had accepted a bid from us,' Dalglish told Sky Sports in 2017.

'So we met [Keane] at a hotel near Stoke. Frank Clark phoned me a day later and said, "What are you doing?" I told him, "Well, we have agreed a fee?" He said, "No we've not." So I had to say I was awfully sorry and the parting shot was him telling me Keane was going to United.'[15]

Having headed to Cork following the Hungary friendly, Keane cut a composed figure and even stopped in for a public appearance at Matthews sports store as their summer season began with a 'Time Off For Leisure' launch event. There was some local media attention and when a photograph of him appeared in the following day's *Cork Examiner*, it carried a magnificent tagline: 'One decision Roy Keane is smart about – where to buy his swimwear.'[16]

Keane was at his family home in Mayfield when he received a call from Alex Ferguson on Tuesday 1 June. He wanted to know if he'd signed anything with Blackburn. When Keane told him he hadn't, Ferguson encouraged him to fly to Manchester later in the week and meet him for a chat. Keane's clever SOS had worked. He put the phone down and informed his United-supporting family of what had just happened. 'It was unbelievable, really,' he told Liam Mackey of *The Sunday Press* a couple of months afterwards. 'I was hyper after he rang me, all the family were. It was brilliant.'[17]

But he kept things calm when speaking to the press and revealing his upcoming meeting.

'United are interested in me so I'll go and listen to what they have to offer,' Keane said. 'I'm keeping an open mind. I don't want to rush into anything. United approached me so I'll sit down and talk to them.'[18]

United had managed to stay on Forest's good side by seeking their blessing to speak with Keane, who was in Manchester by Thursday morning. Ferguson, who had travelled to Oslo to watch England suffer a 2–0 World Cup qualifying defeat to Norway the previous evening, invited Keane to his house for lunch, where he and his assistant, Brian Kidd, tempted him over a game of snooker, dangling the carrot of UEFA Champions League football – given that United had been crowned league champions in May – and what his potential signing would do for the club's chances of success in Europe's premium competition.

'I'm glad I went over to Manchester, quite a bit has been achieved,' Keane said upon his return, though he hardly kept a low profile and went to watch his brother Denis feature for Temple United in the AUL Intermediate play-off against Ballincollig. 'I'm going to think things over for a few days. Ferguson said what a great club United are and he also set out the goals his club is now facing as they prepare to compete in the European Cup.'[19]

The discussions were put on hold as Ferguson holidayed for a few days and Keane had a pair of back-to-back World Cup qualifiers to contend with. As he arrived at the Forte Crest Dublin Airport Hotel ahead of a flight to Riga and a meeting with Latvia, he revelled in the attention and media frenzy. Bombarded with questions regarding his meeting with Ferguson and whether he was going to sign with United or Blackburn, he mischievously toyed with reporters and had them hanging on his every word – of which there weren't many.

'Well,' he began. 'There have been other enquiries.'

The press pack asked him how sure he was of his next destination.

'Ninety-nine per cent,' he said. 'I will say which club between our matches in Latvia and Lithuania.'[20]

Newspaper headlines declared Keane's transfer saga 'a soap opera', though he wasn't showing any adverse effects. In fact, he was thriving. In Riga, he was easily his team's best player and combined with Denis Irwin to set up an opening goal for John Aldridge, while he also hit the woodwork in the second half, after McGrath had headed home to assure another three points.

Afterwards, as the Irish squad made their way back to Dublin, the accepted story was that despite the Ferguson conversation, Keane would still sign for Blackburn. By that stage, they had submitted an official bid of £3.5 million – the only club to do so. But Forest stood firm, with manager Frank Clark going on the offensive.

'Roy's going nowhere until we get the £5 million at which we value him,' he said. 'He seems to be under the misapprehension that he can sign for anybody he likes. But that is not true. He is under contract to us and he won't be leaving until we get the price we want. It [£3.5 million] is still not enough – and nobody has come remotely near what we want for Roy.'[21]

Keane was forced to embarrassingly back-pedal and informed the press that confirmation of his future would have to come *after* the crucial clash with Lithuania in Vilnius.

And, in a way, he was true to his word.

Returning to Dublin with the Ireland squad after a hard-fought but crucial 1–0 victory, he went out to celebrate. He spotted a familiar face and over a few drinks at the bar, Noel Spillane quizzed him on his next move. Keane played along.

'It was like a game of questions and answers,' Spillane says. '"It's United, isn't it?" But he didn't confirm. Then it was, "A three, four or ten-year contract?" He didn't confirm that either. "A British record?" He's smiling away but no confirmation. So we said goodnight and he jumped in a taxi. And I was wondering how I could verify the United move. It was the early hours of the morning so I said, "There's only one thing for this." So I ring the Ireland team hotel and ask for Denis Irwin, who was Roy's room-mate. And he answers! I ask him about the United transfer and he says, "This is the first I've heard about it – he's said nothing to me."'

The story was light, but Spillane felt he had enough, especially as Forest chairman Fred Reacher had confirmed United's official approach. A quote from Keane and details about Alex Ferguson phoning the family home in Mayfield the previous weekend added some weight to the copy, so Spillane filed a couple of hundred words and went to bed.

'The following morning I was getting the train back to Cork and Roy was with me,' he says. 'We were getting closer to the city and he says, "The stuff we were talking about last night, you didn't write that, did you?" So I said, "I did, it's on the back of the *Echo* tonight." And he looks at me and says, "What?" He was furious. I tried to calm him down but we pulled in to Kent Station, he hopped off and made a bee-line for the newspaper stand. He picked up a copy of the paper and says, "Fuck it." He turned to me and said, "And fuck you too." But I was driving him home and had the car parked outside. He was fuming. I dropped him off in Mayfield and it was "Good luck, kid. All the best." Door slam.'

It turned out that Keane was front-page news too. Alongside updates on Aer Lingus' perilous financial situation and a planned one-day work stoppage by Bus Éireann, Spillane's story had also been carried on the front of *The Cork Examiner*.

'I'm waiting on one more telephone call today, but that's all I'm prepared to say,' was the only fresh line from Keane, while it was also revealed Ferguson spoke to his mother, Marie, over the phone and said he would 'see her shortly'.[22] Spillane also noted that Keane planned to have his future sorted before heading to Portugal on a two-week holiday a few days later.

The story prompted confirmation from Keane that United was his preferred destination.

'It was the hardest decision of my career, but money isn't everything,' he said. 'United have a proud tradition and everyone wants to play for them.'[23] But there were a couple of problems. Firstly, United were enthused by Keane's declaration of intent but were aware of the small print in his Forest contract and had no interest in forking out £5 million for his services.

'Keane's done himself no harm by stating that he wants to come to Manchester United,' Ferguson said. 'It shows he's got ambition. I'm delighted with that type of attitude. But a £5m fee for a twenty-one-year-old lad is totally unrealistic. Everyone wants to get as much as they can when they're selling and Forest are no exception. It's in Keane's contract that he can move for £3.5m in October, so why should the fee suddenly be £5m?'[24]

Also, Keane was facing the fallout from having turned down Blackburn. He'd phoned Dalglish to break the news and was met with an understandably seething reaction. Keane later described how Dalglish asked him where he was going on holiday.

'We'll find you and sue you.'[25]

Keane was already in the southern Algarve as Dalglish fumed to reporters, when there was indeed a brief mention of legal action pertaining to what Blackburn felt was Keane's 'verbal agreement' with the club. 'Roy Keane gave me his word on three separate occasions that he would be joining Blackburn Rovers,' Dalglish said.[26]

Ultimately, the club relaxed that stance, aware of their financial clout and how they could seduce both Keane and Forest with substantially better packages than United. Also, they remained the only team to have submitted a formal offer to Keane's employers. 'We certainly do not feel we are out of the hunt,' their secretary John Howarth commented.[27]

By the time Keane returned from Portugal, Arsenal had officially entered the fray and were granted permission from Forest to speak with him. But Keane politely turned them down – as did a collection of other central midfielders, including Andy Townsend and QPR's Andy Sinton.

Keane found himself in purgatory and was growing increasingly tired of waiting. He wanted to sign for United, but they remained locked in a stand-off with Forest over the price and, for a while, there seemed a genuine possibility that he would begin the new season at the City Ground as the Premier League champions attempted to play hardball. 'We are trying to sign Keane,' United chairman Martin Edwards said. 'But I'm not going to be blackmailed on deadlines. We have said to Forest that we will pay the £3.5m, and now it is up to them. We will wait until October if we have to. I don't think there is any way we will raise our bid.'[28]

Edwards and United seemed completely unaware that if Keane was signed in October, he couldn't be registered until the latter stages of the UEFA Champions League – the very competition Ferguson had carefully teased him with during their fateful game of snooker at his house. And the ignorance reflected a strategy that had been strange from the start.

United were extremely late to the table, even though Ferguson subsequently maintained Keane was a long-time target. He chased a central midfielder in the summer of 1992, but it was Andy Townsend who was top of his list. And while Ferguson later spoke of how swiftly United moved to land Keane, Blackburn had spoken to him six months before them. It seemed the real catalyst for igniting Ferguson's chances of landing Keane was Blackburn's mishandling of the entire situation.

'Clough was trying to get Neil Webb back in the summer of 1991,' Ferguson said in RTÉ's *Have Boots, Will Travel* documentary. 'He was out of my plans, to be honest. He'd fallen behind a bit. I said he was available but we'd like Keane as part of the deal. Cloughie dismissed that. And it went on and on like that for a long time, actually, until the season Forest went down. Once they were relegated, we moved in quickly. Frank Clark was astonished this meeting [with Dalglish] had taken place. So he said I had his permission to speak to Roy.'

Considering what had happened at United a year earlier, it was remarkable that they found themselves frantically entering the race for Keane so late.

Ferguson had wanted striker Alan Shearer, then of Southampton, prior to the 1992/93 season getting underway. But he found out from a tabloid newspaper that Shearer had been granted permission to speak with Blackburn. When Ferguson arranged a conversation with him, the striker asked him pointedly, 'Why haven't you been interested in me before now? Kenny Dalglish was phoning me regularly.'[29]

But this time United had a player who wished to join them. Even though the price tag led to a frustrating impasse.

'You get one of them that comes along – not in a lifetime but maybe every ten years – that you just say, "Well, we're not losing him,"' Ferguson said later. 'Every time he played against us or every time I saw him, he was such a competitive lad … and an unbelievable engine – up and down the field. So you knew that he was a Manchester United player just looking at him.'[30]

Still, however, they waited.

In mid-July, Keane reluctantly reported for pre-season training with Forest, and Frank Clark suggested he would face the prospect of reserve football if he was still there come the start of the campaign. But the relegated side had already spent big by signing Stan Collymore and Colin Cooper for a combined fee of £3.9 million and needed to finalise the departures of both Keane and Nigel Clough, who had agreed terms with Liverpool, to balance the books.

And, just a few days later, Forest announced a deal had been confirmed with United and that Keane, pending a successful medical, would sign over the weekend. But late on Friday night, he was still at his house in Scarrington and hadn't heard anything.

'I'm just sitting here waiting for the phone to ring,' he told Noel Spillane.[31]

By that stage, Keane had dispensed with the services of Brendon Batson and brought in Michael Kennedy, a London-based solicitor who had been advising David O'Leary for years, to hammer out the financial details with United.

And things moved fast.

The following day, Saturday 17 July, he was in Manchester for his medical. A record English fee of £3.75 million had been agreed between Forest and United on a four-year contract worth £1.4 million. Blackburn had offered £1.6 million but Keane didn't mind. A substantial loyalty bonus from Forest that totalled around £650,000 and was negotiated as part of his final contract, cushioned things greatly.

'He is one of the biggest signings we have made in my years at the club,' Ferguson gushed to reporters. 'He has all the attributes Bryan Robson had as a young player. It is difficult to say how good a player he can become, but he has magnificent potential. He has all the strengths of a really top player and he is a stage ahead of Bryan at twenty-one, because he is already an established international. I wanted Roy from the first time I saw him play for Forest against us in 1990. The players wanted him too and that was important for me. They told me how highly they rated him.'[32]

There was little time for Keane to enjoy the moment. He was immediately included in United's squad for a pre-season tour to South Africa and was due to depart for Johannesburg on Tuesday evening. But others celebrated on his behalf.

'I'm relieved it's all come to a head,' his father, Mossie, told reporters.'I am proud, yes, but I don't shout about it. In saying that, everyone comes over to me to talk about Roy and now that the news has come out, it will be a dream going into town tonight. Roy has been telling me that running onto the Old Trafford pitch is magic. There's no doubt about it that United are the biggest club in the world. I don't care what they say about the likes of Juventus because if I went out to China and asked a young fella there did he know about Manchester United, he'd tell me, "Ah, Man U".'[33]

Keane muddled the audition a little bit, and was evidently nervous at his unveiling. 'It should be called Magic United,' he said, in a mealy-mouthed attempt to find the right platitude. 'I have always been a supporter of the club since I was a youngster,' he lied, before eventually finding some rhythm. 'Everything about the club appeals to me. This is not a move about money. I'm only twenty-one and that doesn't matter. United are simply the best and biggest club in Britain.'[34]

Of course, there were already concerns.

Under a headline of 'Keane faces a new set of problems', the *Sunday Independent* was quick to reference his 'highly-publicised off-duty escapades' while at Forest and noted how Keane would do well to learn from Paul McGrath and Norman Whiteside, whom Ferguson had unceremoniously dumped owing to their extra-curricular activities, 'should he be tempted to stray from the straight and narrow'.[35]

But the English press focused on football matters.

This would be a considerable step up. The pressure would intensify. And the consequences would be far worse should things go awry. The path was a well-worn one, the scars still carried by the likes of Garry Birtles, Peter Davenport and Neil Webb, who had all swapped the City Ground for Old Trafford.

'It really is a different world to the one he's been used to,' Webb told *Shoot* magazine in the 14 August issue. 'People expect so much of you both on and off the pitch. You find yourself in the limelight all the time. And I really didn't enjoy the experience at all. Roy is certainly going to have to adapt accordingly. He could easily get dragged in to the glamour world and his football could suffer as a result.'

Still, there was an excitement at what lay ahead. In the UK, Keane had been deemed – for a considerable time – an exceptional player. And some of his peers even felt United could merely be a stepping stone.

'I think Keane is one of the few players in England who would almost certainly be guaranteed success if they joined an Italian club,' said David Platt. 'British-style midfielders do well in Italy – look at the track record of people like Liam Brady – and Roy has all the equipment to emulate him. I think he has chosen well for the moment but, at twenty-one, he can do four years at Old Trafford and still be young enough to make his mark in Italy.'[36]

Keane had met the United players already, Ferguson having dragged him into the dressing rooms to introduce him.

'They were all in the bath so it was a bit awkward,' Keane said. 'I couldn't just go over and shake hands with everyone. The manager said, "This is

Roy" and I said "Howya, lads" and a voice from the bath went, "Oh, lend us a fiver, would you Roy?" That was it, that was my start, the first words any player ever said to me at Manchester United.'[37]

Certainly, there was an anxiety. The price tag was a worry. His fitness, too, having only managed a couple of days' conditioning with Forest. There was the quality of the United squad and how he'd fare. Would he embarrass himself? Would he be out of his depth? And how did the players really feel about him? Where would he play? Alongside Ince? Instead of Robson?

'In a sense, it's like starting all over again,' Keane said. 'What I've done for three years at Forest has virtually gone out the window. This is a new start for me now and it's going to be hard. I know how hard it will be. I will have to prove myself all over again. But I think I'm ready for it.'[38]

NOTES

1 The First Half

1   Tommy Dunne, phone interview, 20 June 2019. All subsequent quotes from Tommy Dunne come from this interview, unless indicated otherwise.
2   Richie Purdy, phone interview, 28 June 2019. All subsequent quotes from Richie Purdy come from this interview, unless indicated otherwise.
3   Noel Spillane, interview, Cork, 1 May 2019. All subsequent quotes from Noel Spillane come from this interview, unless indicated otherwise.
4   Darren Barry, phone interview, 9 July 2019. All subsequent quotes from Darren Barry come from this interview, unless indicated otherwise.
5   *Evening Herald,* 9 May 1988.
6   *Sunday Independent,* 22 May 1988.
7   *Evening Herald,* 17 May 1988.
8   *The Irish Press,* 13 October 1988.
9   Keane, Roy, *Keane: The Autobiography* (Penguin, London, 2002), p. 10.
10 *Have Boots, Will Travel,* dir. Colm O'Callaghan. RTÉ 1, 30 June 1997.
11 Redknapp, Harry, *A Man Walks On To a Pitch: Stories from a Life in Football* (Ebury, London, 2014), p. 285.
12 Brian Brophy, phone interview, 4 November 2019. All subsequent quotes from Brian Brophy come from this interview, unless indicated otherwise.
13 Barry Lloyd, phone interview, 9 October 2019. All subsequent quotes from Barry Lloyd come from this interview, unless indicated otherwise.
14 Jamie Cullimore, phone interview, 29 May 2019. All subsequent quotes from Jamie Cullimore come from this interview, unless indicated otherwise.
15 *The Irish Press,* 18 May 1991.
16 *Evening Echo,* 20 April 1991.
17 Keane (2002), p. 79.
18 *Ibid.,* p. 14.
19 *The Cork Examiner,* 2 February 1990.
20 *The Sunday Times,* 12 May 1991.

2 All Out In the Open

1   *Reeling in The Years,* RTÉ 1, 18 October 1999.
2   *The Irish Press,* 17 August 1989.
3   *Sunday Independent,* 20 August 1989.
4   *The Irish Press,* 17 August 1989.
5   Tony Gorman, phone interview, 19 June 2019. All subsequent quotes from Tony Gorman come from this interview, unless indicated otherwise.

6   John Donegan, phone interview, 13 June 2019. All subsequent quotes from John Donegan come from this interview, unless indicated otherwise.

7   Larry Mahony, phone interview, 12 August 2019. All subsequent quotes from Larry Mahony come from this interview, unless indicated otherwise.

8   Fergus McDaid, email interview, 20 November 2019. All subsequent quotes from Fergus McDaid come from this interview, unless indicated otherwise.

9   *The Cork Examiner,* 17 August 1989.

10   Aidan Smith, phone interview, 18 June 2019. All subsequent quotes from Aidan Smith come from this interview, unless indicated otherwise.

11   *The Cork Examiner*, 7 November 1989.

12   Ted Streeter, phone interview, 18 November 2019. All subsequent quotes from Ted Streeter come from this interview, unless indicated otherwise.

13   Keane, Roy, *The Second Half* (Weidenfeld and Nicolson, London, 2014), p. 119.

3 Never Too Late

1   *The Cork Examiner*, 20 November 1989.

2   *Ibid.*, 4 December 1989.

3   Graham Brereton, phone interview, 4 July 2019. All subsequent quotes from Graham Brereton come from this interview, unless indicated otherwise.

4   *Daily Mail*, 30 July 2007.

5   Keane (2002), p. 19.

6   *Daily Mail*, 30 July 2007.

7   *The Independent*, 15 May 1991.

8   *Have Boots, Will Travel*, 30 June 1997.

9   *Ibid.*

10   *The Cork Examiner,* 21 February 1990.

11   *Ibid.*, 3 March 1990.

12   *Irish Independent*, 23 March 1990.

13   *The Observer*, 10 January 1993.

14   *Have Boots, Will Travel,* 30 June 1997.

15   *The Telegraph*, 14 May 2014.

4 Lion's Den

1   *Evening Herald*, 3 May 1990.

2   *Have Boots, Will Travel*, 30 June 1997.

3   *RTÉ News*, 2 February 1993, RTÉ Archives.

4   *Irish Independent*, 27 July 1990.

5   *Evening Herald*, 27 July 1990.

6   Keane (2002), p. 36.

7   *Ibid.*, p. 23.

8   Ian Kilford, phone interview, 27 August 2019. All subsequent quotes from Ian Kilford come from this interview, unless indicated otherwise.

9   Robert Bruton, phone interview, 15 October 2019. All subsequent quotes from Robert Bruton come from this interview, unless indicated otherwise.

10   *Shoot*, 6 November 1993.

11   *Have Boots, Will Travel*, 30 June 1997.

12 *Bandy & Shinty*, Issue 5, 2017, p. 14.
13 Keane (2002), p. 28.
14 *Ibid.*, p. 19.
15 *Ibid.*, p. 26.
16 Brian Rice, phone interview, 4 June 2019. All subsequent quotes from Brian Rice come from this interview, unless indicated otherwise.
17 *Have Boots, Will Travel*, 30 June 1997.
18 *Lancashire Telegraph*, 13 August 2010.
19 Steve Chettle, phone interview, 12 March 2019. All subsequent quotes from Steve Chettle come from this interview, unless indicated otherwise.
20 Clough, Brian, *Cloughie: Walking On Water. My Life* (Headline, London, 2002), p. 156.
21 *The Telegraph*, 4 January 2003.
22 *Have Boots, Will Travel*, 30 June 1997.
23 *Irish Examiner*, 27 June 2015.
24 Keane (2002), p. 32.
25 *Irish Examiner*, 1 October 2011.
26 *Nottingham Evening Post*, 29 August 1990.
27 *Ibid.*
28 *Ibid.*, 30 August 1990.

5 The Stage Door

1 Clough (2002), p. 77.
2 Wilson, Jonathan, *Brian Clough: Nobody Ever Says Thank You* (Orion, London, 2011), p. 96.
3 *Extra Time with Ron Atkinson*, ITV, 21 February 2000.
4 Jonathan Wilson, phone interview, 28 May 2019. All subsequent quotes from Jonathan Wilson come from this interview, unless indicated otherwise.
5 *The Athletic*, 14 October 2019.
6 Craig Bromfield, 'Roy Keane's League Cup Semi – The Third Leg' (May 2019), available at https://youtu.be/gViHocSKu0U.
7 *Nottingham Evening Post*, 30 August 1990.
8 Duncan Hamilton, phone interview, 2 April 2019. All subsequent quotes from Duncan Hamilton come from this interview, unless indicated otherwise.
9 Pearce, Stuart, *Psycho* (Headline, London, 2000), p. 146.
10 Wilson (2011), p. 377.
11 Toddy Örlygsson, phone interview, 22 April 2019. All subsequent quotes from Toddy Örlygsson come from this interview, unless indicated otherwise.
12 Keane (2002), p. 34.
13 *RTÉ News*, 3 February 1993, RTÉ Archives.
14 *The Observer*, 24 February 1991.
15 Clough (2002), p. 245.
16 *Irish Independent*, 15 September 1990.
17 NFFCTube, 'My Forest Story: Steve Hodge' (June 2016), available at https://youtu.be/1et89rtZIJg.
18 Hodge, Steve, *The Man With Maradona's Shirt* (Orion, London, 2010), p. 209.
19 *The Telegraph*, 14 May 2014.

20   Hodge (2010), p. 160.
21   Pearce (2000), p. 165.
22   *The Guardian*, 22 September 1990.
23   *The Irish Press*, 29 September 1990.
24   *Irish Independent*, 29 September 1990.
25   *Roy Keane: As I See It*, dir. Paul Doyle Jr (2002), available at https://youtu.be/75erCnwFmKg.
26   *The Sunday Times*, 30 September 1990.
27   *The Guardian*, 30 September 1990.
28   *Roy Keane: As I See It*, 2002.
29   Hodge (2010), p. 208.

6 Circus Act

1   *The Cork Examiner*, 10 October 1990.
2   Hodge (2010), p. 210.
3   Paul Stewart, phone interview, 13 August 2019. All subsequent quotes from Paul Stewart come from this interview, unless indicated otherwise.
4   *The Times*, 29 October 1990.
5   *Evening Herald*, 29 October 1990.
6   *Evening Echo*, 20 December 1990.
7   *The Cork Examiner*, 29 November 1990.
8   *Ibid.*, 12 October 1990.
9   *Evening Herald*, 19 September 1990.
10   *Ibid.*, 10 April 1989.
11   *The Cork Examiner*, 29 November 1990.
12   Hodge (2010), p. 207.
13   *Nottingham Evening Post*, 31 August 1990.
14   *The Observer*, 30 December 1990.
15   *The Telegraph*, 14 May 2014.
16   *The Cork Examiner*, 29 November 1990.
17   *Sunday Independent*, 6 January 1991.
18   *The Times*, 5 January 1991.
19   *Ibid.*
20   *The Cork Examiner*, 12 January 1991.
21   *Ibid.*
22   *Ibid.*
23   Train 2B Smart Juniors, 'Roy Keane on Brian Clough', (26 August 2017), available at https://youtu.be/Dkd4ZMo_W7Q.
24   *Inside the Mind of Roy Keane*, dir. Ross Wilson. Channel 4, 7 January 2003.
25   Hodge (2010), p. 217.
26   *The Cork Examiner*, 1 February 1991.
27   *The Times*, 11 March 1991.
28   *Evening Herald*, 8 March 1991.
29   *The Observer*, 10 March 1991.

7 A Charming Young Man

1   *Evening Herald*, 20 March 1991.
2   *Ibid.*, 29 March 1991.
3   *The Independent*, 11 April 1991.
4   *The Cork Examiner*, 13 April 1991.
5   *Evening Herald*, 13 April 1991.
6   *Irish Independent*, 15 April 1991.
7   *The Cork Examiner*, 30 April 1991.
8   *Irish Independent*, 1 May 1991.
9   *Ibid.*, 2 May 1991.
10 *The Irish Press*, 1 May 1991.
11 NFFCTube, 'My Forest Story: Steve Hodge' (June 2016), available at https://youtu.be/1et89rtZIJg.
12 *Evening Herald*, 14 May 1991.
13 NFFCTube, 'My Forest Story: Steve Hodge' (June 2016), available at https://youtu.be/1et89rtZIJg.
14 Hamilton, Duncan, *Provided You Don't Kiss Me: 20 Years with Brian Clough* (Fourth Estate, London, 2007), p. 214.
15 Hodge (2010), p. 226.
16 Keane (2002), p. 45.
17 Hodge (2010), p. 210.
18 NFFCTube, 'My Forest Story: Steve Hodge' (June 2016), available at https://youtu.be/1et89rtZIJg.
19 'Roy Keane on first year at Forest 1990–1991' (May 1991), https://www.youtube.com/watch?v=tEb0cqfyAN8 (accessed July 2019).
20 *Ibid.*
21 BBC, 18 May 1991, https://youtu.be/uTsajS2M5f0.
22 Clough, Brian, *Clough: The Autobiography* (Corgi, London, 1994), p. 271.
23 Hamilton (2007), p. 213.
24 *The Guardian*, 23 January 2014.
25 *Irish Independent*, 20 May 1991.
26 *Herald Sun*, 20 May 1991.

8 Back Up The Ladder

1   *Evening Echo*, 5 August 1991.
2   *The Cork Examiner*, 29 July 1991.
3   *Irish Independent*, 22 May 1991.
4   'Jack Charlton interview', BBC, available at https://www.youtube.com/watch?v=jUytT6uHe_U&feature=youtu.be.
5   *The Guardian*, 22 February 1991.
6   *Irish Independent*, 22 May 1991.
7   *Evening Herald*, 23 May 1991.
8   *RTÉ News*, 22 May 1991, RTÉ Archives.
9   *Irish Independent*, 3 June 1991.
10 'Jack Charlton Talks About Roy Keane', https://www.youtube.com/watch?v=9z-RqZRtAS3U (accessed August 2019).

11   Keane (2002), p. 50.
12   *Irish Independent*, 10 June 1991.
13   Kingsley Black, phone interview, 8 March 2019. All subsequent quotes from Kingsley Black come from this interview, unless indicated otherwise.
14   *Irish Independent*, 14 June 1991.
15   Clough (2002), p. 247.
16   *The Observer*, 8 December 1991.
17   Mark Reid, phone interview, 24 June 2019. All subsequent quotes from Mark Reid come from this interview, unless indicated otherwise.
18   *The Cork Examiner*, 29 July 1991.
19   *The Times*, 13 June 1991.
20   *The Sunday Times*, 25 August 1991.
21   *Irish Independent*, 27 August 1991.
22   *Evening Herald*, 28 August 1991.
23   *Sunday Independent*, 8 September 1991.
24   *The Irish Press*, 12 September 1991.
25   *The Cork Examiner*, 10 September 1991.
26   Pearce (2000), p. 286.
27   *The Independent*, 29 August 1991.
28   *Ibid.*, 15 September 1991.
29   *The Guardian*, 16 September 1991.
30   *The Independent*, 15 September 1991.
31   Warren Barton, interview, Los Angeles, USA, 10 February 2019. All subsequent quotes from Warren Barton come from this interview, unless otherwise indicated.
32   *The Guardian*, 16 September 1991.
33   *Irish Independent*, 17 September 1991.
34   *Evening Herald*, 4 October 1991.
35   *Ibid.*, 10 October, 1991.
36   *Ibid.*
37   *The Cork Examiner*, 14 October 1991.
38   *Ibid.*

9 VIP Lounge

1   *The Independent*, 28 November 1991.
2   *Ibid.*, 27 November 1991.
3   *The Times*, 28 November 1991.
4   *The Independent*, 28 November 1991.
5   *The Cork Examiner*, 26 November 1991.
6   *Ibid.*, 28 November 1991.
7   AFP, 14 December 1991.
8   'Nigel Clough red card v Spurs 1991' (27 August 2008), available at https://youtu.be/CoSuxGsoM7Q.
9   Steve Campion, phone interview, 20 August 2019. All subsequent quotes from Steve Campion come from this interview, unless indicated otherwise.
10   *The Cork Examiner*, 25 January 1992.
11   *Daily Mail*, 24 February 1992.

12   *Ibid.*, 8 February 1992.
13   ITV, 1 March 1992, available at https://youtu.be/f3eOxrm-evs.
14   *The Cork Examiner*, 3 March 1992.
15   *Daily Mail*, 2 March 1992.
16   *The Cork Examiner*, 3 March 1992.
17   Craig Bromfield, 'Roy Keane's League Cup Semi – The Third Leg' (May 2019), available at https://youtu.be/gViHocSKu0U.
18   *Daily Mail*, 2 March 1992.
19   *The Times*, 4 March 1992.
20   *Daily Mail*, 9 March 1992.
21   *The Cork Examiner*, 25 March 1992.
22   *Ibid.*
23   *Evening Standard*, 31 March 1992.
24   *The Times*, 3 April 1992.
25   *Evening Standard*, 3 April 1992.
26   *The Independent*, 19 April 1992.
27   *Sunday Independent*, 3 May 1992.

10 Trading Places

1   *The Cork Examiner*, 6 June 1992.
2   Keane (2002), p. 61.
3   Portsmouth FC, 'Macca on … Roy Keane's Rolex', (14 November 2013), available at https://youtu.be/DLPGMEsAiNw.
4   John Toal, phone interview, 28 August 2019. All subsequent quotes from John Toal come from this interview, unless indicated otherwise.
5   *Evening Herald*, 15 August 1992.
6   *Irish Examiner*, 1 October 2011.
7   *Evening Herald*, 17 August 1992.
8   *The Independent*, 17 August 1992.
9   Clough (2002), p. 239.
10   *The Cork Examiner*, 22 September 1992.
11   Clough (2002), p. 239.
12   *The Independent*, 22 September 1992.
13   *The Times*, 22 September 1992.
14   Lovejoy, Joe, *Glory, Goals and Greed: Twenty Years of the Premier League* (Mainstream, Edinburgh, 2011), Chapter 4.
15   *The Times*, 22 September 1992.
16   Clough (2002), p. 248.
17   Pearce (2000), p. 144.
18   *The Independent*, 19 October 1992.
19   *The Cork Examiner*, 28 October 1992.
20   *Daily Mail*, 5 October 1992.
21   *The Observer*, 15 November 1992.
22   *Mail on Sunday*, 8 November 1992.
23   *Ibid.*

11 Fancy Dress

1   *Irish Independent*, 3 November 1992.
2   *The Cork Examiner*, 14 November 1992.
3   *Ibid.*
4   *Irish Independent*, 19 November 1992.
5   *Ibid.*
6   *Sunday Independent*, 22 November 1992.
7   *Ibid.*, 1 December 1992.
8   *Daily Mail*, 20 November 1992.
9   *The Observer*, 15 November 1992.
10 Eddie O'Hare, interview, Cork, 1 May 2019. All subsequent quotes from Eddie O'Hare come from this interview, unless indicated otherwise.
11 *The Cork Examiner*, 11 December 1992.
12 *Ibid.*
13 *Ibid.*, 10 December 1992.
14 *Ibid.*, 12 December 1992.
15 *The Independent*, 7 December 1992.
16 *Press Association*, 11 December 1992.
17 BBC, 12 December 1992, available at https://youtu.be/kwFOzs_dXyg.
18 *The Independent*, 20 December 1992.
19 *The Cork Examiner,* 21 December 1992.
20 Brendon Batson, phone interview, 12 April 2019. All subsequent quotes from Brendon Batson come from this interview, unless indicated otherwise.
21 *The Irish Times*, 22 December 1992.
22 *Press Association*, 9 January 1993.
23 Hamilton (2007), p. 35.
24 *The Cork Examiner*, 9 January 1993.
25 *Press Association*, 29 December 1992.
26 *The Guardian*, 29 December 1992.

12 We Could Have Been So Good Together

1   BBC Sport, https://www.bbc.com/sport/av/football/47031761.
2   *Press Association*, 9 January 1993.
3   *The Times*, 21 January 1993.
4   *Daily Mail*, 29 January 1993.
5   *Evening Herald*, 8 February 1993.
6   *Daily Mail*, 1 February 1993.
7   *RTÉ News*, 3 February 1993, RTÉ Archives.
8   *Daily Mail*, 1 February 1993.
9   *Evening Herald*, 13 February 1993.
10 The42, 24 March 2017.
11 *The Cork Examiner*, 19 February 1993.
12 Robert Rosario, phone interview, 12 April 2019. All subsequent quotes from Robert Rosario come from this interview, unless indicated otherwise.
13 *The Irish Times*, 5 March 1993.
14 *Evening Herald*, 13 March 1993.

15   *The Independent*, 17 March 2008.
16   *Press Association*, 14 March 1993.
17   *The Observer*, 21 March 1993.
18   *The Times*, 24 March 1993.
19   *Nottingham Evening Post*, 25 March 1993.
20   Hamilton (2007), p. 211.

13 After The Lord Mayor's Show

1   *The Cork Examiner*, 24 April 1993.
2   *Press Association*, 11 April 1993.
3   *The Cork Examiner*, 13 April 1993.
4   *RTÉ News*, 3 February 1993, RTÉ Archives.
5   Wilson (2011), p. 542.
6   *The Cork Examiner*, 27 April 1993.
7   *The Sun*, 27 April 1993.
8   *Daily Mail*, 3 May 1993.
9   *The Cork Examiner*, 14 May 1993.
10   Clough (2002), p. 249.
11   *Mail on Sunday*, 23 May 1993.
12   *The Cork Examiner*, 25 May 1993.
13   *The Irish Times*, 25 May 1993.
14   *The Times*, 31 May 1993.
15   *Irish Daily Mirror*, 16 August 2017.
16   *The Cork Examiner*, 31 May 1993.
17   *Irish Examiner*, 19 August 2017.
18   *Daily Mail*, 2 June 1993.
19   *Ibid.*, 5 June 1993.
20   *Irish Independent*, 7 June 1993.
21   *Press Association*, 14 June 1993.
22   *The Cork Examiner*, 18 June 1993.
23   *The Times*, 18 June 1993.
24   *Press Association*, 22 June 1993.
25   Keane (2002), p. 83.
26   *Evening Herald*, 23 June 1993.
27   *The Irish Press*, 24 June 1993.
28   *Press Association*, 15 July 1993.
29   Ferguson, Alex, *Managing My Life* (Hodder and Stoughton, London, 2000), p. 322.
30   'Fergie's Dream Team', Granada Sports, 1994, available at https://www.youtube.com/watch?v=UJ8Lz0RuIZE.
31   *The Cork Examiner*, 17 July 1993.
32   *The Times*, 19 July 1993.
33   *Evening Herald*, 17 July 1993.
34   *Press Association*, 19 July 1993.
35   *Sunday Independent*, 18 July 1993.
36   *The Irish Times*, 20 July 1993.
37   *Irish Examiner*, 19 August 2017.
38   *Ibid.*

BIBLIOGRAPHY

Books

Clough, Brian, *Clough: The Autobiography* (Corgi, London, 1994)

Clough, Brian, *Cloughie: Walking On Water. My Life* (Headline, London, 2002)

Ferguson, Alex, *Managing My Life* (Hodder and Stoughton, London, 2000)

Hamilton, Duncan, *Provided You Don't Kiss Me: 20 Years with Brian Clough* (Fourth Estate, London, 2007)

Hodge, Steve, *The Man With Maradona's Shirt* (Orion, London, 2010)

Keane, Roy, *Keane: The Autobiography* (Penguin, London, 2002)

Keane, Roy, *The Second Half* (Weidenfeld and Nicolson, London, 2014)

Lloyd, Larry, *Hard Man, Hard Game* (John Blake, London, 2009)

Lovejoy, Joe, *Glory, Goals and Greed: Twenty Years of the Premier League* (Mainstream, Edinburgh, 2011)

Marples, David, *The History Boys: Thirty Iconic Goals in the History of Nottingham Forest* (Pitch Publishing, Sussex, 2018)

Moynihan, Michael, *Crisis and Comeback: Cork in the Eighties* (Collins Press, Cork, 2018)

Pearce, Stuart, *Psycho* (Headline, London, 2000)

Redknapp, Harry, *A Man Walks On To a Pitch: Stories from a Life in Football* (Ebury, London, 2014)

Shipley, John, *The Nottingham Forest Miscellany* (The History Press, Oxford, 2011)

Taylor, Daniel, *Deep into the Forest* (Breedon, Stoke on Trent, 2009)

Taylor, Daniel and Owen, Johnny, *I Believe In Miracles: The Remarkable Story of Brian Clough's European Cup-winning team* (Headline, London, 2015)

Wilson, Jonathan, *Brian Clough: Nobody Ever Says Thank You* (Orion, London, 2011)

Interviews

Barry, D., phone interview, 9 July 2019

Barton, W., Los Angeles, 10 February 2019

Batson, B., phone interview, 12 April 2019

Black, K., phone interview, 8 March 2019

Brereton, G., phone interview, 4 July 2019

Brophy, B., phone interview, 4 November 2019

Bruton, R., phone interview, 15 October 2019

Campion, S., phone interview, 20 August 2019

Chettle, S., phone interview, 12 March 2019

Cullimore, J., phone interview, 29 May 2019
Donegan, J., phone interview, 13 June 2019
Dunne, T., phone interview, 20 June 2019
Gorman, A., phone interview, 19 June 2019
Hamilton, D., phone interview, 2 April 2019
Kilford, I., phone interview, 27 August 2019
Lloyd, B., phone interview, 9 October 2019
Mahony, L., phone interview, 12 August 2019
McDaid, F., email interview, 20 November 2019
O'Hare, E., Cork, 1 May 2019
Örlygsson, T., phone interview, 22 April 2019
Purdy, R., phone interview, 28 June 2019
Reid, M., phone interview, 24 June 2019
Rice, B., phone interview, 4 June 2019
Rosario, R., phone interview, 12 April 2019
Smith, A., phone interview, 18 June 2019
Spillane, N., Cork, 1 May 2019
Stewart, P., phone interview, 13 August 2019
Streeter, T., phone interview, 18 November 2019
Toal, J., phone interview, 28 August 2019
Wilson, J., phone interview, 28 May 2019

Documentaries

Have Boots, Will Travel, dir. Colm O'Callaghan (1997)
Inside the Mind of Roy Keane, dir. Ross Wilson (2003)
Roy Keane: As I See It, dir. Paul Doyle Jr (2002)

Newspapers and Magazines

Bandy & Shinty
Daily Express
Daily Mail
Daily Mirror
Evening Echo
Evening Herald
Evening Standard
Herald Sun
Irish Examiner
Irish Independent

Lancashire Telegraph
Mail on Sunday
Nottingham Evening Post
Press Association
Shoot
Sunday Independent
The Athletic
The Cork Examiner
The Guardian
The Independent

The Irish Press
The Irish Times
The Observer
The People
The Scotsman
The Southern Star
The Sun
The Sunday Times
The Telegraph
The Times

Websites

AFP.com
NFFCTube.com
rssf.com

Soccerbase.com
The42.ie
TheAthletic.com

TheCityGround.com
Transfermarkt.com
YouTube.com

ACKNOWLEDGEMENTS

In this line of work, so much comes down to the kindness of strangers. People who pick up the phone and answer a litany of questions when they are well within their rights to tell you where to go.

To all of the contributors here, I owe so much. Their insights and expertise were invaluable. I hope I've done them justice.

Eddie O'Hare allowed me access to a remarkable collection of his unpublished Keane images, which was a real treat and helped immeasurably.

Familiar faces also played their part.

Special thanks to Dave Hannigan and Mark Rodden who offered wise words, suggestions and encouragement.

A firm handshake to Stephen Finn, who was a good friend through the entire process and always full of great ideas.

Similarly, Danny Taylor was an early jolt of positivity and came through on many other things too.

Adrian Russell and Niall Kelly have provided me with a unique platform at The42. Their trust and support, particularly throughout this project, meant a great deal.

Tony Leen and Colm O'Connor at the *Irish Examiner* have given a wonderful home to so much of my writing, no matter how curious the subject matter. I'll be forever grateful.

There are countless others who stepped in to assist at various points. Heartfelt thanks to Paul Rowan, Plunkett Carter, Pat Bowdren, Eoin Luc O'Ceallaigh and Andy van der Linde.

Some, such as Aoife Savage, Allison Follett-Campbell, Chris Young and Cody Royle, simply allowed me the time and space to step away from a laptop and talk, while John Doyle's continued mentorship is something I treasure deeply.

Thomas Doyle at the RTÉ Archives proved an enormous help, as did the staff of Nottingham Central Library.

This book would not have happened without the enthusiasm of Mercier Press. Patrick O'Donoghue championed the idea from our first phone call, while editor Noel O'Regan was meticulous in his craft. Wendy Logue, Sarah O'Flaherty and Deirdre Roberts were patient and dutiful and saw it carefully across the finish line.

I asked Nike Dewoolkar for a cover design. Instead, he delivered a work of art. I'm incredibly thankful to him for investing so much time and creative energy in this and for putting up with my relentless notes.

Much love to Sarah for the snap.

Thanks to Dad, and the entire O'Callaghan clan, for always being there.

Jimmy and Irene were constant supporters and although I bored them to tears with relentless updates, they never once complained. Huge thanks to them and the rest of the Fay family.

Finally, to my wife, Lyndsey, whose strength, determination and electricity drives me every day, I owe everything.

ABOUT THE AUTHOR

Eoin O'Callaghan is an award-winning sportswriter and broadcaster. He has written extensively for a host of publications including *The Guardian*, *The Independent*, *The Athletic*, the *Irish Examiner* and The42, while also serving as a football columnist for Yahoo Sports. As a TV host, reporter and commentator, he has worked with Fox Sports, BBC, RTÉ and Setanta Sports, and he also created, executive-produced and starred in *Celtic Soul*, a critically acclaimed documentary which screened across twenty-three cities in ten different countries and received a theatrical release in Ireland and the UK. He's covered a litany of high-profile sports events, including World Cups, UEFA Champions League finals, Ryder Cups and Olympic Games.